Implementing Mastery Learning

Second Edition

Thomas R. Guskey
University of Kentucky

Wadsworth Publishing Company
I(T)P® An International Thomson Publishing Company

Belmont • Albany • Bonn • Boston • Cincinnati • Detroit • London • Madrid • Melbourne • Mexico City • New York • Paris • San Francisco • Singapore • Tokyo • Toronto • Washington

GOMEZ

Education Editor: Sabra Horne
Assistant Editor: Claire Masson
Editorial Assistant: Louise Mendelson
Print Buyer: Karen Hunt
Permissions Editor: Jeanne Bosschart
Copy Editing, Composition, & Illustration: S. M. Summerlight
Design: Robin Gold / Forbes Mill Press
Cover Design: Carron Design
Printer: Malloy Lithographing, Inc.

Printed in the United States of America
1 2 3 4 5 6 7 8 9 10

For more information, contact Wadsworth Publishing Company:

Wadsworth Publishing Company
10 Davis Drive
Belmont, California 94002 USA

International Thomson Publishing Europe
Berkshire House 168-173
High Holborn
London, WC1V 7AA, England

Thomas Nelson Australia
102 Dodds Street
South Melbourne 3205
Victoria, Australia

Nelson Canada
1120 Birchmount Road
Scarborough, Ontario
Canada M1K 5G4

International Thomson Editores
Campos Eliseos 385, Piso 7
Col. Polanco
11560 México D.F. México

International Thomson Publishing GmbH
Königswinterer Strasse 418
53227 Bonn, Germany

International Thomson Publishing Asia
221 Henderson Road
#05-10 Henderson Building
Singapore 0315

International Thomson Publishing Japan
Hirakawacho Kyowa Building, 3F
2-2-1 Hirakawacho
Chiyoda-ku, Tokyo 102, Japan

Library of Congress Cataloging-in-Publication Data

Guskey, Thomas R.
Implementing mastery learning / Thomas R. Guskey. – 2nd ed.
p. cm.
Includes bibliographical references and indexes.
ISBN 0-534-25872-7
1. Mastery learning. I. Title
LB1031.4.G87 1997
371.3'9–dc20 95-48263

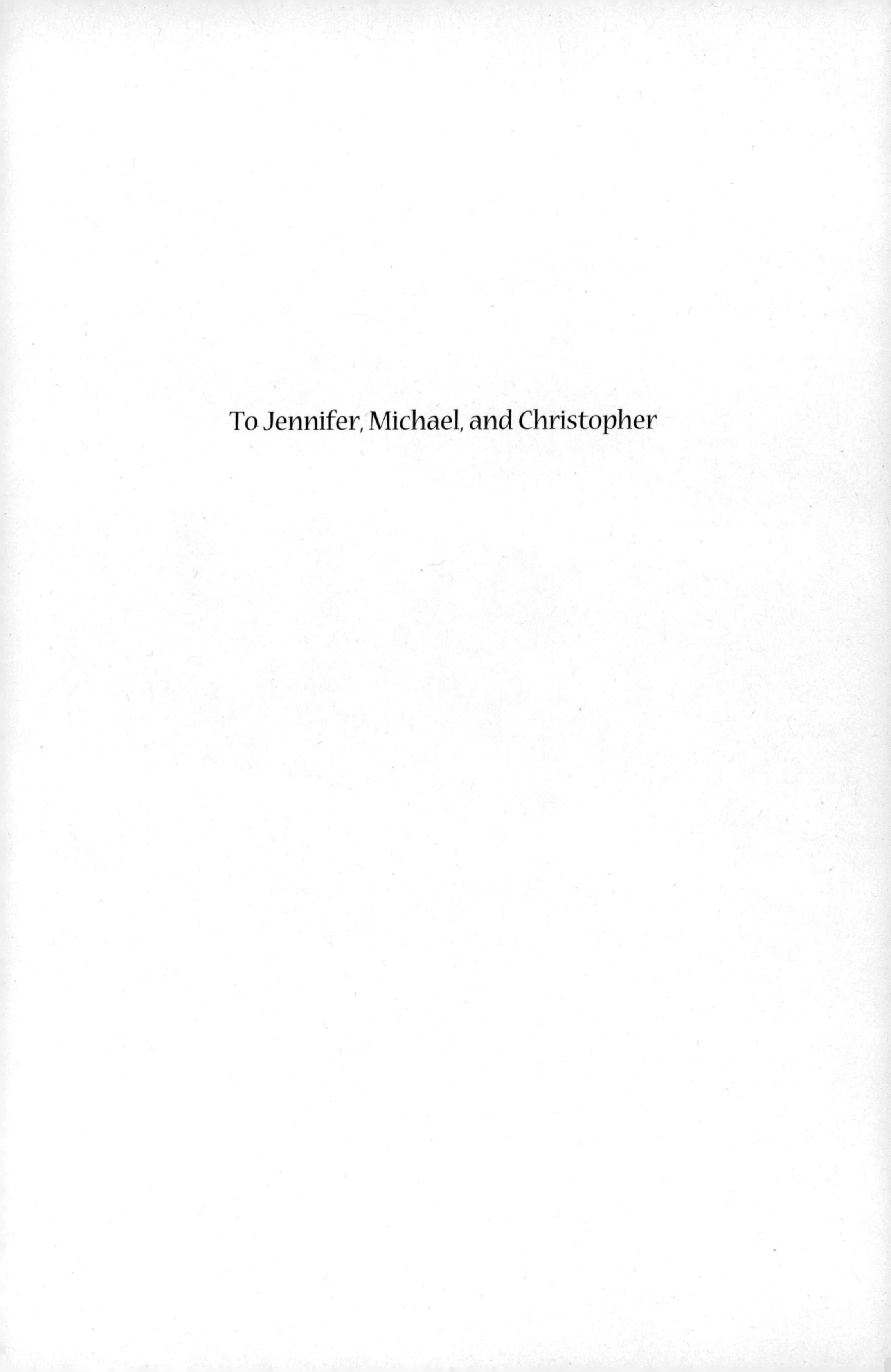

To Jennifer, Michael, and Christopher

Contents

Foreword

Implementing Mastery Learning becomes available to teachers, school administrators, and other persons concerned with the improvement of schooling at a most opportune time. Much attention in recent years has been taken up with concern about school achievement and school standards. The many proposals to improve schools involve money, time, new requirements, new curricula, and changes in the school bureaucracy. Very few of the proposals speak to what happens in the teaching and learning process. It is safe to say that unless there are changes in teaching and learning processes in classrooms, there will be little or no improvement in school learning. This book is primarily about the improvements in student learning that have been and can be brought about by teachers and students at all levels of education, from the elementary school to the graduate and professional school levels.

Professor Guskey has been involved in research on mastery learning as well as on its application in classrooms at all educational levels. He is one of the most eminent experts on mastery learning in the world. During the past two decades, he has helped schools in over forty states and several foreign countries make use of these ideas in their classrooms. Based on his extensive experiences in the use of mastery learning in all types of schools, he has written a book that is likely to appeal to teachers in this country and throughout the world. One hopes that this book, supplemented by appropriate professional development experiences, will enable teachers and their students to use these ideas in both the teaching and learning processes.

The modern notions about mastery learning were introduced in a paper of mine published in 1968. However, the basic underlying ideas have been known for over 2,000 years by leading educators from the time of Plato and Socrates to that of Morrison and Washburne in the early years of the twentieth century. Most of the great historic exemplars of teaching methods made use of *practice trials* or *assessments* in which teachers and pupils cooperated to correct errors and reinforce more appropriate responses. These were followed by *evaluation trials* or *examinations* used for grading and other judgmental purposes. Many of the critics of mastery learning have pointed to this and have stressed that most good teachers are already using some form of mastery learning. It is my fervent hope that this book by Professor Guskey will convince most of its readers that they have already been using these basic ideas and that they should continue doing so–but perhaps a bit more carefully and systematically.

For many years, my graduate students have been interested in mastery learning and its positive contributions to school achievement as well as to the learners' feelings about themselves and school learning. In more recent years, my students' interest in these ideas has been intensified by the results of three separate lines of educational research.

The first major finding is repeated evidence of very high relationships between the achievement of students at grade 3 and their achievement at grades 10 or 11, seven or eight years later. The correlation of the same students' achievement measured at grade 3 and at grade 11 is over +.80, suggesting that the rank order of students in the same school remains virtually the same for almost 90 percent of the students; that is, students' achievement in the early grades has a powerful deterministic effect on their achievement throughout their elementary and secondary school experiences.

A second finding is that the academic self-concept of most students tends to be relatively positive during the first two years of school. But each year thereafter, the top third or fourth of the students in terms of achievement become more positive about school and about themselves, while the bottom third or fourth of the students become more negative about school and themselves. By the end of the eighth grade, the top students feel very adequate about themselves in school and desire more education, while the bottom fraction of the students have feelings of great inadequacy in school and desire to quit school and school learning at the first opportunity. There are many long-term consequences of these increasingly positive or negative academic self-concepts on the students' view of the school, their peers, their family, and even themselves.

A third finding is that student achievement under one-to-one tutoring learning conditions is much higher than student achievement under conventional teaching conditions with one teacher to about thirty students. In studies done by several of my graduate students, the average student under tutoring achieves at a level that is above 98 percent of the students taught under conventional group instructional conditions. This research demonstrates that most students' learning potential is much greater than we normally find under group instructional conditions. While mastery learning is not as effective as one-to-one tutoring, it does enable a large proportion of students to learn any school subject to a very high level. The general finding is that the average student under mastery learning exceeds the level of learning of about 85 percent of the students learning the same subject under conventional instructional conditions–*even with the same teacher.*

The determinism of the school achievement pattern from grade 3 to grade 11, and the corresponding high and low academic self-concepts of the high and low achievers, raise fundamental questions about the effect of school achievement on the ego and mental health of students. There is evidence that mastery learning procedures used effectively during the first two or three years of school can be very successful in raising the level of achievement of the entire class. If mastery learning is also used during the next four or five years, the achievement and academic self-concept of the students will continue to be very positive. We speculate that even if mastery learning is not used during the next few grades, more of the fourth and fifth graders will continue to learn well. However, the main point is that achievement and affect interact, and if students are to feel good about themselves and to enjoy school learning, they must be given positive evidence of their success in school learning. Mastery learning can provide this.

Even more effective learning can be developed with some combination of *mastery learning* and the support of the *home environment, improved curricula,* or *student support systems.* More recent research suggests that some combinations of these alterable variables result in positive learning and positive affect equal to that obtained under one-to-one tutoring conditions. In the near future, it is likely that much more will be known about group learning conditions that are as effective for most students as the best of one-to-one tutoring conditions.

Benjamin S. Bloom

Preface

When *Implementing Mastery Learning* was first published in 1985, it was heralded as the first practical guide available to teachers who were interested in using these ideas. Back then, mastery learning was already well established as a highly effective instructional process. Studies on effective schools and the characteristics of effective teaching consistently pointed to mastery learning as an integral part of successful teaching and learning at all levels of education. *Implementing Mastery Learning* offered educators the most current evidence on these ideas and provided a step-by-step outline of how the mastery learning process could be efficiently used in a variety of teaching situations.

Education, however, is a dynamic field. Each year studies of teaching and learning expand our professional knowledge base and extend our understanding of educational processes. And each year the quality of those studies gets better and their implications for practice are clearer.

Over the past twelve years, we have learned a great deal about mastery learning. Numerous articles have been published that clarified educators' understanding of the process, and several syntheses of mastery learning research have been conducted. Several new books on mastery learning became available, notably *Building Effective Mastery Learning Schools,* by Block, Efthim, and Burns (1989), and *Improving Student Achievement Through Mastery Learning Programs,* by Levine and Associates (1985). We also saw more frequent and more systematic efforts to implement mastery learning throughout the United States and around the world. These efforts were spurred by the use of more effective professional development models, advances in technology, and the growing use of performance-based assessments. All of this made clear that we needed an updated edition of *Implementing Mastery Learning.*

Like the first edition, this edition of *Implementing Mastery Learning* is designed to be a practical guide for those who are interested in applying mastery learning in modern classrooms. It outlines in a step-by-step fashion how this process can be efficiently used in a variety of teaching and learning situations at many different levels. But in addition, this edition presents what we have learned from the last decade of implementation efforts. It also describes the results of the most recent research on mastery learning and outlines the implications of that research for practice. Most important, it shows how the ideas of mastery learning can be practically implemented in modern classrooms, keeping in mind the growing complexities of the group-based classroom environment. Many new practical suggestions for improving teaching and learning in general are also offered.

As was true twelve years ago, mastery learning remains basically an instructional process. It involves organizing instructional activities, providing students with regular information or feedback on their learning progress, offering guidance and direction to help students correct their individual learning difficulties, and providing extra challenges for students who master the important concepts quickly. Most teachers find that mastery learning allows them to help nearly all of their students become successful in learning and gain the many positive benefits of that success. Thus the ideas in this book will be valuable for beginning teachers as they prepare to enter the classroom, as well as for experienced teachers who wish to enhance the effectiveness of their teaching.

Implementing mastery learning requires three primary steps: (1) planning for mastery learning, (2) managing mastery learning in the classroom, and (3) evaluating mastery learning. The tasks and procedures involved in each step are discussed in this book in the sequence most commonly followed by teachers who implement the process. Although some chapters or chapter sections may not be relevant to every reader, the book as a whole provides a fairly complete framework of both the theory and practice of mastery learning.

The first few chapters outline the history and development of mastery learning, as well as discuss the major tasks that must be accomplished when planning for its implementation. These tasks are generally accomplished before classroom applications actually begin. The chapters offer suggestions for introducing the essential elements of mastery learning and for making the best use of available instructional resources. Often teachers find that elements of mastery learning are already part of their regular teaching procedures. As they understand the mastery learning process better, most discover that they can apply these elements more systematically and intentionally, and therefore enhance the overall effectiveness of their teaching.

The next chapters discuss various managing strategies and ways of adapting mastery learning procedures to fit a variety of approaches to instruction and teaching styles. Teachers who are fairly well acquainted with mastery learning, or who are at a school where mastery learning is being used, may want to turn directly to these chapters. However, it still may be useful to review the earlier chapters to ensure a clear understanding of the development and planning that are typically associated with mastery learning.

Later chapters consider the evaluation of learning outcomes within mastery learning classes and also look at overall evaluations of mastery learning programs. The general learning-to-learn skills associated with mastery learning are also covered.

The primary purpose of this edition of *Implementing Mastery Learning* is exactly the same as that of the earlier edition: to help make mastery learning better understood and more widely available to teachers and educators at all levels. To accomplish this, I again divide the book into two major parts. The first offers a comprehensive discussion of the mastery learning process and the steps involved in its implementation. The second provides sample units designed for teaching particular topics or themes in a mastery learning format. These samples are drawn from a variety of grade levels and academic disciplines. They are included not necessarily as exemplary models, but as working examples that help clarify the descriptions and explanations of earlier chapters. Occasional reference to these samples should make discussions in the first part of the book more relevant and meaningful.

Chapter 1 presents the history of mastery learning, its essential elements, and the major steps involved in its application. The basic principles that underlie mastery learning are outlined, together with how these principles are translated into prescriptions for classroom practice. Also considered are the particular aspects of mastery learning that give it such broad appeal, various misinterpretations of mastery learning, and the relationship of mastery learning to performance-based approaches to education.

Chapter 2 focuses on planning for the implementation of mastery learning and, specifically, techniques for outlining intended learning goals or objectives. The chapter also describes the important decisions that need to be made regarding what we want students to learn and be able to do as a result of their involvement in any instructional unit. Although clarifying these decisions is challenging, it is an essential step in successfully implementing mastery learning.

Chapter 3 centers around procedures for checking on students' learning progress through the use of diagnostic "formative" assessments. These assessments are broadly defined to include a variety of procedures for gathering information on students' learning. They include both traditional assessments and a wide variety of alternative assessment formats. Steps are outlined for developing these assessment procedures, ensuring they match the intended learning goals and objectives, and checking on their validity.

Chapter 4 points out the importance of providing students with regular feedback on their learning progress and discusses various techniques that can be used to help students remedy their individual learning problems. This chapter also addresses the use of technology in implementing mastery learning and the critical importance of providing enrichment activities to broaden and extend the learning of faster learners. It is generally agreed that the process of helping students identify and then correct their learning errors, while extending the learning experiences of fast learners through enrichment, are the most crucial aspects in the successful application of mastery learning.

Chapter 5 reviews the development of "summative" examinations and assessments. Unlike the diagnostic formative assessments, these examinations and assessments are culminating demonstrations of what students have learned and are typically used to assign grades or certify competence. They also are broader in scope than are individual formative assessments. Discussions in this chapter focus on the development of summative assessments, the relationship between these evaluative assessments and the diagnostic formative assessments, and important issues related to grading in mastery learning classes.

Chapter 6 discusses the classroom application of mastery learning. It describes the major approaches to classroom implementation, as well as procedures for taking advantage of the positive aspects of each. Methods are outlined for involving students and parents in the mastery learning process, for motivating students to do well on the formative assessments, and for dealing with common problems such as time and grading. We also point out some of the rewards and satisfactions that teachers derive from using mastery learning.

To determine how well the mastery learning process works, or if its use is truly worthwhile in a particular setting, we need some form of overall evaluation. Chapter 7 considers the kinds of information and the types of comparisons that can be useful in making these judgments. We also consider the results of several syntheses of mastery learning research and the implications for practice of this significant research base. Being able to assess the benefits of mastery learning's use is important for both teachers and administrators, especially when they are considering further involvement or expansion.

Chapter 8 focuses on the implementation of mastery learning programs on a school- or district-wide level. We look at the characteristics of successful implementation plans and specific procedures for maintaining program quality. The chapter also considers how mastery learning complements other instructional innovations, promising additions to the mastery learning process, and various prospects for the future of mastery learning in schools.

We begin the second part of the book with Chapter 9. Each chapter in this part contains a sample unit developed by a teacher or group of teachers who currently use mastery learning in their classes. Chapters 9 and 10 are units developed for use in elementary grades. Chapters 11 and 12 contain intermediate or middle-grade units on goal setting and first-level algebra. High school language arts and foreign language (Spanish) units are illustrated in Chapters 13 and 14. All of these chapters include a brief description and critique of the unit, an outline of learning goals or objectives for the unit, and two parallel formative assessments. Also included are corrective activities and suggestions for enrichment or extension activities. Again, these units are offered as practical illustrations, as developed by regular classroom teachers, of some of the ideas discussed in the first part of the book.

In developing the first edition of *Implementing Mastery Learning,* I had a lot of help from others who came before me. Their excellent work and uncompromising dedication were a constant inspiration to me. The same is true of this edition. In many ways, I feel as Albert Einstein did when he wrote, "A hundred times every day, I remind myself that my inner and outer life are based on the labors of others, living and dead, and that I must exert myself in order to give in the same measure as I have received." Like Einstein, I owe a great deal to those who went before me, helped me along the way, and continue to influence my work.

Most particularly, I am indebted to Professor Benjamin S. Bloom. Professor Bloom was my teacher and advisor during my years of graduate study at the University of Chicago. Since then, we have worked together on several projects and remain in close contact. These experiences have greatly influenced the way I think about teaching and learning, and the way I approach the problems we face in education. But, in addition to the gifts of his wisdom and careful reasoning, perhaps the most important gift Benjamin Bloom gave to me was an inexhaustible enthusiasm for education and immense confidence in the potential of educators. I count myself especially fortunate to know him as an inspiring mentor, a valued colleague, and a very dear and cherished friend.

I am also indebted to Professor James H. Block of the University of California at Santa Barbara, and Professor Lorin W. Anderson of the University of South Carolina. Jim and Lorin were early pioneers in efforts to operationalize the theory of mastery learning. Their ideas and the friendship we share have been extremely valuable.

Several individuals read earlier versions of the manuscript and offered many valuable suggestions. They include Lorin Anderson; Robert Burns of the University of California at Riverside; Janet L. Emerick of the Lake Central School Corporation (St. John, Indiana); and Mary Kay Hunt, principal of Lakeside Elementary School in the Metropolitan School District of Warren Township (Indianapolis, Indiana).

In addition, I owe much to the teachers and school administrators with whom I have been privileged to work over the last twenty years in efforts to implement mastery learning. These educators have helped me to be aware of the practical implications of our educational theories and the necessity of addressing difficult application issues. Their commitment and dedication to helping all students learn excellently are a constant inspiration.

A very special thanks is owed to the talented teachers whose work is represented in the latter chapters of this book. They include Mary Kay Hunt (Chapter 9), Donna Bowar (Chapter 10), Erica Chamberlain and Betty Arnold (Chapter 11), Janet Slavin (Chapter 12), Glen David Young (Chapter 13), and Cecile Baer (Chapter 14). Without their contributions, this work would not have been possible.

Finally, I owe a great deal to my family and special friends. They help me keep my work and myself in perspective, which is sometimes difficult, and help me find the patience that I lose from time to time. Perhaps most important, they keep me ever mindful of what is *really* important in life.

T. R.G.
Lexington, Kentucky

Introduction

If you want to try an interesting experiment, wander into a third-grade classroom sometime and ask one of the children, "Tell me, who are the brightest students in this class?" Almost always you will quickly be told the names of two or three children. Then ask, "Can you tell me who are the slowest students in the class–the ones who have the most trouble learning?" Again, with little hesitation, two or three children will be named. Finally, ask, "Suppose we were to put all the students in this class in order, from the very brightest to the very slowest–where would you stand?" After a slight pause, you will invariably get a fairly accurate estimate of that child's relative standing among his or her classmates.

That children in the third grade are able to give such accurate estimates of their academic standing is not particularly surprising to me and may not be to you. Despite their small size and few years, we know that third graders can be unusually clever. What troubles me deeply, however, is that this relative standing among third-grade students is unlikely to change much through their school years. In fact, research has shown that achievement measured in third grade can be used to predict achievement in eleventh grade, eight years later, with an accuracy of 80 percent or better (Bloom, 1964). All that seems to change is the comparative distance between the brightest and the slowest students in the class: Each year that distance grows larger.

As educators, we need to ask ourselves whether this high degree of predictability is simply an unavoidable aspect of the educational process, or whether we have other choices. Is such "determinism" in educational outcomes inevitable, or can we do something to alter these highly predictable results?

Consider, for example, the medical profession. Suppose you were feeling ill and visited a physician. And suppose that after examining you, the physician said, "You are ill. That's too bad, but you are going to die. I can predict this with great accuracy." Few people would be satisfied with that response. We expect those in medicine to do more than simply predict who will live and who will die. The task of those in medicine is to respond to health and medical problems.

Certainly, there are limitations on what they are able to accomplish. But success in medicine is judged by the degree to which prediction is defied–when a disease is cured that might otherwise have resulted in death or when an injury is healed and life is prolonged. The medical profession constantly looks for ways to intervene in biological processes specifically to defy prediction and guarantee a higher quality of health for all individuals.

Similarly, in education, our task should be to find ways to respond to students' learning problems so that learning outcomes become less predictable. Although we also face limitations on what we can accomplish, we too should try to defy prediction. We should be searching for ways to intervene in the educational process in order to guarantee a higher quality of learning for all students.

This idea is shared by the majority of beginning teachers. When they first enter the classroom, most teachers are confident that they can provide excellent instruction for all of their students. They generally have great enthusiasm and strongly believe that they will be able to reach every child with their teaching. But within a short period of time, these beliefs fade. Often they come to be regarded as naive delusions. Psychological survival seems to compel teachers to lower their sights (Harris & Associates, 1992; Pajack & Blase, 1989). When asked a few years later about their classroom "successes," these now-seasoned teaching veterans typically name two or three students who became excited about learning and made far greater progress than might have been expected or predicted. Such students, however, are exceptions. They are not the rule. Furthermore, they generally represent a small minority of the hundreds of students a teacher might face.

The effects of the high degree of predictability in education and the seeming determinism in student learning outcomes are well known. A few students in each class consistently learn well. These students are rewarded for their efforts, feel good about themselves, and develop a sense of pride and self-confidence. Generally, they like school, their teachers, and learning. Many more students, however, consistently learn less well, receive few rewards, and develop a sense of inadequacy in learning situations. Often they begin to feel incapable of learning, or at least of learning well. These students thus become handicapped in a society that increasingly depends on the ability to learn. They fail to develop skills that may be necessary for their survival in our increasingly complex world.

In recent years, research on teaching and learning has shown that there are ways we can intervene in the educational process to defy the predictability of learning outcomes. Several studies have shown that when students are taught in a way that is appropriate for their needs and when they receive help in overcoming individual learning difficulties, virtually all of them learn well (Bloom, 1976, 1988). Under these kinds of instructional conditions, learning outcomes become less predictable. How well students learn cannot be estimated because of the strong influence of the intervening instructional conditions.

Research studies also have shown that most teachers can provide appropriate instruction and help students overcome their individual learning problems when the teachers work with students in a one-to-one tutorial situation. When they are responsible for a single student, most teachers are able to help that student reach a very high standard of learning (Anania, 1981; Bloom, 1984a, 1984b). Unfortunately, that level of individual attention is rarely possible. In most school situations, learning takes place in a classroom where a teacher is responsible for the learning of not one, but twenty-five or more students. The problem thus becomes one of translating the elements of appropriateness and individualized help into the classroom setting, where instruction is primarily group-based.

Regardless of the level at which they teach, virtually all teachers are concerned with the appropriateness of their instruction. They know, for instance, that different students learn in different ways, and while one approach to teaching will be appropriate for some students, it is likely to be inappropriate for others. Most teachers would like to provide more individualized instruction and help for their students. But the constraints and demands of the classroom environment make individualization hard to accomplish. When attending to the individual needs of one student, the needs of twenty-four or more others are left temporarily unattended, and disruptions are likely to occur. In addition, most programs designed to "individualize instruction" require that learning be student-paced–that each student work at his or her own pace through a planned sequence of lessons. When students determine their own instructional pace, however, there is no guarantee that any but the most highly motivated, self-directed students will learn the important concepts within the time available. And all students may need to learn those concepts well in order to succeed at the next higher level of learning. Together, these management difficulties and curriculum demands make individualization extremely difficult and impractical in most classroom situations (Bangert, Kulik, & Kulik, 1983; Horak, 1981; Rothrock, 1982).

If we truly wish to alter the high degree of predictability in learning outcomes, an approach to teaching and learning that provides more appropriate instruction and individualized help seems essential. At the same time, however, such an approach must be sensitive to the constraints and demands of the actual classroom environment. In other words, the approach must be applicable in the typical classroom in which one teacher is responsible for twenty-five or more students. It must also be applicable in classes where the curriculum is fairly well fixed and only a limited amount of instructional time is available.

For many teachers, the teaching and learning process known as mastery learning provides just such an approach. Mastery learning combines much of what we know about effective teaching and learning in a set of sound and useful instructional practices. Basically, these practices involve procedures for planning and organizing instruction, along with strategies for giving students regular feedback on their learning that can be used to correct individual learning errors. In essence, mastery learning provides teachers with a better way to individualize teaching and learning within a group-based classroom.

Mastery learning is certainly not an educational panacea. It will not solve all of the problems that a teacher faces. But in a wide variety of settings, teachers have found that mastery learning can help many more of their students learn excellently. Mastery learning allows teachers a stronger and more powerful influence on the learning of their students (Guskey, 1980a, 1985b). Furthermore, it gives them a way to break the traditional lockstep procedures of highly predictable learning outcomes.

Programs designed to help teachers implement mastery learning are operating today in schools throughout the world. For example, large-scale programs are working in urban, suburban, and rural school districts throughout the United States (Anderson, 1994; Benjamin, 1981; Fiske, 1980; Vickery, 1987), as well as in Asia (Hau-sut, 1990; Kim, 1969; Wu, 1994), Australia (Chan, 1981), Europe (Dyke, 1988; Langeheine, 1992; Mevarech, 1985, 1986; Reezigt & Weide, 1990, 1992), and South America (Cabezon, 1984). Although some of these programs are still in the early stages of development, others have been expanded to include hundreds of teachers and thousands of students.

Mastery learning has great appeal among teachers in these school systems for two principal reasons. First, mastery learning allows teachers to pass along the benefits of learning success to more of their students than ever before. When successful in learning, students develop a sense of pride and well-being. They feel good about themselves and find school an enjoyable place to be. Success energizes them, and they become more engaged. They also feel more confident of themselves in future learning activities. Under more traditional approaches to teaching, only a handful of students attain these rewards.

Second, mastery learning does not require dramatic changes in a teacher's instructional techniques. In fact, most teachers find that it blends well with their current teaching practices and can be easily adapted to differences in classes and students. The application of mastery learning is quite flexible. In most cases, it can be used without any alteration in school policy, class scheduling, or classroom arrangements.

Today, excitement over mastery learning continues to grow. Many of the most recent reform and restructuring efforts include the implementation of mastery learning ideas. In addition, each day more teachers discover the important and positive influence they can have on their students' learning through mastery learning. The evidence for this comes not from educational laboratories, but from actual classrooms in all parts of the world. This evidence demonstrates that the effectiveness of nearly every teacher can be enhanced through the use of mastery learning. And, in many cases, the differences that result in student learning outcomes are tremendous (Kulik, Kulik, & Bangert-Drowns, 1990a; Walberg, 1985).

The enthusiasm about mastery learning has led several advocates to call for its rapid expansion and immediate large-scale implementation. In most instances, however, mastery learning programs are expanded at a slower and more gradual rate. Although some teachers find this frustrating, it is easy to understand if we consider the basic nature of most mastery learning programs.

Experience has taught teachers and school administrators to be wisely cautious of any new idea or innovation. Education is flooded with innovations that may be sound in theory but have no practical utility in the classroom. Many such innovations create more problems for teachers than they solve. For this reason, mastery learning programs are typically begun on a small scale and expanded only after successful results are verified by teachers in that school or school system. Once positive results are attained and the program gains credibility, however, its expansion is often rapid. In New York City's public schools, for example, the mastery learning program began with only twelve teachers taking part in a brief summer workshop. Four years later, mainly because of the positive results reported by teachers from all parts of the city, more than six hundred teachers volunteered to participate in a similar workshop in order to become involved in the program.

Another important explanation for mastery learning's relatively slow expansion is that it is not simply a package of educational materials that can be bought and applied in any classroom. Mastery learning is an instructional process. It involves teaching that is carefully planned with consideration of students' needs, along with procedures for identifying and then correcting students' individual learning difficulties. Expansion of this kind of process is bound to occur at a more gradual and measured pace than an innovation that depended only on the dissemination and use of materials.

The implementation of mastery learning certainly can be facilitated by carefully developed educational materials. In fact, several commercial publishers have refashioned their instructional materials in a format that is appropriate for mastery learning, and many teachers find these quite useful. In addition, the curriculum staffs of many school systems have developed instructional packages to aid teachers in the planning and organization involved in mastery learning.

Other school systems have employed teams of experienced mastery learning teachers to prepare similar packages.

Although materials and instructional packages are helpful when mastery learning is first implemented, it is teachers' thoughtful and sensitive use of the process that is crucial to the success of any mastery learning program. Even with materials organized in a mastery learning format, teachers still must critically review the materials, make judgments about their appropriateness, and make changes or additions depending on their students' needs. No collection of instructional materials is teacher-proof. None can be indiscriminately applied in a classroom and result in successful learning for all students. As R. J. Murnane points out, "A necessary condition for effective teaching may be that teachers adapt instructional strategies and curricula to their own skills and personalities, and to the skills, backgrounds, and personalities of their students" (1981, p. 26).

Critical judgment, sensitivity, and individual adaptation by the teacher are essential for mastery learning's successful application, just as they are for any approach to teaching and learning. We hope that the ideas presented in these pages will be helpful to those engaged in the important task of making these judgments and adaptations.

As indicated earlier, mastery learning is neither an educational cure-all nor the most ideal of all instructional conditions. If resources were available to pair each student with an excellent tutor, then undoubtedly all students would learn well and attain a high level of achievement. But those kinds of resources simply are not available. With mastery learning, however, many teachers find that they can come a little closer to offering students that ideal. Most find that mastery learning allows them to have a more powerful and more positive influence on learning, regardless of their students' characteristics. They are better able to pinpoint individual learning problems and help students overcome their specific difficulties, thus altering the lockstep procedures that lead to highly predictable learning outcomes. While mastery learning does not offer a solution to all of the problems that teachers face, it does offer a set of useful ideas and practical techniques that can be used by teachers to help more of their students become highly successful in learning and thus gain the positive benefits of that success.

Part I

The Mastery Learning Process

1

The History and Development of Mastery Learning

Throughout history, teachers have struggled with the problem of how to make instruction more appropriate for their students. By improving the quality and appropriateness of their instruction, many teachers believed that virtually all of their students might be able to learn quite well. This optimistic perspective about teaching and learning can be found in the writings of such early educators as Comenius, Pestalozzi, and Herbart (Bloom, 1974). This perspective is also the basic premise that underlies mastery learning.

Mastery learning was developed as a way for teachers to provide higher quality and more appropriate instruction for their students. The guiding theory held that nearly all students would be able to learn quite well and truly "master" any subject under these more favorable learning conditions. And, indeed, the tremendous improvement in student learning from modern classroom applications of mastery learning has confirmed this theory. As a result, mastery learning has generated great interest and enthusiasm among educators around the world.

This chapter explores the history and development of mastery learning. It describes the essential elements of this process and compares mastery learning with other strategies for individualizing instruction. The distinctions between mastery learning and performance-based or results-based education also are discussed. Finally, the major steps involved in implementing mastery learning are outlined, as well as the qualities of mastery learning that make it so appealing to teachers at all levels.

John B. Carroll's "Model for School Learning"

Although the roots of mastery learning can be traced to the days of the early Greeks, a major factor that influenced the development of current versions of mastery learning was the publication of "A Model for School Learning" by Harvard University professor John B. Carroll. In this 1963 article, Carroll challenged long-held notions about student *aptitude.* He pointed out that student aptitude had traditionally been viewed as the *level* to which a child could learn a particular subject. Children with high aptitude would be able to learn the complexities of that subject, while children with low aptitude would be able to learn only the most basic elements. When aptitude is viewed in this way, children are seen as either good learners (high aptitude) or poor learners (low aptitude).

Carroll instead argued that student aptitude more accurately reflects an index of *learning rate;* that is, all children have the potential to learn quite well but differ in the time they require to do so. Some children are able to learn a subject quickly, while others take much longer. When aptitude is viewed as an index of learning rate, children are seen not simply as good and poor learners, but rather as fast and slow learners.

Carroll proposed a model for school learning based on this alternative view of aptitude. He believed that if each child were allowed the time needed to learn a subject to some criterion level, and if the child spent that time appropriately, then the child would probably attain the specified level of achievement. But if not enough time were allowed or if the child did not spend the time required, then the child would learn much less. Thus the degree of learning attained by a child can be expressed by the following equation:

$$\text{Degree of learning} = f\left(\frac{\text{time spent}}{\text{time needed}}\right)$$

In other words, the degree of learning is a function of the time a child actually spends on learning, relative to the time he or she needs to spend. If the time spent were equal to time needed, then the learning would be complete and the equation would equal 1. However, if the time spent were less than the time needed, then the learning would be incomplete by that proportion.

Carroll further identified the factors that he believed influenced the time spent and the time needed. He believed that both elements were affected by characteristics of both the learner and the instruction. Specifically, he believed that the time spent was determined by a learner's perseverance and the opportunity to learn. *Perseverance* is simply the amount of time a child is willing to spend actively engaged in learning, and *opportunity to learn* is the classroom time allotted to the learning. In other words, time spent is determined by the child's persistence at a learning task and the amount of learning time provided. On the other hand, Carroll believed that the time needed was determined by the child's learning rate for that subject, the quality of the instruction, and the child's ability to understand the instruction. Thus:

$$\text{Degree of learning} = f\left\{\frac{\begin{array}{c}\text{Perseverance}\\ \text{Opportunity to learn}\end{array}}{\begin{array}{c}\text{Learning rate}\\ \text{Quality of instruction}\\ \text{Ability to understand}\\ \text{the instruction}\end{array}}\right\}$$

Again, a child's *learning rate* is a measure of the time required by the child to learn the concepts or material under ideal instructional conditions. If the *quality of the instruction* were high, then the child would readily understand it and would probably need little time to learn. However, if the quality of the instruction were not as high, then the child would have greater difficulty understanding and would require much more time to learn. In other words, the quality of the instruction and the child's *ability to understand the instruction* interact to determine how much time is needed for the child to learn the concepts or material.

Carroll's article was a significant contribution to learning theory. It set forth new guidelines for research into the concept of aptitude and identified the specific factors that influence learning in school settings. His ideas about learning rate also prompted the development of a host of new "individualized instruction" programs that allowed students to progress through a series of learning units at their own, self-determined pace. Two of the most popular of these "continuous progress" programs were Individually Prescribed Instruction (IPI), which was developed at the University of Pittsburgh (Glaser, 1966; Scanlon, 1966), and Individually Guided Education (IGE), which was developed at the University of Wisconsin (Klausmeier, 1971; Klausmeier et al., 1968). Carroll himself, however, did not address the problem of how to provide sufficient time or how to improve instructional quality. These issues were left unresolved.

Benjamin S. Bloom's "Learning for Mastery"

During the 1960s, Benjamin S. Bloom of the University of Chicago was deeply involved in research on individual differences, especially in terms of learning. He was also interested in ways to improve the teaching and learning process.

Bloom was impressed by the optimism of Carroll's perspective on learners and particularly by the idea that students differ in terms of the time required for complete learning rather than their ability to learn. If aptitude was indeed predictive of the time a child would require to learn, Bloom believed it should be possible to set the degree of learning expected of each child at some mastery performance level. Then, by attending to the instructional variables under the teacher's control–the opportunity to learn and the quality of the instruction–the teacher should be able to ensure that each child attain that specified level. In other words, Bloom believed that given sufficient time and appropriate instruction, virtually all students could learn.

Bloom observed that in most traditional classroom settings, all students are provided with the same opportunity to learn and the same quality of instruction. But while these are probably appropriate and sufficient for some students in the class, it is likely they will be less so for others. Those students for whom the instruction is appropriate typically learn quite well and master the concepts or material. Those for whom the instruction is less appropriate generally learn less well. If, however, the instructional situation could be altered to provide more appropriate opportunities to learn and a more appropriate quality of instruction for each student, then a majority of students in the class, perhaps as many as 90 percent, might be expected to learn well and attain mastery.

To determine how this might be practically achieved, Bloom first considered how teaching and learning take place in typical group-based classroom settings. He observed that most teachers begin their instruction by dividing the concepts and material they want students to learn into smaller learning units. These units often are sequential and correspond, in many cases, to chapters in the textbook used in teaching. Following instruction on the unit, a quiz or test is administered to students that covers the unit's important concepts. To the teacher, this test is an evaluation device that determines who learned those concepts well and who did not. Based on the results from this test, students are sorted into categories and assigned marks or grades. To the students, on the other hand, this test signifies the end of instruction on the unit and the end of the time they need to spend working on those concepts. It also represents their one and only chance to demonstrate what they learned. After the test is administered and scored, marks are recorded in a grade book, and instruction begins on the next unit, where the process is repeated.

When teaching and learning proceed in this manner, only a few students usually learn the unit's concepts and material well. In fact, Bloom found that even the best teachers were well pleased if half of the students in a class received an A or a B on a unit quiz (more than 80 percent correct).

If the learning units are sequential–that is, if concepts from one unit are built on and extended in the next unit–then students who fail to master the first unit

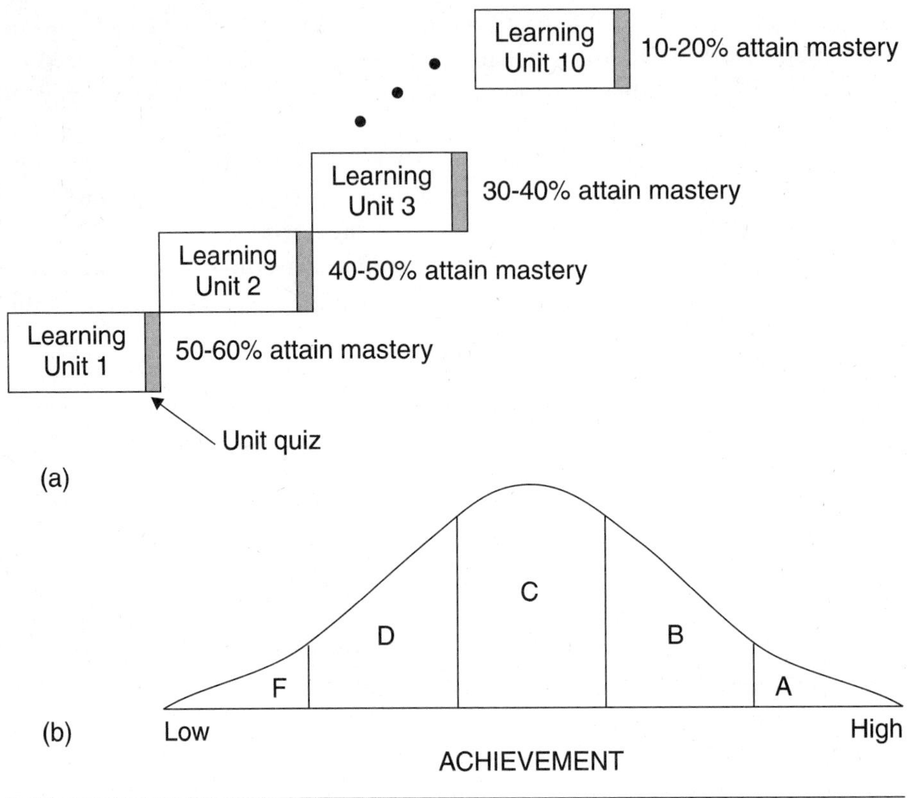

Figure 1.1 (a) Instructional sequence and (b) achievement distribution curve in most traditional classrooms

are unlikely to master the second unit. In addition, some students who do master the first unit will do less well on the second. Hence the number of students who master the second unit is likely to be less. As this process continues, a smaller number of students masters each subsequent unit. By the end of the term or marking period, only about 20 percent of the students in the class usually have mastered what the teacher set out to teach. Under these conditions, the distribution of achievement among students at the end of the instructional sequence looks much like a normal bell-shaped curve, as shown in Figure 1.1.

Seeking a strategy that would produce better results, Bloom drew from two sources of information. The first was knowledge of the ideal teaching and learning situation in which an excellent tutor is paired with an individual student. In this regard, Bloom also considered the work of early pioneers in individualized instruction, especially Washburne (1922) and his Winnetka Plan, and Morrison (1926) and his University of Chicago Laboratory School experiments. When considering this work, Bloom tried to determine what critical elements of one-to-one tutoring and individualized instruction might be transferred to group-based instructional settings. The second source from which he drew was descriptions of the learning strategies employed by academically successful students, most particularly the work of Dollard and Miller (1950). Here Bloom sought to identify the activities of high-achieving students that distinguish them from their less successful counterparts in group-based learning environments.

The Basis of Mastery Learning

1. Tutoring and individualized instructional techniques
2. Learning strategies of successful students

Bloom saw organizing the concepts and material to be learned into small learning units and checking on students' learning at the end of each unit to be useful instructional techniques. He believed, however, that the quizzes and tests typically used by teachers did little more than show for whom the initial instruction was or was not appropriate. If these checks on learning were instead accompanied by a feedback and corrective procedure, then they could serve as valuable learning tools. In other words, instead of using these checks solely as evaluation devices marking the end of each unit, Bloom recommended they be used to diagnose individual learning difficulties (feedback) and prescribe specific remediation procedures (correctives).

This type of feedback and corrective procedure is precisely what takes place when an individual student works with an excellent tutor. If the student makes an error, the tutor first points out the error (feedback), and then follows up with further explanation and clarification (corrective). Similarly, academically successful students typically follow up the mistakes they make on quizzes and tests, seeking further information and greater understanding so that their errors are not repeated.

With this in mind, Bloom outlined a specific instructional strategy to make use of this feedback and corrective procedure, labeling it "learning for mastery" (Bloom, 1968) and later simply shortening it to "mastery learning" (Bloom, 1974). By this strategy, the concepts and material students are to learn first are organized into instructional units. For most teachers, a unit is composed of the concepts presented in about a week or two of instructional time. Following initial instruction on the unit, a quiz or assessment is administered to students. But instead of signifying the end of the unit, this assessment is used as part of the learning process and is designed primarily to give students information, or feedback, on their learning. In fact, to emphasize its new purpose, Bloom suggested it be called a *formative* assessment, meaning "to inform or provide information." A formative assessment identifies for students precisely what they already have learned well and what they need to learn better.

Included with the formative assessment are explicit suggestions to students on what they might do to correct their learning difficulties identified by the assessment. Because these suggested corrective activities are specific to each item or set of prompts within the assessment, students need to work only on concepts not yet mastered. In other words, the correctives are "individualized." They may point out additional sources of information on a particular topic, such as the page numbers in the course textbook or workbook where the topic is discussed. They may identify alternative learning resources such as different textbooks, learning kits, alternative materials, video or audio tapes, or computerized instructional lessons. Or they may simply suggest sources of additional practice, such as study guides, independent or guided practice activities, or collaborative group activities. With the feedback and corrective information gained from a formative assessment, each student has a detailed prescription of what more needs to be done to master the unit's concepts or learning goals.

Assessment Information or "Feedback"

1. What students are expected to learn
2. What each student has learned well
3. What each student needs to learn better

When students complete their corrective activities, usually after a class period or two, they are administered a second formative assessment. Bloom stressed that this second assessment should be parallel but not identical to the first assessment; that is, it covers the same concepts and learning goals but is not composed of exactly the same problems or questions. This ensures that students learn those important concepts rather than simply memorize the answers to specific questions.

There are two major reasons for this second assessment. First, it is used to verify whether or not the correctives were successful in helping students overcome their individual learning difficulties. But second, and more important, a second formative assessment offers students a second chance at success. Hence it serves as a powerful motivational device.

The Second, Parallel, Formative Assessment

1. Ensures that the corrective activities were successful.
2. Gives students a second chance at success.

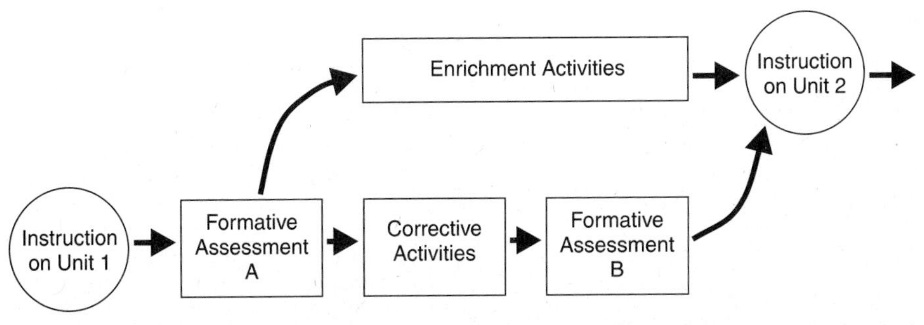

Figure 1.2 The process of instruction under mastery learning

On the first formative assessment, some students will undoubtedly demonstrate that they learned the concepts in the unit very well. For these students, the initial instruction was highly appropriate and they do not need corrective activities. To ensure that these students' learning progress is not interrupted, Bloom recommended that special enrichment or extension activities be provided to broaden these students' learning experiences. Enrichment incorporates exciting and challenging learning activities that may be developed or self-selected by students. They might involve special projects or reports, academic games, or any of a variety of complex thinking tasks. Figure 1.2 illustrates this instructional process.

Bloom believed that combining formative assessment with the systematic correction of individual learning difficulties would provide all students with a more appropriate quality of instruction than is possible under more traditional approaches to teaching. He recognized that with careful planning, a teacher's initial approach to teaching is likely to be appropriate for many, and perhaps even most, students in the class. But because of individual differences among students, that approach also is likely to be inappropriate for some. Corrective procedures make other, hopefully more appropriate, approaches available to those students so that a much larger portion of students learns well and reaches high levels of achievement.

Bloom believed that by providing students with these more favorable learning conditions, nearly all could learn excellently and truly master the unit concepts and material (Bloom, 1971a, 1976). As a result, the distribution of achievement among students would look more like that in Figure 1.3 (page 10). Note in this figure that grading standards have not been changed in any way. The same level of achievement is used to assign grades. But under mastery learning conditions, 80 percent or more of the students in a class reach the same high level of achievement that only about 20 percent do under more traditional approaches to instruction.

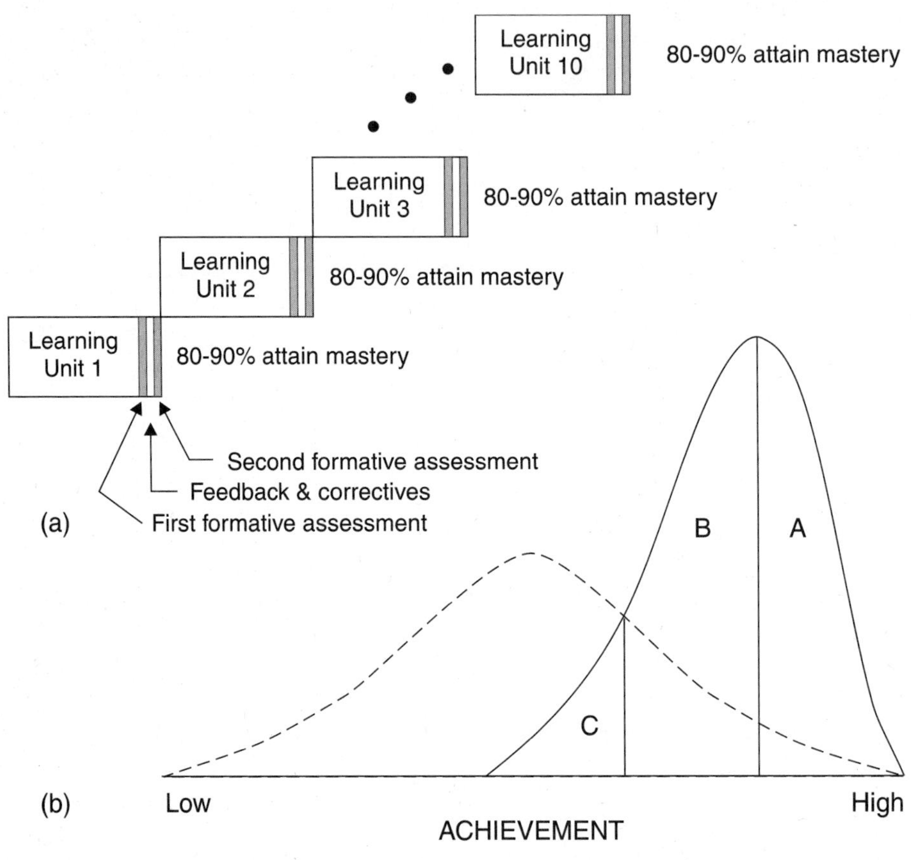

Figure 1.3 (a) Instructional sequence and (b) achievement distribution curve in a mastery learning classroom

The Essential Elements of Mastery Learning

Since Benjamin Bloom first set forth his ideas, mastery learning's popularity has grown steadily. A great deal has been written about it in theory and practice, and the process has been widely implemented (e.g., Block, 1971, 1974; Block & Anderson, 1975; Block, Efthim, & Burns, 1989; Levine et al., 1985). Because of its popularity, however, the name "mastery learning" has become a buzz phrase in education. It is attached to a variety of programs, materials, and curricula, many of which have little to do with Bloom's ideas. As a result, the characteristics of programs labeled "mastery learning" vary greatly from setting to setting (Burns, 1987). In addition, educators interested in applying Bloom's ideas often have difficulty finding a concise description of the essential elements of mastery learning and the specific changes required for successful implementation.

In recent years, two elements have been described as essential in implementing mastery learning (Guskey, 1987a). Although the actual appearance or format of these elements may vary, they serve a specific purpose in a mastery learning classroom and most clearly differentiate mastery learning from other instructional approaches. These two essential elements are (1) the *feedback, corrective, and enrichment process;* and (2) *congruence among instructional components,* or *alignment.*

Feedback, Correctives, and Enrichment

To use mastery learning, a teacher must offer students regular and specific information on their learning progress. Furthermore, that information must be both diagnostic and prescriptive; that is, the information or feedback students regularly receive should (1) reinforce precisely what was most important for them to learn in each unit of instruction, (2) recognize what students learned well, and (3) identify the specific concepts on which students need to spend more time. To be effective, this feedback also must be appropriate for students' level of learning.

As Bloom noted, however, feedback alone will not help students greatly improve their learning. For significant improvement to occur, feedback must be paired with specific corrective activities.

Correctives offer students explicit guidance and direction on how they can correct their learning errors and remedy their learning problems. But, most important, the correctives must be different from the initial instruction. Simply having students go back and repeat a process that has already proven unsuccessful is unlikely to yield better results the second time. Therefore, corrective activities must offer instructional alternatives to students. Specifically, they must present the concepts differently and involve students in learning differently than did the initial teaching. This means the correctives should incorporate different learning styles, learning modalities, or forms of intelligence (Armstrong, 1994; Carbo, Dunn, & Dunn, 1986; Gardner, 1983; McCarthy, 1987). In addition, corrective activities should be effective in improving performance. A new or alternative approach that does not help students overcome their learning difficulties is inappropriate as a corrective and ought to be avoided.

In most group-based applications of mastery learning, correctives are accompanied by enrichment or extension activities for students who attain mastery from the initial teaching. Enrichment activities provide these students with exciting opportunities to broaden and expand their learning. To be effective, these enrichments must be both rewarding and challenging. In general, they are related to the subject or topic being studied, but they need not be tied directly to a particular unit's content. Hence enrichment offers an excellent means of engaging students in challenging, higher level activities such as those designed for the gifted and talented (see Figure 1.4 on page 12).

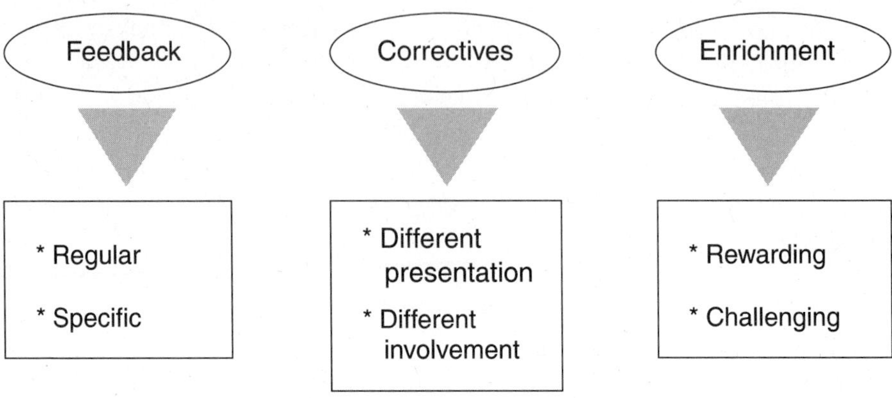

Figure 1.4 Characteristics of feedback, correctives, and enrichment in a mastery learning classroom

As we will see in Chapter 4, this feedback, corrective, and enrichment process can be implemented in a variety of ways. In some mastery learning classes, teachers use short, paper-and-pencil quizzes as formatives to give students feedback on their learning progress. But a formative assessment can be any device teachers use to gain evidence about their students' learning progress. Thus essays, compositions, projects, reports, performance tasks, skill demonstrations, and oral presentations can all serve as formative assessments.

Following a formative assessment, some teachers divide their classes into separate corrective and enrichment groups. While the teacher directs the activities of students engaged in correctives, enrichment students work on self-selected, independent enrichment activities that provide opportunities for them to extend and broaden their learning. Other teachers team with colleagues and exchange students, so that while one teacher oversees corrective activities the other monitors enrichments. Still other teachers engage students in cooperative learning activities in which students work together in teams to ensure that all reach the mastery level. The entire team may receive special awards or credit if all members attain mastery on the second formative assessment (Guskey, 1990a).

Feedback, corrective, and enrichment procedures are crucial to the mastery learning process, for it is through these procedures that mastery learning "individualizes" instruction. In every unit taught, students who need extended time and opportunity to remedy learning problems get them through correctives. Furthermore, students who learn quickly or for whom the initial instruction was highly appropriate are provided with opportunities to extend their learning through enrichments. As a result, all students are provided with favorable learning conditions and more appropriate, higher quality instruction.

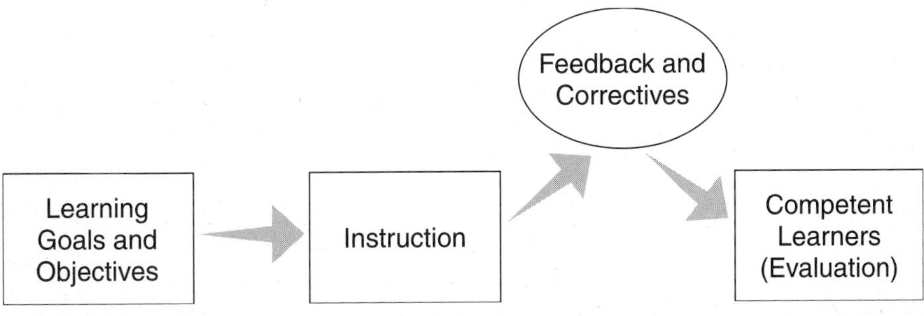

Figure 1.5 Major components in the teaching and learning process

Congruence Among Instructional Components or Alignment

Feedback, correctives, and enrichment are extremely important, but they alone do not constitute mastery learning. To be truly effective, they must be combined with the second essential element of the mastery learning process: congruence among instructional components or alignment.

The teaching and learning process is generally perceived as having three major components. To begin, we must have some idea of what students are to learn–that is, the learning goals or objectives. This is followed by instruction that, hopefully, results in competent learners: students who have learned well and whose competence can be assessed through some form of evaluation. Mastery learning adds an additional component, the feedback and corrective component, that allows teachers to determine for whom the initial instruction was appropriate and for whom an alternative must be planned. Through these alternatives, it is likely that more students will learn well and be competent at the end.

Although essentially neutral with regard to what is taught, how it is taught, and how the results are evaluated, mastery learning does demand consistency and alignment among these instructional components (see Figure 1.5). For example, if students are expected to learn higher level skills such as those involved in application, analysis, or synthesis, then mastery learning stipulates that instructional activities must be planned to give students opportunities to actively practice those skills. It also requires that students be given specific feedback on their learning of those skills, coupled with directions on how to correct any learning errors. Finally, procedures for evaluating students' learning also should be based on those skills.

Although congruence among instructional components is essential for mastery learning, it is actually an essential component of effective teaching and learning at any level (Cohen, 1987). Suppose, for example, that a language arts teacher offers students feedback on their learning through short, multiple-choice quizzes on grammar and punctuation, but then evaluates their learning in terms of the clarity and precision with which they organize ideas in written compositions. In this case, although students receive regular feedback, it clearly is not congruent with the procedures used to evaluate their learning. Students may know the rules of grammar and punctuation but be unable to apply those rules in their writing. Or they may prepare a composition with perfect grammar and punctuation but receive a low mark because of inadequate content or poor organization.

In a mastery learning class, the feedback students receive should always be congruent with the specified learning goals or objectives and the procedures used to evaluate their learning. If students' writing skill, organization of ideas, and writing content are the criteria by which their learning is to be evaluated, then they should receive diagnostic feedback based on those criteria and prescriptive guidance to correct whatever learning difficulties they may be experiencing.

This element of congruence among instructional components has led some critics to dismiss mastery learning as simply "teaching to the test." But the important question in this regard is, what forms the basis for teaching? If a test is the basis of teaching, and if what is taught is determined primarily by that test then, indeed, one is "teaching to the test." Under these conditions, the content and format of the test dictate not only what is taught but also how it is taught. Proponents of "measurement-driven instruction" advocate such an approach provided, of course, that the tests address truly worthwhile learning standards (Popham, 1987; Popham, Cruse, Rankin, Sandifer, & Williams, 1985).

With mastery learning, however, the desired learning goals or objectives are the basis of teaching. In most cases, these are determined by the teacher. In using mastery learning, teachers simply ensure that their instructional activities and procedures for evaluating student learning match what students should learn. Thus, instead of "teaching to the test," mastery learning teachers are more accurately "testing or assessing what they teach."

Admittedly, identifying the desired learning goals or objectives requires that teachers make crucial decisions. They must decide, for example, what concepts or skills are most important for students to learn and most central to students' understanding of the subject. But all teachers also must recognize that they are already making these decisions. Every time a quiz is administered, a paper is graded, a task is assessed, or an evaluation of learning is made, teachers communicate to their students what they consider to be most important. The use of mastery learning simply compels teachers to confront these decisions more directly, thoughtfully, and intentionally.

The Essential Elements of Mastery Learning

1. Feedback, correctives, and enrichment
2. Congruence among instructional components (alignment)

Mastery Learning and Personalized Systems of Instruction

Despite continual clarification, questions still frequently arise about how mastery learning differs from other strategies for individualizing instruction. The most common questions concern the difference between mastery learning and personalized systems of instruction (PSI). Although researchers have always recognized the distinction between these two approaches (Block & Burns, 1976; Kulik, Kulik, & Bangert-Drowns, 1990a), many education textbooks, particularly in the area of educational psychology, continue to confuse them (see Guskey, 1994a, for examples).

Table 1.1 (page 16) outlines the major differences between Bloom's mastery learning model (Bloom, 1968, 1971b) and F. S. Keller's personalized system of instruction model (Keller, 1968). These differences are also summarized briefly below, primarily to clarify issues that will be important in future discussions.

The PSI model is an individually based, student-paced approach to instruction in which students typically learn independently of their classmates. It is essentially an extension of programmed instruction that includes a personal or social element. In other words, feedback in a PSI classroom is provided by people–usually student proctors–rather than by a computer or a designed set of instructional materials. Students typically work at their own pace and move on to new material only after they have demonstrated perfect mastery of each unit. In addition, students may retake mastery tests at the end of each unit any number of times without penalty. Those who do not pass the mastery test repeat the original instructional unit and retake the test when they believe they are prepared.

The teacher's role in a PSI classroom is primarily to give individual assistance as needed. Occasional class presentations are seen as vehicles of motivation rather than as sources of critical information. Thus carefully designed, self-instructional materials or computer programs, which are often organized in "learning modules," are essential to a successful PSI program (Kulik, Kulik, & Cohen, 1979; Thompson, 1980).

The mastery learning model, on the other hand, is typically a group-based, teacher-paced approach to instruction in which students learn, for the most part,

Characteristic	Model: Mastery Learning	Model: Personalized Systems of Instruction
Basis of instruction	Group	Individual
Pace of instruction	Teacher-determined	Student-determined
Primary source of instruction	Teacher, supplemented by materials	Materials, supplemented by teacher
Standard of mastery	80–90%	100%
Number of retake assessments per unit	One (typically)	As many as needed for mastery
Correctives	New and different approach	Repetition of original material
Major applications	Elementary and secondary levels	College level

Table 1.1 Major differences between mastery learning and personalized systems of instruction

cooperatively with their classmates. Mastery learning is designed for use in the typical classroom situation where instructional time is relatively fixed and a teacher has charge of twenty-five or more students. The model can be adapted, however, to an individually based, student-paced format in situations where instructional time and format are less restricted.

In a mastery learning classroom, the pace of the original instruction is determined primarily by the teacher. Support for this idea comes from studies that show that younger elementary students and those with low entry abilities generally lack the self-discipline, motivation, and self-direction to be good managers of their own learning (Raiser, 1980; Ross & Rakow, 1981). Furthermore, if left on their own to determine an appropriate instructional pace, many students suffer "procrastination effects" that can stifle their progress (Lamwers & Jazwinski, 1989; Sherman, 1992).

Also, in mastery learning classrooms a high but not perfect level of performance (that is, usually 80 to 90 percent correct) is required of students on each formative assessment. This procedure stems from the recognition that (1) not all learning is perfectly sequential for all learners; (2) the assessments themselves may be less than perfect–that is, they may contain items that are poorly worded or scoring criteria that are somewhat ambiguous; and (3) perfect performance may be an unrealistic or unnecessary expectation. The role of the teacher in a mastery learning classroom is different as well. With mastery learning, the teacher is an instructional leader and learning facilitator who directs a variety of group-based instructional methods together with accompanying feedback and corrective procedures.

In terms of applications, the mastery learning model is generally more flexible than the PSI model. Teachers are usually encouraged to adapt mastery learning to their personal teaching style, classroom situation, and students' specific needs. Both models have seen widespread use since their development. While most PSI programs have been implemented at the college or university level, however, the majority of mastery learning programs have been implemented in elementary and secondary schools where greater variation is typically seen among students in terms of their educational needs and learning styles.

Mastery Learning and Performance-Based Education

Mastery learning is also confused with performance-or results-based education (O'Neil, 1993; Towers, 1992). Although these approaches to educational reform have much in common with mastery learning, especially philosophical premises, there are important differences. Viewing each from a historical perspective helps clarify the distinction (Guskey, 1994b).

Performance-Based or Results-Based Education

Although some theorists suggest that performance-based or results-based approaches are recent developments (Brandt, 1992), their guiding principles were elegantly set forth in the 1940s by Ralph W. Tyler in his classic book, *Basic Principles of Curriculum and Instruction*. Tyler (1949, p. 1) emphasized that those engaged in the process of developing any curriculum and plan of instruction must answer four fundamental questions: (1) What educational purposes should the school seek to attain? (2) What educational experiences can be provided that are likely to accomplish these purposes? (3) How can these educational experiences be effectively organized? (4) How can we determine whether these purposes are being attained?

Tyler's Four Fundamental Questions

1. What educational purposes should the school seek to attain?
2. What educational experiences can be provided that are likely to accomplish these purposes?
3. How can these educational experiences be effectively organized?
4. How can we determine whether these purposes are being attained?

Although Tyler regarded the specification of educational purposes as synonymous with defining "educational objectives," he considered objectives to be broadly defined conceptions of what we want students to learn and be able to do. He saw them as the building blocks of any curriculum and the central issue in the first of his four fundamental questions. Tyler recognized, however, that "in the final analysis, objectives are matters of choice and they must, therefore, be considered value judgments of those responsible for the school" (1949, p. 4).

In the 1960s and early 1970s, Tyler's notions of educational objectives became associated with behavioral approaches to instruction. These approaches were referred to as "objective-based education" (Baker, 1970) and were popularized because of the "back to basics" movement that was then dominant in American education. Under objective-based approaches, complex learning tasks were broken down into smaller, more basic skills, which then were arranged in an appropriate "scope and sequence" for students to learn (Quilling & Otto, 1971; Rude, 1974).

The seemingly mechanistic and reductionist nature of behavioral approaches soon fell out of favor among mainstream educators, however, and attention turned to defining "educational competencies" and "competency-based education" (Spady, 1978; Spady & Mitchell, 1977). Competencies were defined as "indicators of successful performance in life-role activities" (Spady, 1977, p. 10) and were popular among curriculum development specialists during the mid-1970s. Although Tyler undoubtedly would have considered competencies to be one type of objective, the term was more palatable to educators concerned with the perceived rigidity of objective-based approaches.

With the advent of competency testing and other criterion-referenced measurements in the latter 1970s, many educators focused on establishing "minimum or essential competencies." These were curriculum standards required of all students and were designed to address public demand for accountability in education. But this focus on minimum competencies left other educators worried that students' higher level capabilities would be neglected.

In searching for a label for these significant, higher level capabilities, a variety of options was considered. Researchers at the Northwest Regional Educational Laboratory advocated "goal-based education" (Blum, 1981; Blum & Butler, 1981) to focus attention on more advanced learning. Goals were considered broader in context and more cognitively complex than more narrowly defined "objectives" or "competencies."

Another group loosely linked to the American Association of School Administrators came upon the word *outcomes*. Benjamin Bloom first used the word as a subheading in his original description of the mastery learning process (Bloom, 1968, p. 10). Outcomes were defined by Bloom as the desired results from any teaching and learning process. They were the purposes a school sought to attain, as Tyler stated in the first of his four fundamental questions. And because the term *outcomes* was untainted by previous use or misuse, it would not be interpreted with the same narrowness that had come to be associated with objectives and competencies. Hence the label "outcome-based education" was born in the late 1970s and early 1980s (Mitchell & Spady, 1978).

Like objectives, competencies, and goals, outcomes were variously defined. The more simple definitions focused exclusively on curriculum and Tyler's first fundamental question, "What educational purposes should the school seek to attain?" Boysen, for example, defined an outcome as "what students are expected to demonstrate" (1992, p. 10). Others offered more detailed definitions that also hint at Tyler's fourth question dealing with assessment: "How can we determine whether these purposes are being attained?" Spady, for example, defined an outcome as "a culminating demonstration of the entire range of learning experiences and capabilities that underlie it in a performance context that directly influences what and how it is carried out" (1992, p. 7).

In recent years, outcome-based approaches to educational reform have been criticized by those who question the process by which outcomes are identified and assessed, and by those who feel the outcomes held for students are too low or unclear (Chion-Kenney, 1994; Guskey, 1994c; O'Neil, 1994). As a result, alternative approaches have developed under new labels such as "standards-based," "proficiency-based," "performance-based," and "results-based" education. Despite the varying definitions and labels, however, performance-based or results-based approaches obviously focus primarily on curriculum and assessment, Tyler's first and fourth fundamental questions. His second and third questions concerning instruction generally are not addressed.

Mastery Learning

As noted earlier, most forms of mastery learning today can be traced to Benjamin S. Bloom's pioneering work in the late 1960s. Bloom, a former student of Tyler, recognized the importance of the curriculum issues in Tyler's first fundamental question and the assessment issues in Tyler's fourth. His earlier work in developing the Taxonomies of Educational Objectives (Bloom, Engelhart, Furst, Hill, & Krathwohl, 1956; Krathwohl, Bloom, & Masia, 1964) brought increased clarity and precision to educators' efforts in addressing these issues. In developing mastery learning, however, Bloom focused on the instructional issues involved in Tyler's second and third fundamental questions: "What educational experiences can be provided that are likely to accomplish these purposes?" and "How can these educational experiences be effectively organized?"

Bloom proposed mastery learning as a theory and philosophy about teaching and learning that was linked to a set of practical instructional strategies.

These strategies were designed to give teachers the means to have more of their students learn effectively and excellently whatever was taught (Bloom, 1968).

Note, however, that in developing mastery learning, Bloom set aside curriculum issues. He acknowledged, of course, that curriculum is extremely important. He also strongly encouraged educators engaged in curriculum development to focus on more complex, higher level learning skills. Even though these skills are harder to teach and more difficult to learn, Bloom emphasized that they are retained much longer and are more useful in students' later lives (Bloom, 1978). Nevertheless, Bloom saw mastery learning to be neutral with regard to curriculum. He believed that the instructional strategies of mastery learning would be useful to educators regardless of their curriculum decisions.

A Powerful Tandem

Viewed from this historical perspective, the distinction between performance- or results-based education and mastery learning is clear. Although known by various names, performance-based education is principally a curriculum reform model with definite implications for the assessment of student learning. As such, it directs the attention of educators to Tyler's first and fourth fundamental questions: "What educational purposes should the school seek to attain?" and "How can we determine whether these purposes are being attained?" Mastery learning, on the other hand, is principally an instructional process designed to help teachers enhance the quality of their teaching so that more students learn excellently. As such, it focuses on Tyler's second and third fundamental questions: "What educational experiences can be provided that are likely to accomplish these purposes?" and "How can these educational experiences be effectively organized?"

So while performance-based education and mastery learning are conceptually and theoretically linked, they are clearly distinct. They focus on different educational issues and address different educational concerns. Equally clear, however, is their potential if used in combination.

The finest list of learning goals or standards in the world, even if accompanied by valid assessment tools, represents a wish list at best. It will have little impact on student learning in the absence of effective instructional practices (Guskey, 1994d). At the same time, highly effective instructional strategies must be paired with a thoughtfully planned curriculum. Having students learn well is of little value if what they learn is trivial or unimportant. Only when a thoughtful curriculum is combined with effective instructional practices will true improvement in education become possible. Hence, the combination of performance-based education and mastery learning is likely to prove very powerful. Together they address all four fundamental educational questions posed by Tyler a half century ago.

Major Steps in Implementing Mastery Learning

As mentioned in the Introduction, the tasks involved in implementing mastery learning are usually divided into three steps: (1) planning for mastery learning, (2) managing mastery learning in the classroom, and (3) evaluating in mastery learning. Planning usually takes place before classroom applications begin, while managing and evaluating are focused classroom activities.

The initial planning step involves several tasks. These are outlined in Figure 1.6. First, teachers must review their curriculum and instructional materials to

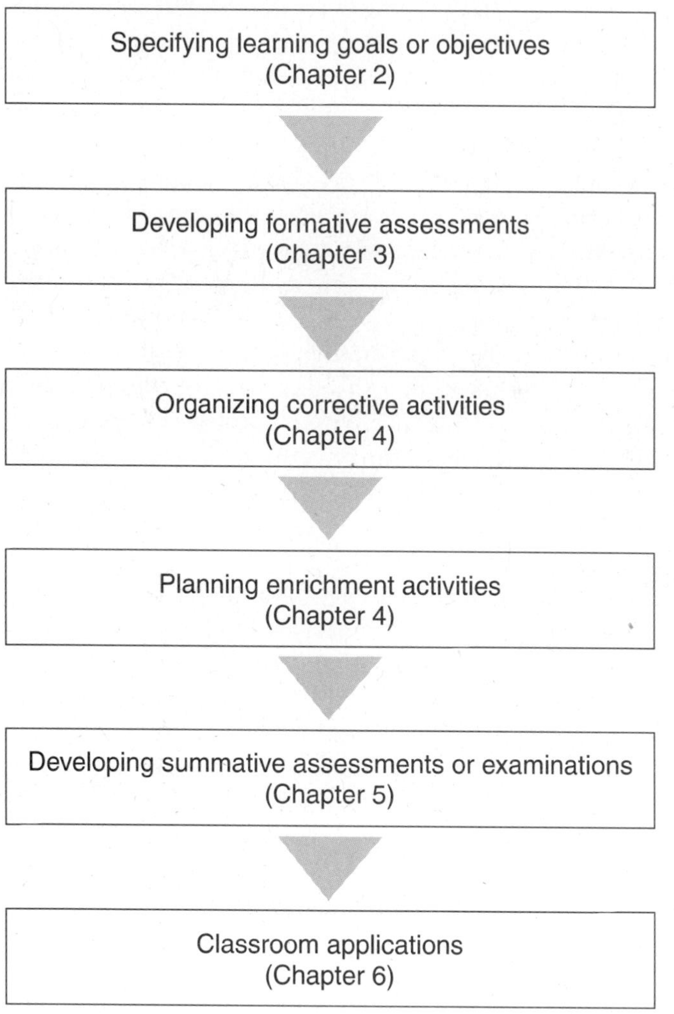

Figure 1.6 Tasks in planning for the implementation of mastery learning

decide what concepts or ideas are most important for students to learn and at what level. This reviewing and decision-making process is sometimes referred to as *valuing* (Block & Anderson, 1975). It involves making judgments about what new concepts and information are important for all students to learn well. It also requires that decisions be made about whether students should be able simply to recall those concepts, apply them in new and different contexts, or synthesize them in meaningful ways.

These decisions are typically outlined in a table of specifications (Bloom, Hastings, & Madaus, 1971; Bloom, Madaus, & Hastings, 1981). These tables are the main topic of Chapter 2. Unlike a lesson plan, a table of specifications lists what is to be taught, but not necessarily how. It also helps to clarify the criteria that will be used to assess or evaluate students' learning and the particular sequence of instruction that might best assist students in attaining mastery. A table of specifications thus serves to enhance the congruence and consistency between what is taught and what evidence will be gathered to verify student learning.

The next tasks in planning involve the development or organization of formative assessments, corrective and enrichment activities, and summative examinations. Again, a formative assessment is basically a diagnostic instrument or process used by the teacher to assess learning. It is also a principal aid in planning corrective measures to remedy learning errors. As such, formative assessments can take many forms. Some are short, objective quizzes made up of matching, multiple-choice, or completion items. Others take the form of essays, compositions, skill demonstrations, projects or reports, performance tasks, or oral presentations. Any one or combination of these assessment forms is appropriate, so long as performance criteria are clearly defined and communicated to students. These and other aspects of formative assessment are discussed in Chapter 3.

Corrective and enrichment activities also may take a variety of forms and usually vary from one unit to the next. For instance, correctives may involve alternative materials or resources, peer or cross-age tutoring, computer-assisted lessons, or any type of learning activity that allows for differences in sensory or motivational preferences. Enrichment activities may also include tutoring, special projects, problem-solving exercises, or any learning activity that is both stimulating and rewarding for fast learners. A variety of useful corrective and enrichment activities are described in Chapter 4.

The effectiveness of the correctives in helping students overcome their learning difficulties is typically determined through the use of a second formative assessment. This second assessment is parallel in form to the first formative assessment for the unit, but it usually is not identical; that is, it covers the same concepts and material as the first assessment but asks questions in a slightly different way or format. If, on the other hand, the formative assessment takes the form of a composition or skill demonstration, then the scoring criteria or rubric would be identical for both formatives. In this case, the correctives would involve simply revising and refining what was done on the first assessment.

If the correctives have been successful in helping students remedy their learning difficulties, then almost all students will demonstrate their mastery on the second formative assessment. This second assessment also becomes a powerful motivational device by showing students directly that they can improve their learning and become successful learners.

Finally, there is the development of a summative examination or assessment. This examination is a culminating demonstration of what students have learned. Typically, it is broader based and wider in scope than any of the individual formative assessments, and it is usually administered after several units of instruction. It is designed to assess the criterion goals or outcomes of the course and often is used as a basis for certifying competence or assigning grades. Summative examinations are the focus of Chapter 5.

After deciding what is important for students to learn and organizing or developing the formative assessments, correctives, and enrichment activities, the teacher's attention focuses on managing and coordinating mastery learning within the classroom. Management tasks include informing students and their parents of the intentions and procedures of mastery learning, and then administering the cycle of instruction → diagnostic assessment → correctives or enrichment → second diagnostic assessment. Managing the corrective and enrichment activities is probably the most challenging aspect of this process. The teacher must make decisions about how much class time versus out-of-class time to allow for correctives, what kinds of corrective activities will work best, and how to encourage students' active engagement in correctives. Other decisions involve determining whether students who have mastered the concepts from the unit should be asked to aid those who have not, or whether they should be engaged in some other form of enrichment or extension activity. In addition, teachers must ensure that enrichment is a rewarding and challenging learning experience, rather than simply a requirement to complete more and harder problems.

Any one corrective or enrichment activity is unlikely to work all of the time. Most teachers find that variation is necessary to maintain students' interest and motivation. In most cases, about 10 percent more time is needed in the learning unit for the corrective and enrichment process, with somewhat more time needed during the early stages of implementation and less later on. Time issues and other specific application concerns are considered in Chapter 6.

After managing the implementation of mastery learning over a series of units, the teacher's final step is to evaluate the final competence of students by administering a summative examination or assessment. At this time, too, the teacher should consider how the procedures might be revised in future implementation efforts. Ideally, close to 80 percent of students in a class should attain the high level of achievement that was previously attained by only about 20 percent. Although relatively few teachers gain results this dramatic when they first implement mastery learning, nearly all realize startling improvements over past results (Block, Efthim, & Burns, 1989). Most also find that improvements steadily increase as they become more comfortable with the process and adapt it to more closely fit their students' needs (Guskey, 1982a, 1985b).

The Role of the Teacher Using Mastery Learning

Because of mastery learning's flexibility in classroom applications, it is not unusual to find two teachers in the same school teaching the same subject at the same grade level and applying mastery learning in different but equally effective ways. Their applications, of course, will have many common elements. For instance, both are likely to follow a similar sequence of teaching their lessons and involving students in learning as they think best, checking on student learning through some type of formative assessment, providing correctives paired with a second assessment for students who need additional assistance, and offering enrichment to extend the learning of students for whom the initial instruction was highly appropriate. But the teachers may be quite different in how they engage students in learning during their initial instruction, the type of formative assessment employed, how the corrective process is carried out, how the correctives are checked, and the type of enrichment activities employed. This flexibility in mastery learning's application has contributed to its widespread acceptance among teachers at all levels.

In addition, mastery learning principles can be broadly applied. Most teachers can see how mastery learning might be used to teach subjects that are structured and hierarchical, such as some topics in mathematics. But mastery learning is equally effective in subjects that are less structured, such as language arts or social studies, or when the focus of instruction is likely to be on higher level skills, such as problem solving, drawing inferences, deductive reasoning, or creative writing (Arredondo & Block, 1990; Mevarech, 1985, 1991; Soled, 1987).

In teaching creative writing, for example, the teacher must first be able to describe, in some detail, the difference between compositions that are and are not creative. If that difference cannot be clearly described, then what is the teacher to teach? Describing that difference is an essential prerequisite to teaching the higher level skills associated with creative writing. Furthermore, as soon as that difference is described, a basis is established for offering students feedback on their writing, as well as guidance in correcting their errors and making revisions. The result is that the composition that is not creative becomes more like one that is. In other words, a basis is established for using mastery learning, even in an advanced, highly complex subject such as creative writing.

In a writing class, students' compositions serve as the formative assessments. They are submitted to the teacher and evaluated in terms of criteria the teacher has taught. In some cases, fellow students may offer diagnostic feedback following directions from the teacher. Compositions are then returned to students with suggestions for revision based on the specified criteria. Corrective activities would involve helping students make their revisions, using different techniques than those employed in the initial teaching. Once completed, the revised compositions are submitted to the teacher as the second formative assessment.

Related to the flexibility and broad application of mastery learning is the fact that, unlike most other new approaches to teaching and learning, mastery learning does not require teachers to make major changes in their current methods of instruction. Instead, it is a practical tool that can be used with the instructional skills and talents that a teacher has already developed. Teachers are usually encouraged to adapt mastery learning, particularly the use of the feedback and corrective elements, to the unique characteristics of their classroom situations and students.

These aspects of mastery learning make it tremendously appealing to experienced teachers who are often the best judges of what will and will not work well in their classrooms. Such teachers generally have a wide repertoire of instructional tactics and are quite resourceful in drawing on them. In many cases, elements of the mastery learning process are already a part of their regular teaching practices. As they become more familiar with mastery learning, most teachers find that they are able to apply these elements in a more purposeful and systematic way to enhance the overall effectiveness of their teaching (Guskey, 1980b, 1987a).

Even though mastery learning can be easily adapted to a wide variety of teaching styles and instructional methods, its use still implies an important change in the teacher's classroom "role." In many traditional classroom settings, learning is a highly competitive endeavor in which students compete with one another for the few scarce rewards (high grades) that are given out by the teacher. This is especially true when students are graded "on the curve," or in terms of their relative standing among classmates. These norm-referenced standards–that is, comparing each student's progress to her or his classmates'–tend to intensify a sense of competition among students. They quickly recognize that helping a classmate might jeopardize their own chances for "success." Under these conditions, the teacher serves mostly as a rule maker and director of the competition, the one who is primarily responsible for making judgments, evaluations, and classifications of students.

With mastery learning, however, learning becomes much more cooperative than competitive. Students' learning is evaluated in terms of criterion-referenced standards–that is, based on what they have learned and are able to do–rather than their relative standing among classmates. For students, this means that it is no longer detrimental for one student to help another. In fact, teachers often find that peer tutoring and other forms of cooperative learning begin to occur spontaneously in mastery learning classrooms (Guskey, 1980a, 1990a). Under these conditions, the students and teacher are both on the same side, and out to "master" what is to be learned. Thus the teacher becomes more of an instructional leader and learning facilitator, and less of a competition manager. This change in role is another appealing aspect of mastery learning to most teachers.

Mastery learning will certainly not solve all of the problems teachers must face, but it has proven to be a way in which teachers can greatly increase the number of students who learn–and learn very well–the important concepts they set out to teach. In addition, mastery learning has the advantages of being an instructional process that is adaptable and that blends well with the professional skills teachers have already developed and refined.

Summary

Mastery learning was developed by Benjamin S. Bloom to help teachers provide a higher quality of instruction for more of their students. In deriving the process, Bloom extended the ideas of John B. Carroll's theoretical learning model. He also drew on knowledge of the elements of one-to-one tutoring and successful individualized instructional programs, as well as the learning strategies employed by successful learners. The process he outlined included procedures for (1) providing students with regular feedback on their learning progress, and (2) then pairing that feedback with specific corrective activities designed to help students remedy their individual learning difficulties. Through the careful use of these feedback and corrective procedures, and enrichment activities to extend the learning of fast learners, Bloom believed that 80 percent or more of the students in a class could attain the same high level of achievement that only 20 percent attain under more traditional instructional methods.

There are two essential elements in mastery learning that serve specific purposes. The first is the feedback, corrective, and enrichment process. The second is congruence among instructional components, or alignment. These two elements show that mastery learning is both flexible and broad in its applications and, as a result, highly appealing to teachers at all levels. These elements also distinguish mastery learning from other approaches to individualization, and they show how it can be meaningfully combined with various performance-based education models.

Mastery learning is usually implemented through a careful process of organization and planning, followed by specific procedures for classroom application and student assessment or evaluation. Mastery learning does not challenge teachers' professionalism or academic freedom but instead offers a useful instructional tool that can be flexibly applied in a variety of teaching situations. Although it is not an educational cure-all, mastery learning significantly increases the positive influence teachers can have on student learning.

Questions for Discussion

1. What changes in perspective might a teacher need to make to be successful in implementing mastery learning? Explain.
2. What obstacles might stand in the way of a teacher who wants to implement mastery learning? How could these be avoided or overcome? How might the teacher contend with those obstacles that cannot be avoided or overcome?
3. Have any of the teachers you have known as a student used elements of mastery learning? If so, which elements? At what level of education? How successful was their use? How might that teacher have been even more successful?
4. Do you think there are some subjects or areas of instruction in which the mastery learning process will not work? Are there certain levels of education at which implementation might be less successful? Explain your answer.

2

Outlining Learning Goals and Objectives

We now turn our attention to the initial tasks in planning for the implementation of mastery learning. The first task is to set out, in specific terms, what students are expected to learn and be able to do as a result of their involvement in a particular learning unit. These expectations are generally referred to as *learning goals, learning outcomes,* or *learning objectives*. They are the main topic of this chapter.

Learning goals and objectives describe the concepts, skills, and abilities that students are to acquire by engaging in learning activities. Specifying goals and objectives requires that a series of important decisions be made about what is essential for students to learn and at what level that learning should occur. While these decisions are fundamental to the use of mastery learning, they are also an integral part of effective teaching in any context. Clearly articulated learning goals and objectives not only serve to focus instructional activities, but also add precision to procedures for assessing or evaluating students' learning. In mastery learning, they further serve as a basis for developing formative assessments and planning feedback and corrective activities.

Some educators argue that the specification of learning goals and objectives restricts students' acquisition of knowledge by narrowing the focus of learning to only those ideas, concepts, and performance skills the teacher feels are important. As they correctly point out, a great deal of learning takes place in the absence of directed teaching.

Nevertheless, teaching is, by definition, a purposeful and intentional activity. To engage in teaching implies helping students develop specific insights and understandings. And, as others (Bruner, 1960; Flavell, 1971; Polya, 1973; Prawat,

1989) have noted, if students are to develop these insights and higher level cognitive skills, they must be involved in instruction that emphasizes the organization of knowledge and important connections to other knowledge. Thus even those who advocate a "constructivist" view of learning (Prawat, 1992a) and who see teaching as inducing conceptual change in students rather than infusing knowledge into a vacuum (Brophy, 1992) recognize the importance of clarity and focus in teaching.

The process of identifying instructional goals also need not be solely a teacher-dominated activity. It is certainly possible, and in many cases advisable, to involve students in the process of specifying learning goals and objectives. Although students' perspectives may be limited because of their lack of experience or insufficient knowledge base, considering their input in these decisions helps illustrate that learning is a shared experience in which students are active participants, not simply passive recipients. Furthermore, involving students in this process can add authenticity to the goals that are ultimately specified.

Still other educators argue that the purpose of teaching is not to help students acquire knowledge, but to help them develop certain *cognitive strategies.* These strategies are also referred to as *learning skills, cognitive skills,* or *heuristics.* They are guides or mental maps to the solution of problems. To some educators, these cognitive strategies are the principal goal of instructional activities. Others consider such strategies an interim step between students' abilities and the true instructional goal, which might be to have students construct meaning from text or solve complex problems (Rosenshine, 1993). In either case, clear specification of that goal remains of critical importance.

To assist teachers in making decisions about what is important for students to learn and at what level, many school districts have developed curriculum guides or curriculum frameworks. In addition, many commercial publishers provide lists of the particular learning goals or objectives their materials are designed to help students attain. These frameworks and lists of learning goals vary widely in their quality and detail. Still, most teachers find them helpful in selecting learning materials and the methods of instruction that best fit their students' needs. Some commercial materials even include tests or other assessment devices for checking on students' learning progress. These, too, not only can be useful, but also can help reduce the amount of preparation time required of teachers.

Unfortunately, few commercial materials are universally applicable. Refinements and adaptations are usually necessary to meet the needs of particular groups of students or the instructional preferences of different teachers. Therefore, along with considering the decisions that need to be made in outlining learning goals and objectives, in this chapter we will also consider procedures for reviewing and adapting the learning goals and materials that may be already available.

The Importance of a Structure for Learning

Generally, when scholars or researchers reach a certain level of sophistication in a subject, they are able to see definite relations among the ideas and concepts in that subject. These relations help them understand more complex phenomena and aid them in conducting further study. In many cases, curriculum writers, most of whom are also experts in the subject, assume that the structure of the knowledge in that subject is synonymous with an appropriate structure for teaching and learning that subject. Unfortunately, this is not always true.

For example, several modern mathematics and science curricula were based on the belief that if the sophisticated organizing principles that experts found so helpful could be provided to young people learning the subject, then the young people would find the subject much easier to learn. Researchers quickly discovered, however, that while these organizing principles are useful for specialized scholarship, they are not always useful in helping the majority of students learn the subject. As Bloom, Hastings, and Madaus (1971, p. 12) point out, "The usefulness of a structure for learning has to do with the ability of students to comprehend it and use it as an organizing factor in their learning. There is no relation between the usefulness of a structure for scholars and its usefulness (and meaningfulness) for students."

Students do learn more easily when provided with a structure that helps them relate various aspects of the subject. Such a structure also helps students gain deeper meaning from what might otherwise be a large number of unconnected specifics. For this reason, many teachers take time at the outset of instruction to highlight certain organizational and structural patterns that can help students better assimilate new information or ideas in a subject. Before students read about the French Revolution, for example, the teacher might take time to present the conceptual scheme of a revolutionary movement's phases. These conceptual frameworks are generally referred to as *advance organizers* (Ausubel, 1979, 1980). In most cases, they are simple verbal or visual bridges, provided by the teacher, to help students link their previous knowledge to whatever is to be learned. Research studies on advance organizers show that providing students with such a framework can have a positive effect on both learning and retention (Ausubel, 1963; Luiten, Ames, & Ackerson, 1980; Slate & Charlesworth, 1989; Stone, 1983).

Similarly, investigations on the use of instructional *scaffolds* indicate they can be highly effective as well. Scaffolds are the temporary supports provided by the teacher, or more capable students, to bridge the gap between students' current understandings and the learning goal (Palincsar & Brown, 1984, 1988; Paris, Wixson, & Palincsar, 1986; Tobias, 1982). Scaffolding reduces the complexities of problems for students by breaking the problems down into manageable chunks that students have a real chance of solving. Essentially, it reduces the demands of the problem and allows students "to participate at an ever-increasing level of competence" (Palincsar & Brown, 1984, p. 122). Scaffolds include providing simplified problems, modeling by the teacher, and thinking aloud explanations as the teacher solves the problem. Scaffolds are then generally withdrawn as students become more competent and independent, although students may continue to rely on them or may even request them when particularly difficult problems are encountered (Rosenshine, 1993; Rosenshine & Meister, 1992).

A structure for learning should thus provide students with a mechanism they can use to better understand the instruction and to organize the concepts they are learning. It should also provide students with a way to move from one level of learning to another. Keep in mind, however, that a structure for learning is based primarily on learning or pedagogical considerations and may not be the same as an expert's or scholar's view of the field.

Organizing Learning Units

Developing or organizing an appropriate structure for learning generally involves three elements.

1. The final learning goal must be specified. This goal is usually defined as a competent learner who has truly mastered those concepts and understandings that are part of the unit and who is able to demonstrate appropriately what was learned.
2. The final learning goal must be analyzed to identify the steps that are necessary to reach the goal.
3. The steps must be ordered in a meaningful sequence to facilitate learning and provide for steady and regular progress toward the goal.

Although these three elements may seem implicit in all teaching, one or more is often neglected. For instance, the daily burdens of teaching can sometimes distract a teacher's perspective from the final learning goal. As a result, instructional efforts lose their focus and cohesion. Similarly, concentrating solely on the goal without careful attention to the separate steps required to reach that goal can result in frustration for both teachers and students. Both the final goal and the sequence of steps required to reach that goal need to be kept in mind for teaching and learning to be effective.

The process of analyzing a learning goal and then organizing the steps necessary to reach that goal is a natural part of most teaching and learning activities. Consider, for example, how you might teach a child to play tennis. You would probably begin with a mental picture of the child playing tennis: approaching the ball, swinging smoothly, and returning the ball to the other court. This is the goal you would hope to attain at the end of the learning process.

From that mental picture you would begin by dividing the components of that final learning goal into various steps. You would probably think about adjusting the racket to the child's size and strength, adjusting the child's grip for backhand and forehand returns, explaining to the child the importance of watching the ball, and showing the child how to move to the ball to make the backswing, return, and follow-through, and then recover for the next return. You would also need to demonstrate serving, as well as explain the rules of the game and how to keep score.

Given this breakdown, you would then decide on an appropriate sequence of learning steps. You might decide to order the steps in terms of difficulty or complexity. The most basic elements, such as watching the ball, would be presented before more complicated steps, such as an appropriate follow-through. Then, as you begin teaching, you would want to make sure the child is actively engaged, while you watch for any special problems the child may be experiencing. These you would try to correct as they appear. You would also try to be aware of individual differences among children and adapt your teaching to those differences. For example, some children play well using a traditional stance while others do better with a more open stance. In addition, you would probably make a point of complimenting the child whenever progress was evident and providing reassurances at other times. And, of course, you would want to emphasize the enjoyable aspects of the game and give the child opportunities to experience these whenever possible.

This example illustrates the process that takes place in most effective teaching and learning situations. The learning goal, or what is sometimes referred to as the *summative goal,* is first analyzed in terms of the parts that need to be learned or mastered. Those parts are then organized and arranged in a meaningful sequence of learning steps. Care is taken to ensure that each step is understood, practiced, and mastered while progress is made toward that final goal and adaptations are made for individual differences among students.

Similarly, to begin the use of mastery learning, a teacher must first identify the final learning goal and define the specific steps that need to be mastered to reach that goal. Many teachers do this regularly as a part of their instructional planning; that is, they start with a mental picture of a competent learner at the end of an instructional sequence and then divide the concepts and skills that must be learned over the year or term to reach that goal into smaller segments or steps. Each step is then considered a "learning unit."

The delineation of learning units is somewhat arbitrary in many cases. Ideally, learning units should be determined by natural breaks in the subject material or by content elements that make a meaningful whole. Therefore each unit might not cover exactly the same amount of content or exactly the same number of concepts or skills. Textbook publishers usually use these natural breaks to divide the content of a particular subject. For this reason, chapters in textbooks often represent appropriate learning units.

Instructional time is another critical element in determining learning units. A learning unit should contain the knowledge, concepts, and skills that can be presented in a week or two of classroom time. Generally, learning units at the high school or college level are longer and cover more material than those in the elementary grades. A unit in a high school course may last more than two weeks and cover fifteen or twenty important concepts. An early elementary school unit, on the other hand, seldom lasts more than a week and may cover a single concept or skill. If learning units are made too short, however, then the learning can become fragmented, and generalizations or higher level skills will be difficult to build. But if units are too long, then students who fall behind because of particular learning problems may have great difficulty catching up. Thus not only the content but also the pace of instruction and the kinds of students involved in the learning need to be considered in determining appropriate learning units.

Identifying learning units involves thoughtful judgment on the part of teachers. But all teachers do this already as part of their instructional planning. Many use textbooks or curriculum frameworks in making these decisions, and all give some consideration to instructional time. The key, therefore, is not to alter decisions that have already been made, but simply to approach those decisions with careful thought and a clear vision of the final learning goal.

Tables of Specifications

Once the sequence of learning units is clearly delineated, the next task is to specify the learning objectives of each unit. To do this, a teacher must first identify the new concepts and material that will be presented in each unit.

Many teachers develop detailed outlines of the new material they plan to present and often consider this material to be the objective of the unit. They might describe, for example, the political, economic, and social factors that led to the American Civil War, or the similarities and differences between equilateral, isosceles, and right triangles. But even though detailed outlines of new material can be particularly useful in teaching, they say nothing about what students might be expected to do with that material. For instance, should students simply know these factors and definitions, or should they be able to explain them in their own words, to cite specific examples, or to see how these factors and definitions apply in new problem situations? The answers to these questions will have clear implications for both how the unit is taught and how student learning will be assessed.

In specifying learning objectives for a unit, therefore, we must consider not only the material or content students are expected to learn, but also the specific skills and understandings they will be expected to develop in relation to that content. In other words, we need to be clear about what students will be expected *to do* with what they have learned. These skills and understandings indicate the ways we would like students to be able to think, act, or feel about the material, and about themselves, about others, and so forth. What students are expected to do with the material is just as important to consider as the material itself.

Another factor that needs to be considered in specifying learning objectives is the level of generality (Gronlund, 1995). Teachers sometimes describe their expectations for student learning in explicit and highly detailed ways. This practice was especially popular during the 1970s and 1980s when teachers were required to "teach to objectives." In developing their learning objectives, many teachers would begin with the phrase, "The student will be able to. . . ." They would complete the phrase with a verb selected from the Taxonomy of Educational Objectives (Bloom et al., 1956) that described the particular skill they hoped students would acquire. Their objective would end with a description of the content related to that skill.

Stating objectives so narrowly and in such specific detail can reduce instruction to a lockstep type of training program. The flexibility, creativity, and spontaneity of both teachers and students are often restricted, and learning can become regimented. The teacher who feels compelled to address as many as three or four such minutely defined objectives during each class session has little time for anything else.

In more recent years, emphasis has shifted away from such narrowly defined objectives and toward descriptions of broadly defined proficiencies, competencies, or goals. Many educators today, for instance, want their students "to develop the skills and understandings necessary to become life-long learners." Broad definitions such as these offer a "big picture" view of what an excellent educational program should provide. Unfortunately, they offer little instructional guidance to practically minded classroom teachers who must be concerned with daily lessons and unit plans.

Ideally, learning objectives should fall somewhere between these two extreme positions on the generality continuum; that is, they should be specific enough to provide focus for both teaching and the assessment of student learning. At the same time, they should be broad enough to enhance a teacher's flexibility in selecting instructional methods and materials (Gronlund, 1995).

We have found that one useful and efficient way to accomplish this balance is to outline the new concepts and skills students are expected to attain through their involvement in a learning unit in a simple two-dimensional table. This table is sometimes called a "mastery chart" or a "content map." More generally, it is referred to as a *table of specifications*.

A table of specifications is basically an outline of the learning goals and objectives for a unit. As such, it serves two important functions. First, it adds precision and clarity to teaching. The information on the table should be precise enough to convey exactly what is intended in the instruction and clear enough that students can be helped to fully understand what they are expected to learn.

Many teachers go through a similar specification process as a regular part of their class preparations. But too often what is expected of students is never made clear until the test or assessment is administered. In these instances, students are required to guess what is important and what is inconsequential in each unit. Although some students are good at guessing what they are expected to learn, many others are not. For those who are not, learning soon becomes a frustrating experience. Specifying the goals and objectives for learning in a clear and precise way, and then clearly communicating these to students, not only eliminates much of this guesswork but also helps organize and focus teaching and learning activities.

The second function of a table of specifications is to serve as a guide for consistency between learning goals and objectives, and procedures for checking on students' learning progress. Although this kind of consistency is critically important for learning, it too is often neglected or given only cursory attention. For example, many classroom teachers stress that they want their students to develop higher cognitive skills such as the ability to make applications, analyses, or syntheses. However, the vast majority of classroom quizzes and tests tap only those skills that are easiest to assess, such as knowledge of the definitions of terms or specific facts.

A table of specifications can be used as a guide in preparing a wide variety of assessment and evaluation procedures. In this way, it can help to guarantee consistency between the important goals and objectives, and the procedures used for checking on students' learning (see, for example, the sample tables in Chapters 9 through 14).

Functions of the Tables of Specifications

1. Add precision and clarity to teaching.
2. Provide consistency between learning goals and assessments.

Steps in Developing a Table of Specifications

The first step in preparing a table of specifications is to address the question, "What should students learn from this unit?" In other words, what new concepts or material are to be introduced in the learning unit that are important for students to learn? What are the new terms, facts, relations, procedures, understandings, and so forth that are explained, defined, illustrated, or otherwise presented in the unit?

Usually, textbooks and other learning resources are relatively clear in signaling when new material or concepts are being introduced and can be a useful guide in answering these questions. Changes in print or color, comments in the margins (particularly in teachers' editions of textbooks or curriculum guides), and summaries at the end of chapters often are helpful in identifying new content. Still, textbooks need not be a teacher's only guide. At all levels, teachers should feel free to add to, or delete from, what the textbook provides in order to better fit students' needs.

The next step is to address the question, "What should students be able to do with what they learn?" The answer involves determining the particular student skills, abilities, or understandings that should be paired with the new concepts and material. For example, will students be required simply to remember or recall the new content, or will we want them to be able to use it in a new or different way?

Questions to Address in Developing a Table of Specifications

1. What should students learn from this unit?
2. What should students be able to do with what they learn?

In specifying their answers to these questions, many teachers find it useful to classify the new elements of content according to some of the categories in *Taxonomy of Educational Objectives, Handbook I: Cognitive Domain* (Bloom et al., 1956). These categories represent a hierarchy of levels that differ in terms of cognitive complexity and difficulty. The lowest levels represent the simplest kinds of learning, while higher levels represent more advanced cognitive skills. The categories that are most useful in a wide variety of subject areas are shown in the table of specifications in Figure 2.1. These levels include:

1. *Knowledge of terms*. Terms are the new words or phrases that students are expected to learn. They may include new vocabulary, names, expressions, or symbols. Students may be expected to know the definitions of these terms, recognize illustrations of them, determine when they are used correctly, or recognize synonyms. Examples would include the terms *factor* and *product* in a mathematics unit on multiplication, or *photosynthesis* in a science unit dealing with plant life. The *knowledge* level here implies simple recognition or recall, and it is generally considered to be the simplest level of student learning. All new words, phrases, names, expressions, and symbols that are to be introduced and explained in the unit are listed in the table under "Terms."

Table of Specifications						
Knowledge of				Translations	Applications	Analyses and Syntheses
Terms	Facts	Rules and Principles	Processes and Procedures			

Figure 2.1 General outline for a table of specifications

2. *Knowledge of facts.* Facts are the specific types of information that students are expected to remember. In general, facts are particular details that are important in their own right or essential for other kinds of learning. Facts include names of persons, events, operations, or other kinds of specific information. Students may be expected to recall particular facts or remember the correct fact when asked about it in a relatively direct manner. Examples are "The Declaration of Independence was signed on July 4, 1776," and "Stephen Crane wrote *The Red Badge of Courage.*" Any new facts in the unit that are important for students to learn and remember should be listed in the "Facts"column.

3. *Knowledge of rules and principles.* Rules and principles concern specific patterns or schemes that are used to organize a subject's major ideas. Generally, they bring together facts or describe the interrelationships among specifics. As such, they are sometimes considered "organizers," "scaffolds," "guidelines," or simply "organizational tools." Students may be expected to know a rule or principle, to remember an illustration of it used during instruction, or to recall situations in which it was applied.

In most cases, rules and principles are more difficult to learn than terms or facts, but they also are retained longer by students. But keep in mind that this category deals only with the *knowledge* of rules and principles, not their application, which is a more complex level. Examples of rules and principles include the "commutative principle" in mathematics and the "rules for subject–verb agreement" in grammar. New rules and principles in a unit should be listed in the table.

4. *Knowledge of processes and procedures.* In many subjects, students are expected to know the particular steps involved in a certain process or procedure. Frequently, these steps must be recalled in a specific sequence. For example, students may be expected to know the specific patterns of character development used in a novel, the appropriate order of steps in a mathematics problem-solving task, or the sequence of events necessary to enact legislation in Congress. In cases such as these, students must know that this happens first, this happens second, and so forth.

Processes and procedures often involve many terms or facts and are typically more difficult for students to learn. Any new processes or procedures that are part of the unit should be included in the table. Keep in mind, however, that these are the processes and procedures we want students to learn, *not* the instructional processes or procedures we plan to use in teaching the unit.

5. *Ability to make translations.* Translation involves the transformation of a term, fact, rule, or process from one form to another. In making a translation, students express particular ideas or concepts in a new way or take phenomena or events in one form and represent them in another, equivalent form. As such, translation implies the ability to distinguish, describe, or compute. Students may be expected, for example, to recognize new illustrations of a term, fact, rule, or other matter or to determine whether a new illustration is appropriate.

In general, students employ translation when they put an idea in their own words or recognize new examples of what they have already learned. Translation in this sense should not be confused with translation in foreign language instruction, although they are similar. The specific translation skills students will be expected to learn should also be listed in the table.

6. *Ability to make applications.* Application is the use of terms, facts, principles, or procedures to solve problems in new or unfamiliar situations. Students may be expected to use ideas or concepts learned in one context to solve a problem presented in a new one. Or they may be expected to illustrate their understanding in a unique format or otherwise to demonstrate what they have learned. Remember, however, that if the problem is one that students have encountered previously–except that new data are substituted–then the skill called for is really translation rather than application. Asking students to identify the grammatical errors in sentences written by others, for example, typically involves only translation. But to have students use their knowledge of grammar to write clear and concise sentences of their own would involve application.

The difference between translations and applications also depends on the way particular ideas and concepts are taught. Hence an application for the students of one teacher might be a translation for the students of another, depending on differences in the examples used in class presentations or practices. For this reason, providing specific examples is difficult.

In general, to make applications students must first recognize the essentials for the new problem; determine the facts, rules, procedures, and so forth that are relevant; and then use these to solve the problem. As such, the ability to make applications is a fairly complex behavior and the highest level of learning objective used by most teachers. The application skills that students are expected to develop in a unit should be included in the table.

7. *Skill in making analyses and syntheses.* An even more advanced skill is that of making analyses and syntheses. Analyses generally involve the breakdown

of concepts into their constituent parts and the detection of the relationships among those parts. They require students to explain, infer, or compare and contrast. Syntheses, on the other hand, involve putting together elements or concepts in a way that develops a meaningful pattern or structure. Syntheses often call for students to develop creative solutions within the limits of a particular problem or methodological framework. They typically require students to combine, construct, or integrate what they have learned.

Because of the complexity of these behaviors, analyses and syntheses are sometimes considered only in more advanced grades or in higher level classes. However, some teachers feel that these skills are important, and they try to include practice in these kinds of activities for students at all levels. Examples of analyses are "Distinguish facts from opinions in a communication" and "Identify conclusions and their supporting statements." An example of synthesis is "Write a paragraph that organizes a set of ideas and statements." Those included in a unit as part of students' learning should be described in the table.

Once they become familiar with the table of specifications, teachers generally have little difficulty outlining learning objectives in terms of these categories. Using their textbooks or other learning materials as a guide, most find they are able to answer the first question–"What should students learn from this unit?"–in the first four knowledge level categories. This is because textbooks and other learning resources typically present new material at the knowledge level (Tyson-Bernstein, 1988). In addressing the second question, "What should students be able to do with what they learn?" most also discover they must move beyond what their instructional materials alone provide. Curriculum guides or frameworks often are helpful in making decisions about these more complex cognitive levels, but a teacher's thoughtful and sensitive judgment is essential in the process. The descriptions offered in Figure 2.2 (page 40) are designed to assist in answering these questions and making these decisions.

Relationships Among Learning Objectives

Besides listing the new concepts and understandings that are a part of each unit, and indicating the skills and abilities students are expected to develop in relation to those concepts, the table of specifications can also be used to illustrate relationships *among* concepts. Knowing the definition of a term, for example, may be necessary to understanding a fact pertaining to that term. Or knowing two or three facts may be essential in understanding a particular procedure. Similarly, knowing a procedure is likely to be a prerequisite to being able to apply that procedure in solving a complex problem.

Many teachers find it helpful to illustrate these relationships on the table by drawing connecting lines between related concepts. For instance, lines might be

Table of Specifications						
Knowledge of						
Terms	**Facts**	**Rules and Principles**	**Processes and Procedures**	**Translations**	**Applications**	**Analyses and Syntheses**
New vocabulary Words Expressions Names Phrases Symbols	Specifc information Dates Events Persons Operations	Guidelines Organiza-tional cues Relation-ships	Order of events or operations Patterns Sequences Steps	Classify Compute Describe Discuss Distinguish Identify Interpret Predict Recognize	Construct Demonstrate Illustrate Relate Solve Use	Combine Compare and contrast Develop Infer Integrate Organize Summarize

Figure 2.2 Description of the categories in a table of specifications

drawn from two or three new terms to a fact that incorporates these terms. A line could also be drawn from knowledge of a particular procedure to the application of that procedure. Drawing these lines on the table generally helps the teacher keep these relationships in mind so that they can be developed more fully for students. An example illustrating these relationships for an elementary social studies unit is shown in Figure 2.3.

Subject Area Differences

Learning goals and objectives from nearly any subject can be outlined according to the categories shown in the table of specifications in Figure 2.1. However, all of these categories may not be applicable to a particular subject or particular unit. Some social studies units, for example, may include no new rules and principles. Similarly, many mathematics units include no new terms. Thus some of the categories in a table of specifications for a particular subject or unit may be omitted or left blank. Only those categories that are useful in listing the new concepts and specifying the skills expected of students in relation to those concepts need to be included. These subject differences can be seen by inspecting the tables of specifications in Chapters 9 through 14.

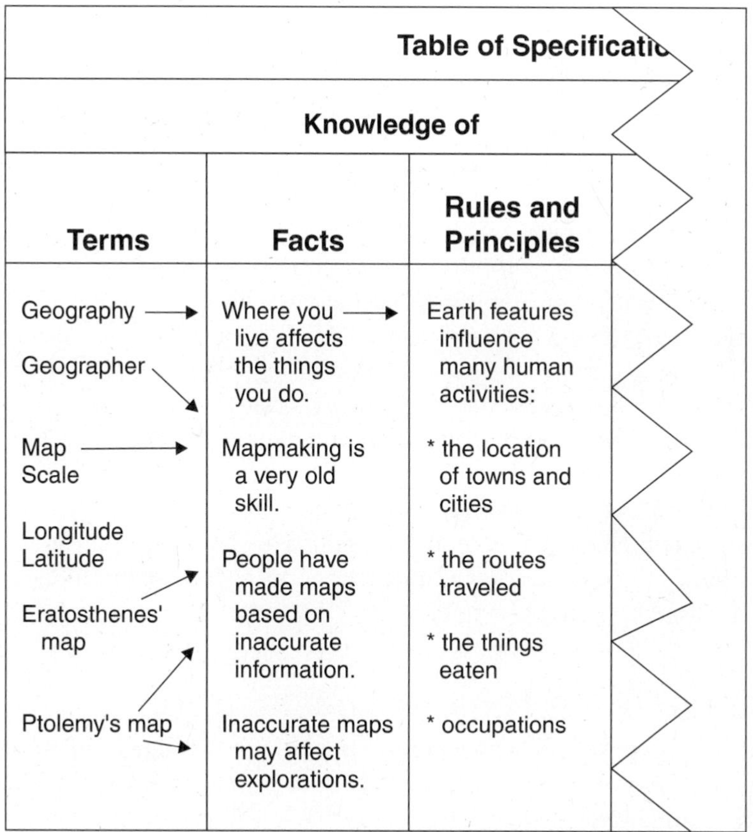

Table of Specificatio[ns]		
Knowledge of		
Terms	**Facts**	**Rules and Principles**
Geography → Geographer	Where you live affects the things you do.	Earth features influence many human activities:
Map → Scale	Mapmaking is a very old skill.	* the location of towns and cities
Longitude Latitude Eratosthenes' map	People have made maps based on inaccurate information.	* the routes traveled * the things eaten
Ptolemy's map	Inaccurate maps may affect explorations.	* occupations

Figure 2.3 Portion of a table of specifications showing related concepts in an elementary social studies unit

The difficulty of preparing a table of specifications also varies somewhat by subject. Some, such as mathematics and science, lend themselves quite easily to this format. Identifying the new terms, facts, rules, and procedures that are part of a mathematics or science unit usually is not difficult. However, subjects such as reading, composition, language arts, and social studies are not as easily categorized. Special adaptations are sometimes necessary for these subjects, as can be seen in the language arts unit in Chapter 11.

Many teachers today, especially at the elementary and middle grade levels, employ *integrated* or *thematic* units of instruction (Drake, 1993; Jacobs, 1989). These units fuse concepts from several disciplines to allow teachers to teach important ideas or understandings more effectively. For example, a teacher might use problems from science to provide a context for the knowledge and skills that students are learning in mathematics. Similarly, learning in a social studies unit might be enhanced by having students read particular pieces of literature from the period of time or region they are studying. For teachers who use interdisciplinary units, the table of specifications is an effective tool for both illustrating relationships across the disciplines and helping students develop a more meaningful context for their learning.

Regardless of whether units are subject-specific or interdisciplinary, it remains important to clearly specify the new concepts and ideas that are important for students to learn, and the skills students are expected to develop in relation to those concepts. For instance, in helping students develop their skills in drawing inferences, a necessary first step is to specify the various components that are a part of the process of drawing inferences and how students should use those components. Clarifying precisely the characteristics that distinguish students who can draw appropriate inferences from those who cannot also will be important. Finally, but perhaps most important, the teacher must consider a variety of methods to help students who are having difficulty drawing appropriate inferences to acquire that skill. This kind of specification not only can enhance the organization of instruction, but also can help students become more focused in their learning efforts.

Adaptations to the Table of Specifications

As teachers become more skilled in developing tables of specifications and more proficient in using them, they often make adaptations to the general format of the table to better suit their teaching style and the needs of their students. Many teachers, for example, add an additional "Review" column to the left side of the table. In this column they list those concepts or ideas that were part of earlier instructional units but still need to be "refreshed" before new information is presented that builds on them. The elements listed in the review column might even come from previous courses or instruction that took place in previous years. Including these elements in the table reminds the teacher to take some time in helping students clarify their understanding of those concepts and in building a solid foundation for the new learning that is to come.

Other teachers combine certain columns on the table to simplify their work. One common combination is a "Terms and Facts" column. This practice is especially popular among teachers in the early elementary grades, where much of the new information students are expected to learn involves specific vocabulary.

Still other teachers divide the table of specifications with horizontal lines to organize the concepts and material from the unit into daily lessons. This is particularly helpful to those teachers who use the table as a guide in developing their daily lesson plans. Organizing the concepts from the unit in this way helps these teachers better relate each lesson to the overall unit objectives. This practice also ensures that each day's learning builds on and extends what came before. Examples of each adaptation can be seen in the units in Chapters 9 through 14.

Adaptations to the Table of Specifications

1. Add a column listing concepts that need to be reviewed.
2. Combine adjacent columns to simplify the table.
3. Use horizontal lines to divide concepts into daily lessons.

Advantages of a Table of Specifications

Most teachers find the process of developing a table of specifications to be somewhat difficult at first, but extremely valuable. It is difficult because it requires teachers to think carefully about what they are teaching and the desired outcomes of their instruction in a different and much more precise way. Being clear and explicit about what we want students to learn and what they should be able to do as a result of their learning can be challenging. For many teachers, however, the process is also revealing.

One major advantage in developing a table of specifications is that it enables teachers to view new concepts and their relationships in a compact form. By making tables of their own or by carefully reviewing prepared tables, teachers can add greater precision to their teaching and more closely match presentations of unit material and activities with learning objectives. A table of specifications can also reveal possible gaps in the instruction. It can show where important elements may have been neglected or where relationships between concepts or ideas need to be emphasized.

A table also helps to solve the problem of generality. If teachers have a collection of narrowly described instructional objectives that they are required to teach, then the table offers a way to combine those and develop the relationships among them in a meaningful instructional unit. But if teachers have a series of broad competencies or goals, then developing a table can clarify the components and skills that students must develop to attain that overall goal.

In addition, a table helps to bridge the gap between learning objectives and goals, and instructional materials. Research on teacher planning shows that most teachers do not focus on learning objectives or goals as they plan their lessons and units of instruction. Rather, they focus on instructional materials and activities (Callaway, 1988). For this reason, most curriculum guides and frameworks generally end up in desk drawers or on book shelves collecting dust.

Teachers who use their instructional materials as a resource in developing tables of specifications establish a direct link between those materials and their instructional goals with students. As a result, most come to see their materials in a less defining and more facilitative role.

At the same time, the process of developing tables of specifications also helps teachers identify shortcomings in their instructional materials. Most textbooks and other instructional resources present new concepts and ideas at the knowledge level only (Tyson-Bernstein, 1988), so teachers who want students to develop the higher level skills of application, analysis, and synthesis must plan instructional activities that go beyond what these materials alone provide.

Still another advantage of developing tables of specifications is that it compels teachers at all levels to move beyond simple knowledge and to consider higher levels of learning for all of their students. Most teachers become uneasy when developing a table if they have not included any higher level skills. The general format of the table makes the absence of such skills in an instructional unit particularly obvious: Blank columns on the right side of the table are difficult to ignore. As a result, even teachers in the earliest elementary grades often begin to include translations, applications, and other higher level skills in the instructional units they plan.

Finally, and perhaps most important, developing a table of specifications is the first step toward establishing consistency or congruence between the learning objectives for a unit and the procedures used to assess student learning. A table can be used as a guide in constructing instruments or procedures to check on students' learning progress or to evaluate the validity of instruments and procedures already on hand. As such, it offers a concise description of the concepts and skills that should be the focus of the assessment devices. These considerations are discussed more extensively in the next chapter.

Advantages of the Table of Specifications

1. Adds precision to teaching.
2. Helps reveal gaps in instruction.
3. Solves the problem of generality in objectives.
4. Helps to bridge the gap between learning objectives and instructional materials.
5. Identifies shortcomings in instructional materials.
6. Compels teachers to engage all students in higher level skills.
7. Helps to establish congruence between learning objectives and assessment procedures.

Pitfalls in Developing Tables of Specifications

As teachers develop tables of specification, they sometimes encounter difficulties that detract from their efforts and make the process unnecessarily difficult. Keeping in mind the purposes of clarity and precision often can prevent these problems from occurring. Still, recognizing them in advance as potential pitfalls will make them easier to avoid and far less serious if they do arise.

One of the most common difficulties is confusion about whether a particular concept or idea should be listed under one or another of two adjacent categories. For example, a certain concept might be considered a fact by one teacher and a principle by another; or a particular skill might be thought of as translation by one teacher but as application by another. Such differences may seem important, but they are usually of little consequence. So long as the concept or skill is included in the table, where it is makes little difference. Major distinctions–for instance, between the knowledge level and the translation or application level–are important, however, and need to be carefully considered.

A second difficulty is encountered by teachers who believe that every unit must include concepts or skills listed in every category on the table. For example, if they find no rules or principles when outlining the important concepts from a unit, then they sometimes believe they must develop some to make the unit complete. But, as mentioned earlier, the content elements and skills that are important for students to learn are likely to differ from subject to subject and from unit to unit within a subject.

The table of specifications format shown in Figure 2.1 was developed for use in a wide variety of subjects and across a wide range of levels. It is intended to be general and broadly inclusive so that its use can be easily understood and applications easily made. At the same time, it is designed to accommodate individual adaptations. Therefore, tables for units that do not include certain categories of concepts or skills, or those that include concepts or skills other than those listed in this format, are simply examples of such adaptations. The tables in the units in Chapters 9 through 14 show this clearly.

A third difficulty comes about when teachers attempt to make their tables of specifications too detailed. Many teachers are so accustomed to developing lists of narrow learning objectives that they fill their tables with long sentences, each beginning with the phrase, "The student will be able to. . . ." Others are so concerned with how they will teach a unit and the learning activities in which they will engage students that they include detailed descriptions of these on their tables. However, none of this is necessary.

A table of specifications is a relatively brief, compact, and yet concise description of what we want students to learn and be able to do as a result of their involvement in a particular learning unit. So long as it communicates that clearly, it has served its purpose well.

Tables of Specifications and Lesson Plans

The process of preparing a table of specifications can greatly add to the clarity of lessons and class activities. In fact, many teachers use the table as a guide while they are teaching. But for most teachers, a table of specifications by itself is insufficient as a lesson plan.

Particularly at the elementary and middle grade levels, most teachers prefer to teach from lesson plans that are fairly detailed. These plans describe not only what will be taught, but also how it will be taught. In preparing these plans, teachers often list the pivotal questions they plan to employ in their presentations or the guiding questions they want to use to stimulate discussion. Sample problems may be illustrated, and specific examples may be listed. Although details such as these are extremely useful in presenting a lesson, they are usually not included in a table of specifications.

A typical table of specifications is brief and describes the learning objectives for an entire unit in a page or two. It is designed to address these two basic questions: (1) What should students learn from this unit? (2) What should students be able to do with what they learn? The first question concerns the content; the second concerns the skills we want students to develop in relation to that content. Note, however, that both are "what" questions. The "how" questions–particularly, "How should this unit be taught?" and "How should student learning be assessed?"–are usually not addressed in the table.

The types of learning described by the objectives in a table of specifications certainly suggest different approaches to teaching and assessment. For example, while drill and recitation may be appropriate techniques for teaching knowledge of terms and facts, they are inappropriate for teaching students the skills involved in making analyses and syntheses (Gagne, 1985; Gagne & Driscoll, 1988). The inclusion of both levels on a table of specifications thus implies that different approaches to instruction and assessment will be used.

Teachers who want a more detailed plan that illustrates specific instructional activities or particular assessment techniques will need to supplement the table of specifications with lesson plans that include further directions and information. Such lesson plans typically describe the activities to be used each day or in each class session. They also directly address the question of "how" the particular learning objectives outlined in the table are to be accomplished.

Additional Benefits of Tables of Specifications

Outlining learning objectives and preparing tables of specifications clearly illustrate the importance of the decisions made by teachers in using mastery learning. Even the process of reviewing tables prepared by other teachers or curriculum specialists requires careful thought and consideration as to what students will be expected to learn. Although we cannot deny the importance of these decisions, we also must realize that these decisions are a fundamental part of all teaching. Judgments about what should be taught, what students should learn, and what students should be expected to do with what they have learned are made by teachers on a daily basis. Developing a table of specifications simply compels teachers to be conscious of those judgments and decisions and to make them in a highly explicit way. As a result, teaching activities can be better organized, more focused, and undoubtedly more successful.

As mentioned earlier, the process of preparing a table of specifications may seem somewhat difficult and cumbersome at first. Generally, this is because making these judgments and decisions in such a specific manner is an unfamiliar experience. The process requires a perspective toward learning objectives and instructional goals that is new for many teachers. However, within a short time, most find that the process becomes much easier. The time required to prepare a table of specifications for a second unit is usually about half that required for the first. A table for a third unit requires even less time.

In addition, most teachers discover that teaching becomes somewhat easier. Clearly specifying what students are to learn and what they are expected to do can save a teacher valuable time and provide a sense of accountability. Furthermore, being well organized allows a teacher to concentrate more fully on the best ways to present new material and on different methods for involving students in the instruction. In this way, a table of specifications is similar to a map used by travelers. It does not limit the pathways that can be taken, but it does enhance the efficiency of the traveling, the enjoyment of the travelers, and the likelihood that all will successfully reach a particular destination.

Other Areas of Goals and Objectives

Most tables of specifications focus on *cognitive* learning goals and objectives, because the primary concern of most teachers is the academic or intellectual skills that students should develop from their involvement in particular learning units. But many teachers also want their students to develop certain attitudes, dispositions, or work habits. These are generally referred to as *affective* goals. Others want their students to develop specific physical skills or abilities. These types of learning goals are referred to as *psychomotor.*

To specify affective or psychomotor learning goals, we must make further adaptations to the table of specifications. In making these adaptations, we find it helpful to consider categories drawn from taxonomies specific to the affective and psychomotor areas. Although such additions or adaptations complicate the table somewhat, they can bring added clarity to learning expectations and greater precision to instructional practices.

The following discussion describes both the affective and psychomotor taxonomies. An excellent and far more detailed summary of these taxonomies can be found in *Measurement and Assessment in Teaching,* by Robert Linn and Norman Gronlund (1995).

Affective Area

The taxonomy for affective goals and objectives (Krathwohl, Bloom, & Masia, 1964) includes five broad categories. Similar to the cognitive categories that are the basis for the table, each successive category in the affective area is slightly more complex and more difficult to develop. The categories that are part of the affective taxonomy include receiving, responding, valuing, organization, and characterization.

1. *Receiving.* This term refers to a student's willingness to pay attention and attend to particular phenomena. Learning objectives at this level range from simple awareness to selective attention. For example, we may want students to listen attentively, to show their awareness of or sensitivity to certain issues, or to attend closely to classroom activities.
2. *Responding.* This category is concerned with active participation on the part of students. At this level, we want students not only to attend to phenomena but also to react to them. Learning objectives here may seek to have students complete their work in a timely manner, participate in class discussions, or show increased interest in the subject by reading additional material outside of class.
3. *Valuing.* This level concerns the worth or value students attach to their learning. It can range from simple acceptance, where students show a desire to improve their own understanding or skill, to more complex commitment, where students actually accept responsibility for their own learning and development.
4. *Organization.* This category brings different understandings, resolves the conflicts between them, and begins to build an internally consistent value system. For example, we may want students to recognize the need for balance between freedom and responsibility in a democracy or to recognize the role of systematic planning in solving problems.
5. *Characterization.* At this level, students are developing patterns of behavior that are pervasive, consistent, and predictable. The major emphasis is that the behavior be typical or characteristic of students. We may, for example, want students to demonstrate self-reliance in working independently or to maintain good health habits.

Although these affective categories are appropriate at all levels of education, they are most prevalent in the elementary grades where teachers are helping students to develop appropriate work habits and interpersonal skills. Similar areas often are included as part of an elementary report card or overall reporting system. If such affective goals and objectives are considered important for students to attain, then they should be noted on the table of specifications.

Categories of Affective Goals or Objectives

1. Receiving
2. Responding
3. Valuing
4. Organization
5. Characterization

Psychomotor Area

The psychomotor area is another area of interest to many educators, especially those in certain technical fields, the performing arts, and physical education. The taxonomy for psychomotor goals and objectives (Harrow, 1972; Simpson, 1972) includes seven categories. Similar to the others, these categories vary in their complexity and difficulty, with each higher level being somewhat more complex than the one before. These categories include perception, set, guided response, mechanism, complex overt response, adaptation, and origination.

1. *Perception.* This level concerns students' use of their senses to guide certain motor activities. It can range from simple awareness to the appropriate selection of sensory cues. For example, we may expect students to relate music to a particular dance step or to recognize the malfunction of a machine by its sound.
2. *Set.* This category refers to students' readiness to take a particular action. It may include mental, physical, or emotional readiness. We may want students to know the appropriate sequence of steps that is necessary to enter data in a computer spreadsheet, for example. Or we may want students to demonstrate the proper body stance for batting a ball.
3. *Guided response.* At this level, the focus is on the early stages of students learning a complex skill. It may include being able to repeat an action demonstrated by the teacher or using adapted trial and error to identify an appropriate response. For example, we may expect students to be able to apply first aid bandages as demonstrated or to determine the best sequence of steps for preparing a meal.
4. *Mechanism.* This level concerns acts for which the learned responses are habitual and the performance is done with some confidence and proficiency.

We may want students to be able to operate a particular piece of machinery successfully and safely. Or we may expect students to be able to enter text at the keyboard with a certain speed and with limited errors.

5. *Complex overt response.* Our concern here is with students' skillful performance of physical acts involving complex movement patterns. Our interest is in quick, smooth, and accurate performance without hesitation and with increased automaticity. For example, we may want students to play a musical instrument skillfully or demonstrate their skill in driving a car.
6. *Adaptation.* At this level, students' physical skills are so well developed that they are able to modify movement patterns to fit special requirements or to meet the demands of particular problem situations. We may, for example, want students to adjust their tennis play to counteract the style of their opponents or to modify their swimming stroke to fit the roughness of the water.
7. *Origination.* This level refers to students creating new movement patterns to fit particular situations or specific problems. The emphasis is on creativity based on highly developed skills. For example, we may want students to create their own musical composition or to design a new dress style.

Categories of Psychomotor Goals or Objectives

1. Perception
2. Set
3. Guided response
4. Mechanism
5. Complex overt response
6. Adaptation
7. Origination

Learning goals and objectives in the psychomotor area generally require students to perform or demonstrate specific physical skills or behaviors. Hence most assessments of student learning in this area must be done on an individual basis. In many technical fields, the performing arts, and physical education, however, these skills and behaviors are the focus of instruction and critical to student learning in each area. When this is the case, the table of specifications should be adapted to include them.

Summary

Having a clear idea of what we want students to learn from a unit and what they should be able to do with what they learn is essential in implementing mastery learning. This is usually accomplished by outlining specific learning goals and objectives. The tasks involved in this process are as follow:

1. Identify specific learning units. Learning units are typically determined by the natural breaks in the subject content, and they usually represent the concepts and material covered in about a week or two of instructional time.
2. Determine the concepts and understandings that are important in each unit. List the new terms to be introduced, the facts to be presented, the rules and principles to be explained, and the processes and procedures to be discussed.
3. Determine what students are to do with the new concepts and understandings in each learning unit; that is, clarify the skills and abilities they are to develop in relation to those new concepts and understandings. Indicate whether students will be expected to know or recall the new concepts, translate them from one form to another, apply them in a new or different situation, or analyze them in a new way.
4. Prepare a table of specifications that summarizes these decisions. A table of specifications outlines the concepts that are part of the unit and the learning outcomes expected of students in relation to that content. It can also serve as a guide in planning instruction and assessing students' learning.
5. Make adaptations to the table of specifications as needed to better suit the unit's topic or subject and the students' learning needs. Consideration of affective or psychomotor goals may be particularly helpful in making these adaptations.
6. Review the table of specifications for gaps or inconsistencies and to ensure that it includes all of the unit's important concepts and understandings.

Activities

1. In a familiar subject area, preferably one you teach, identify a learning unit. If you do not currently teach, consider the concepts presented in this chapter as a learning unit.
2. Using the general format shown in Figure 2.1, construct a table of specifications for the unit.
3. Have a friend or teaching colleague review both the unit and your table of specifications, asking of the table, "Are these the same concepts I would identify as important in this unit?" and "Are these the same skills I would expect of students?"
4. Discuss with your friend or colleague any differences that arise through this review. Although such differences are likely to be few, their clarification can add greatly to the precision and completeness of a table of specifications.

3

Formative Assessment

Now that we have outlined the learning goals and objectives, we need procedures for gathering information on students' learning. In other words, having specified what we want students to learn and be able to do, we need to consider how to assess what they have learned and the skills or proficiencies they have acquired. In mastery learning, this is accomplished through *formative assessment.*

It might seem that before describing ways to assess students' learning we should first consider how best to present new ideas and concepts to students and how best to involve students in learning activities. Appropriate instructional methods and the active engagement of students are certainly crucial to effective teaching and learning. But the mastery learning process is basically neutral with regard to these issues.

As every teacher knows, instruction is a highly complex phenomenon involving many components and a complicated array of interrelationships among those components. It is also a dynamic phenomenon in which teachers interact with their students differently from day to day and week to week (Anderson, Ryan, & Shapiro, 1989). Furthermore, instruction is a highly individualized phenomenon: The effectiveness of any particular method can vary from teacher to teacher. Some teachers, for example, understand discussion methods better than lecture methods and are highly skilled in leading effective class discussions. Other teachers are dynamic and engaging lecturers who involve students better through demonstrations and simulations.

The same instructional behaviors may yield quite different results in different settings and situations; that is, instructional effectiveness tends to be context-specific (Anderson & Burns, 1989). This makes matters even more complex. No evidence supports the notion that there is one "most effective" teaching method, and, despite a multitude of studies on various methods of instruction, no one prescription for teaching has been identified as clearly best (see, for example, Brophy & Good, 1986; Murnane, 1981; Walberg, 1986).

Certain instructional techniques, however, have been found to be superior to others for teaching students particular kinds of skills (Anderson & Burns, 1989; Cooper, 1990; Cruickshank, Bainer, & Metcalf, 1995; Gagne, 1985). For example, the techniques associated with "direct instruction" (Carnine, Grossen, & Silbert, 1995; Rosenshine, 1986, 1987) have been shown to be highly effective in helping students learn a variety of basic skills. Similarly, cooperative learning arrangements (Johnson & Johnson, 1989, 1995; Johnson, Johnson, & Holubec, 1994) and "constructivist" approaches to instruction (Brooks & Brooks, 1993; Forman, 1987) appear to be effective in helping students develop complex problem-solving skills. Still, no single method has proven effective for all levels of skills.

The instructional techniques that work best also vary by subject area. The methods associated with high levels of achievement in mathematics, for instance, appear to be different from those that work best in helping students learn language arts or social studies (Evertson, Anderson, & Brophy, 1978; Stodolsky, 1988). Grade-level differences are also evident in the research (Stallings & Stipek, 1986). Procedures that correlate with learning success in the second grade, for example, differ from those related to high achievement in the fifth grade (McDonald & Elias, 1976). Thus, despite efforts to systematize and mechanize the instructional process, much of teaching obviously still remains craftlike and artistic (Gage, 1978; Rubin, 1985). For these reasons, decisions about teaching methods and instructional activities are best left to teachers to make individually, based upon their experiences and professional expertise.

Highly Effective Teachers

Several general elements, of course, characterize highly effective teachers in any context (Guskey, 1989a). Two of the most recognized are (1) having a clear vision of what students are to learn and (2) having a well-organized plan of how that vision can be accomplished (Bloom, 1982).

The vision of exemplary teachers generally includes definite ideas about curriculum and its content. Most reject the notion that everything in the curriculum or everything in the textbook is equally important. Instead, they focus their instruction on what they consider to be the most central concepts and understandings. These are emphasized during initial presentations and reviewed and reinforced throughout the instructional process (Hunter, 1979, 1982).

Highly effective teachers also have clear ideas about what students should be able to do with those central concepts. Rarely are they satisfied with having students simply memorize details or recall factual information. Rather, they want their students to be able to use those key concepts, see interrelations, and transfer their understanding to other learning situations.

The plans of highly effective teachers typically have two parts. The first focuses on the sequence of steps necessary to realize their vision. This part of the plan specifies the optimal experiences students should have, the most meaningful order of those experiences, the resources necessary to provide them, and procedures for checking on students' progress at regular intervals throughout the instructional sequence. These progress checks are closely tied to the learning goals that students are to attain and are used more to provide feedback to students than for grading or evaluation purposes.

The second part of effective teachers' plans are built-in sets of instructional alternatives. Recognizing that no one approach to teaching a particular concept or topic is likely to work with all students, exemplary teachers consider several ways to present each topic, a variety of examples and illustrations, and different instructional materials. In this way, if one approach falls flat, they can immediately turn to another (Anderson & Jones, 1981; Guskey, 1988b).

An important advantage to having a definite plan and thinking about instructional alternatives before teaching is that it allows teachers to routinize large chunks of what goes on in the classroom (Berliner, quoted in Brandt, 1986). Having considered beforehand many of the problems that might arise, their minds are free to respond to situational dilemmas that frequently occur but which cannot be anticipated.

Finally, highly effective teachers clearly communicate to students both their vision and their plan. Learning in their classrooms is not a "guessing game" for students, but a well-organized set of learning experiences. Students know from the outset what is expected and what procedures will be followed to meet those expectations (Porter & Brophy, 1988).

Two things should be evident from this description of highly effective teachers. First, these individuals are not characterized by a particular type of personality or mind. No rare gift allows these exemplary teachers to communicate more effectively with students than other teachers do, nor are they any more creative. It is not who they are, but what they do in their teaching and in their preparations for teaching that makes them so outstanding. As Csikszentmihalyi and McCormack (1986, p. 418) note in their study of exemplary teachers, "A teacher who presents material in an original manner is not necessarily highly creative, but simply more willing to spend time thinking about how best to convey information to a specific audience." Highly effective teachers have a fairly broad repertoire of tactics and strategies for presenting new concepts and ideas (Anderson & Scott, 1978; Lortie, 1975). From this repertoire, they select the techniques that work best for them and that are most effective for the particular students they are teaching. At the same time, they keep available several alternative approaches that can be called on if their original plan does not bring the results they want.

Second, what these teachers do looks much like mastery learning. The vision they have of what they want students to learn and be able to do reflects the purpose of the table of specification. Their regular efforts to reevaluate the effectiveness of their teaching and to make changes if student learning is not what they believe it ought to be (Guskey & Easton, 1983) reflects the process of formative assessment and correctives. Even though they may not label it as such, it is clear that the instructional practices of effective teachers are closely aligned with mastery learning.

The Purpose of Formative Assessment

With careful planning, the methods or strategies a teacher chooses to initially present new concepts or skills are likely to be appropriate for many, perhaps even most, of the students in a class. Yet because of differences among students in terms of aptitude and learning style, those methods are likely to be inappropriate for some. Because we are interested in having *all* students learn well, we must identify these individuals and the particular learning difficulties they are experiencing. With this information, we can plan instructional alternatives to help these students remedy their problems. This kind of information is gained quickly and systematically through the use of formative assessments.

Assessments serve a variety of functions in the classroom. Some are used to measure students' entry-level skills so that they can be placed appropriately in an instructional sequence. These are generally referred to as "pre-tests" or "placement tests," and they typically are administered before instruction or formal teaching begins. Various forms of assessment are also used by teachers at the end of instruction to evaluate students' learning, certify competence, and assign marks or grades. This type of assessment is usually referred to as *summative assessment.* A third type of assessment is used during instruction to inform instructional decisions and provide immediate feedback to both students and teachers. The main purpose of this kind of assessment is not to place or evaluate students, but to gather specific information on their learning progress. This type of assessment is referred to as *formative assessment.*

Of all the functions of assessment, the formative one is probably the most neglected. The experiences of most teachers and students with assessments are primarily summative–that is, as measurement devices used at the end of the teaching process to document student achievement and assign grades. For this reason, the very mention of the words *assessment* or *test* inevitably prompts nervous questions from students about how much it will count and how many questions will be included. As such, many students view assessment as a consistently negative experience. It serves to make public their shortcomings and learning problems, and seldom is there any opportunity for improvement.

Assessment can serve many valuable instructional purposes, however. But to do so, it must be conceived as a teaching activity in and of itself and not simply as an add-on to the end of the teaching process (Wiggins, 1989, 1992). For this to happen, both teachers and students must understand and experience assessments as formative in nature; that is, they must experience tests and other assessment devices as instructional tools. This is accomplished in mastery learning through the regular use of thoughtfully designed formative assessments.

Formative assessments can take a variety of forms in a mastery learning class. Many are short quizzes composed of multiple-choice, completion, or short-answer questions. But they can also include short essays, writing samples, skill demonstrations, laboratory experiments, or oral presentations. In essence, a formative assessment can be any device or procedure by which teachers acquire evidence on students' learning.

A formative assessment's most important characteristic is that it provide students with precise and immediate feedback on their learning progress. This feedback then can be used to remedy learning difficulties and serve as a guide for the correction of errors or misunderstandings that developed during the original instruction. For this reason, the scores that students attain on formative assessments often are not counted in determining their grade. The primary use of this type of assessment is to check on each student's learning progress and direct further study.

The Relationship Between Tables of Specifications and Formative Assessments

A table of specifications lists the learning goals and objectives for a particular unit. It outlines the concepts and understandings that are part of the unit, together with the specific skills or behaviors that students are expected to develop in relation to those concepts. Generally, these concepts are outlined in some detail in the table. But in most cases, not all of these details are equally important. Some concept elements are undoubtedly essential for students' learning and understanding of the subject, while others may not be. For a formative assessment to be most useful, it should address all of the concept elements in the unit that are important for students to learn. Therefore the first step in constructing a formative assessment, or reviewing one that is already prepared, is to identify those elements in the table of specifications that are essential to learning. This process is generally referred to as *valuing*.

For example, in presenting a science unit, a teacher may discuss the names of particular scientists who worked on an important idea and made significant contributions (e.g., Madame Marie Curie, who won two Nobel Prizes for her work on radioactivity), the dates when they lived (e.g., 1867–1934), the countries in which they were born (e.g., born in Poland but did most of her scientific work in France), and some of the social and political aspects of the time in which they worked (e.g., World War I). All of these details may be listed on the table of specifications. These details also serve to make presentations on the unit much more interesting. But not all are equally important to students' learning.

In determining the elements that are essential for students' learning, the teacher must consider several things. Those elements that form the basis for concepts or ideas developed more fully in later units should, of course, be considered essential. These may be the terms or facts that will be used again in explaining more complex concepts, or they may be the principles or procedures that need to be applied in later problem-solving tasks. In general, if the understanding of a concept from one unit is a prerequisite for learning in a more advanced unit, then that concept is definitely an essential element of the first unit.

Concepts that directly relate to overall course goals or objectives also must be counted as essential. These are the concepts that all students are expected to learn and master as a result of their experiences in the class. Curriculum frameworks and teachers' manuals often outline or highlight the specific concepts or skills that are considered most important in a unit, and many teachers find these resources to be quite helpful. In the end, however, the teacher's judgment remains the most crucial factor in making this determination. That is why this process is referred to as *valuing*: Teachers must determine what is most important or most valuable for students to learn.

Once decisions are made about the essential elements in a unit, they should be specially marked–by underlining, circling, highlighting, or with an asterisk or other special notation–on the table of specifications. In this way, anyone observing the table can get a clear picture of the unit's overall scope as well as the specific elements that are considered most crucial to students' learning.

Each learning unit may have as few as two or three or as many as twenty or twenty-five important concepts, concept elements, or objectives. The number depends on the unit's length, its complexity, and the complexity of the included concepts. Typically, units in the lower elementary grades are shorter and cover fewer concepts than those for upper grades.

Matching Formative Assessments to the Table

The essential concepts or objectives form the basis for developing a formative assessment. Thus the relationship between the table of specifications and a formative assessment is very direct. Making this relationship clear is also a crucial step in bringing about the congruence among instructional components that is essential to mastery learning.

A good formative assessment should contain at least one item, group of items, or prompt for every important concept element or objective in the unit. An easy way to ensure that this occurs is to match the items or prompts in the formative assessment to the table of specifications. To do this, simply ask of each item, "What must students know and be able to do to respond appropriately?" Once this is determined, locating that concept and its associated skill precisely on the table should be easy.

Suppose, for example, that to solve a particular science problem on a formative assessment, students must be able to apply a specific scientific principle. One should be able to go to the table of specifications and find some notation on the use of that principle in solving scientific problems under the "Applications" column.

To illustrate this relationship explicitly, many teachers list the item numbers from the formative assessment directly on the table of specifications, next to the concept elements to which they relate. If the science problem discussed earlier is item 7, for instance, then a small circled "7" would be listed beside that entry under the "Applications" column on the table of specifications. In this way, anyone can see the direct match between the items or prompts on the formative assessment and the concepts and skills identified as important in the table of specifications. Examples of this are shown on the tables of specifications included in Chapters 9 through 14.

Matching each item or prompt on a formative assessment to the table serves two important purposes. First, as mentioned above, it provides congruence and consistency between learning objectives and procedures for checking on students' learning progress. Although usually unintended, discrepancies are not uncommon between a teacher's stated learning objectives and the student assessment procedures employed. When the table of specifications is used as a guide in preparing a formative assessment, however, consistency between objectives and procedures for checking students' learning is ensured.

Second, this matching process enhances thoroughness. Without the detail and precision provided by the table of specifications, important elements in a unit are often missed or neglected on classroom assessment devices. But when a carefully prepared table is used in developing formative assessment procedures, all important objectives are covered and checks on learning progress are both thorough and complete.

Dilemmas in the Matching Process

Two dilemmas are frequently encountered in the above-discussed matching process. The first occurs when the knowledge or skill called for in an item is not included on the table of specifications. In other words, what students must know and be able to do in order to respond appropriately is not described in any column on the table. This may happen because the particular concept called for in that item was simply missed when the table of specifications was being developed. If so, then the concept should be added to the table and the item number placed beside it. Care also should be taken to ensure that instructional activities are planned so that students have opportunities to learn that particular concept and skill.

This lack of description also may occur because the concept addressed by the item is trivial or unimportant. This often happens when formative assessment instruments are part of the instructional materials offered by a commercial publisher to supplement a text or instructional series. Because these assessment devices typically are developed by persons other than the text or series authors, they often do not reflect what is emphasized in the materials or what teachers consider to be the most important elements. Sometimes, too, assessments focus on those elements that are easiest to measure, rather than on what is most important for students to learn. In either case, the items or prompts that focus on these trivial elements should simply be eliminated from the formative assessment.

The second dilemma occurs when important concept elements listed on the table of specifications are not included in the formative assessment. To ensure that this does not happen, remember to look again at the table after all items or prompts are matched to make sure that all of the important concept elements from the unit are covered. If they are not, then develop and add any missing items or prompts to the formative assessment.

Developing Assessment Items and Prompts

Developing assessment questions that measure students' understanding of important concepts or objectives is not easy. The task becomes even more difficult because most teachers have little training in evaluation or assessment techniques (Guskey, 1994d; Stiggins, 1995). Fortunately, the skills involved in developing formative assessments are some of the same skills that are important in developing tables of specifications. Specifically, both require thorough consideration of unit concepts and the skills that students are expected to develop in relation to those concepts. To be appropriate and useful, a formative assessment must measure students' understanding at the cognitive skill level prescribed in the table. An item that checks students' knowledge of a particular principle, for example, will be quite different from one that measures their ability to use that principle in solving a complex problem.

A variety of assessment formats can be used in formative assessments. Each format has both advantages and limitations. Each also varies in its appropriateness, depending on the concepts and skills being measured. To simplify our discussion of these formats, we have divided them into two groups: *traditional* and *alternative*. The types of items or prompts that typically are included in these two categories are:

Traditional Assessments

1. True/false
2. Matching
3. Multiple-choice
4. Completion
5. Essay and short answer

Alternative Assessments

6. Skill demonstrations
7. Oral presentations
8. Task performances and complex problems
9. Compositions and writing samples
10. Laboratory experiments
11. Projects and reports
12. Portfolios
13. Group tasks or activities

Although other assessment formats are available, this list gives some idea of the variety of item types and measurement devices that are appropriate in formative assessments. Several publications outline practical guidelines and specific suggestions for developing items and prompts in each assessment format. The following are excellent references.

Airasian, P. W. (1994). *Classroom assessment* (2nd ed.). New York: McGraw-Hill.

Bloom, B. S., Madaus, G. F., and Hastings, J. T. (1981). *Evaluation to improve learning.* New York: McGraw-Hill.

Gronlund, N. E. (1993). *How to make achievement tests and assessments* (5th ed.). Boston: Allyn & Bacon.

Linn, R. L., & Gronlund, N. E. (1995). *Measurement and assessment in teaching* (7th ed.). Englewood Cliffs, NJ: Prentice-Hall.

Marzano, R. J., Pickering, D., & McTighe, J. (1993). *Assessing student outcomes.* Alexandria, VA: Association for Supervision and Curriculum Development.

Perrone, V. (Ed.) (1991). *Expanding student assessment.* Alexandria, VA: Association for Supervision and Curriculum Development.

Popham, W. J. (1995). *Classroom assessment: What teachers need to know.* Boston: Allyn & Bacon.

Stiggins, R. J. (1994). *Student-centered classroom assessment.* New York: Merrill.

Wiggins, G. P. (1993). *Assessing student performance.* San Francisco: Jossey-Bass.

The following discussion briefly summarizes each type of item and prompt, together with general suggestions for their development. For more detailed explanations and specifications, the references cited above are highly recommended.

Traditional Assessments

Traditional assessment formats include true/false, matching, multiple-choice, completion, and essay or short-answer. They are referred to as *traditional* because they are the assessment formats most familiar to teachers and the ones with which they have had the most experience, both as teachers and as students.

The first three formats–true/false, matching, and multiple-choice–are considered "selected response" formats. This is because students are asked simply to choose the best or most appropriate response from those that are provided. Completion, essays, and all of the alternative assessment formats are considered "supply or production response" formats because they require students to construct or produce their own responses.

Although some contemporary writers discourage teachers from using them, traditional assessment formats are highly appropriate in many circumstances and serve a variety of useful purposes. When well-constructed, even selected response formats can be used to assess students' mastery of content knowledge and their ability to use that knowledge to reason and solve problems (Stiggins, 1995). Whatever format is used, the items must be well constructed and carefully matched to the skill level being addressed.

True/False Items

A true/false item is simply a declarative statement that students must judge to be true or false. For example:

DIRECTIONS: Circle the T in front of each of the following statements you believe to be true and the F in front of those you believe to be false.

T F 1. Shakespeare's Hamlet was the Prince of Denmark.

T F 2. The *Rime of the Ancient Mariner* was written by Herman Melville.

True/false items are relatively easy to write and score. The exception is when students are asked to respond by printing either a T or F. Inevitably, some will offer the response shown below, in the hope it will be read quickly and judged to be whatever response is correct:

F

The solution is simply to print a T and an F before the statement and have students circle their response as in the example above.

Despite their ease in development and scoring, the use of true/false items is limited because they assess only a small bit of information and are generally appropriate only for lower level cognitive skills. Furthermore, students have a fifty-fifty chance of guessing the correct response without any knowledge or understanding of the material. They may also be able to identify an incorrect statement without knowing what is truly correct. Some teachers try to get around this by asking students to correct those statements they determine to be false to make them true. Most assessment experts discourage this practice, however, because it can result in extremely complicated scoring procedures. How should a response be scored, for example, if the student knows the statement is false, but the way in which he or she revises it is also incorrect?

The best true/false items contain a single significant idea and are worded precisely so that they can be judged unequivocally true or false. Avoiding extraneous clues to the answer is always best–particularly words such as *always, never, usually,* and *sometimes*–because these often allow students to select the correct response without truly understanding the concept. Also, avoid using double negatives because they often make statements difficult to interpret. For example, consider the following statement: "You should not teach children to never cross the street before looking both ways." It is false, although not obviously so at first glance.

Matching Items

Matching items typically consist of items or premises listed in one column and responses in another. Students are to match each item with one or, in some cases, more responses. For example:

DIRECTIONS: Match each statement in the left-hand column with a person listed in the right-hand column by placing the appropriate letter in the blank before the statement. A person may be matched with several or none of the statements.

___ 1. Fourth president of the United States	a. George Washington
___ 2. Member of the first cabinet	b. Benjamin Franklin
___ 3. Presiding officer at the Constitutional Convention	c. Alexander Hamilton
___ 4. Refused to attend the Constitutional Convention	d. Thomas Jefferson
___ 5. Proposed the Articles of Confederation	e. John Adams
___ 6. Principal author of *The Federalist*	f. Patrick Henry
___ 7. First vice president of the United States	g. Oliver Ellsworth
___ 8. Proposed the "Connecticut Compromise"	

Source: Bloom, Madaus, & Hastings (1981, p. 191)

Matching items are fairly easy to write and score. They are particularly appropriate with vocabulary lists and can often be used to cover a wider scope of material than true/false items. Like true/false items, however, matching items are generally used to assess lower level cognitive skills and are appropriate only in specific instances–that is, with lists of terms or facts.

The best matching items include only homogeneous material so that all responses are likely alternatives. If, for example, only one premise asks for a date and only one date is included among the responses, it does not require much skill to determine which response is correct. The lists of items also should be kept fairly short, with the brief responses placed on the right-hand side of the page. Because students typically work from left to right on a page, formatting matching items in this way will significantly reduce the time required for assessment.

With matching items, make sure the number of responses is either larger or smaller than the number of premises. If there is a direct, one-to-one correspondence, students will be able to determine the answers to some items simply through a process of elimination. In addition, directions should be provided that specify the basis for matching and indicate that a response may be used once, more than once, or not at all.

Multiple-Choice Items

A multiple-choice item consists of a stem, which presents a problem situation, and several alternatives, which provide possible solutions to the problem. The stem is generally a question or an incomplete statement. The alternatives include one correct answer to the question and several other plausible but incorrect answers that are known as "distracters." The following items are examples.

DIRECTIONS: For each of the questions below, select the best answer. Place the letter of your answer on the blank in front of the item.

____1. Using semantic differential techniques, it was discovered that *good* has slightly male overtones, while *nice* has slightly female ones. This is an example of what kind of word meaning?
a. Explicit
b. Symbolic
c. Conceptual
d. Denotative
e. Connotative

____2. When children first learn a new word, they tend to overextend its use. In learning theory terms, this is very much like ____________.
a. Generalization
b. Discrimination
c. Operant learning
d. Latent learning
e. Cognitive learning

Multiple-choice items have several advantages over other assessment formats. First, they can be constructed so that more than one concept is assessed in a single item. When students answer a multiple-choice item, they must determine not only that one alternative is correct but also that the others are incorrect. Hence a single item can be broad in the scope of material it covers. Second, when multiple-choice items are carefully constructed, they can be used to assess higher level cognitive skills. Translation and application skills in particular often are measured with multiple-choice items. Third, because multiple-choice items are a selection rather than a supply or production type of item, they are quickly and easily scored. For these reasons, multiple-choice items are used in nearly all standardized achievement tests.

Multiple-choice items also can be constructed to provide diagnostic information. Consider, for example, the following mathematics item:

3. 2.3 + .15 = ____.
a. 3.8
b. .38
c. 1.73
d. .245
e. 2.45

One of the most common errors students make in answering a mathematics problem such as this one is adding without first aligning the decimal points. Thus if a student selects alternative *a* or *b,* the teacher can be fairly certain of the error that was made and can offer specific corrective help. Different corrective help would be needed by students who select alternative *c* or *d.*

Good multiple-choice items are probably the most challenging assessment items to construct. Developing plausible but not unfairly misleading alternatives to the correct response is difficult. In addition, more than one correct response often is created. Bloom, Madaus, and Hastings (1981), Gronlund (1993), and Stiggins (1994a) offer helpful suggestions for preparing good multiple-choice items. Some of the most important follow.

1. *The stem of the item should present a single, clearly formulated problem.* The stem of the item should be stated so clearly that students understand the problem without looking at the alternatives. This clarifies the task for students and enhances the validity of the item.
2. *As much of the wording as possible should be placed in the stem.* Putting most of the wording in the stem clarifies the problem, avoids the repetition of material, and reduces the time students need to read the alternatives.
3. *The stem should be stated in positive form whenever possible.* Generally, positively phrased items measure more important learning outcomes than do negatively stated items. Furthermore, being able to identify responses that do not apply provides no assurance that students possess the desired understanding. When negative wording is used, it should always be emphasized with underlining, italics, or all capital lettering.
4. *All alternatives should be grammatically consistent with the stem and parallel in form.* Inconsistencies in tense, articles, or grammatical form among the alternatives can provide clues to the correct response or make some of the incorrect alternatives less effective.
5. *Avoid verbal clues that might enable students to select the correct response or eliminate incorrect alternatives.* Often the wording of an item provides clues to the correct response. Some of the most common verbal clues include:
   a. similarity of wording in both the stem and the correct response;
   b. stating the right answer in textbook language or stereotyped phraseology;
   c. stating the correct response in greater detail (the longest alternative is likely to be the correct one);
   d. including absolute terms in incorrect alternatives (for example, *all, only,* and so on); and
   e. including two alternatives that have the same meaning.
6. *Incorrect alternatives should be plausible and attractive.* If all alternatives are plausible, similar in length, and similar in complexity, then the item will distinguish students who understand the concept from those who do not.

In addition, including common misconceptions or errors among the alternatives can help to identify specific learning difficulties that students are experiencing.

7. *Avoid using the alternative "All of the above" and use "None of the above" with extreme caution.* Including "All of the above" as an alternative allows students to answer the item on the basis of partial information. Students can detect that it is the correct response simply by noting that two other alternatives are correct, or that it is incorrect because one of the alternatives is incorrect. When "None of the above" is used, it may be measuring students' abilities to recognize incorrect responses rather than their understanding of the concept.
8. *The correct response's position should be randomly varied.* The correct response should appear in each alternative position about the same number of times, but without following any particular pattern.
9. *Each item should be independent of the other items in the assessment.* When assembling an assessment, make sure that information given in the stem of one item does not help students answer another item. Furthermore, avoid item chains where the correct response to one item depends on knowing the correct response to an item preceding it. Such chains of interlocking items overly penalize students who are unable to answer the first item in the chain.

Although developing good multiple-choice items can be difficult, their advantages of broad scope and objective scoring make them ideally suited for many subjects. In addition, because most of the standardized achievement tests that students are required to take include multiple-choice items, practice in responding to this type of item on teacher-made tests can help students prepare for those experiences.

Completion Items

There are two general types of completion items: questions or incomplete statements, and problems. With questions or incomplete statements, students are to provide the appropriate words, numbers, or symbols. With problems, especially in mathematics, students are expected provide the complete answer and sometimes show their work in finding the solution. An example of both types is illustrated below:

DIRECTIONS: Complete each statement below by writing the correct word or phrase in the blank. Be sure to use correct spelling.

1. The largest group under which organisms are classified is ____________.
2. All of the plants in an area are referred to as the ____________.

Or, as is common in mathematics:

> DIRECTIONS: Solve each problem and record your answer in the space provided. Be sure to show your work and, in the case of fractions, be sure to reduce your answer to simplest form.
>
> 1. $\begin{array}{r} 53 \\ -17 \\ \hline \end{array}$
>
> 2. $\frac{1}{2} + \frac{2}{3} =$ ___

Completion items are fairly easy to write and sometimes can be used to assess higher level cognitive skills–that is, they can require students to recall correct information rather than simply recognize it. However, they can present some scoring difficulties. Often more than one correct response is possible, particularly if synonyms are available. Other problems arise over spelling errors and the interpretation of unclear written responses. Mathematics problems present the dilemma of partial credit, especially when the solution to a problem involves multiple steps. Because of these problems, completion items are usually restricted to situations where students are specifically asked to recall information, where computation problems are used, or where a selection type of item would make the answer obvious.

The best completion items are stated so that only a single, brief response is possible. The words supplied by students should relate to the main point of the statement and be placed at the end of the statement. Extraneous clues to the answer, such as the use of *a* and *an* or singular or plural verbs, should be avoided. In mathematics problems, the directions should be clear and explicit so that students know exactly what is expected.

Essay and Short-Answer Items

An essay or short-answer item asks students a question or poses a problem that requires them to produce their own written response. Sometimes these are referred to as "open-ended response" items. Generally, students are free to decide how to approach the question or problem, what information to use, and how to organize their response. The following is an example.

> DIRECTIONS: Write an essay comparing the struggle for independence in the United States in the 1700s and Vietnam in the 1900s. Describe and give examples of at least three ways in which these struggles were similar and three ways they were different. Your response will be evaluated in terms of its completeness, the appropriateness of the examples, and the skill with which it is organized. (30 points)

Or in mathematics:

DIRECTIONS: Answer each of the following problems. Make sure to show your work in each step and label your answers.

1. At lunch Monica buys two apples that cost 65¢ each. She gives the cashier two dollars to pay for the apples. Calculate how much change Monica should receive and list a combination of bills, or coins, or bills and coins that would make that amount (15 points).

The major advantage of essay or short-answer items is that they can be used to measure higher levels of cognitive skills. Complex skills such as making analyses or syntheses are sometimes difficult to assess with selection types of items. The open-response format of essay and short-answer items, however, places a premium on students' abilities to produce, integrate, and express ideas and concepts.

At the same time, essay and short-answer items also have their own shortcomings. First, items of this type provide only a limited sample of students' learning. Because of the time required by students to respond to essay and short-answer items, typically only a small number of these questions can be included in an assessment. Hence the learning that can be assessed is confined to relatively few areas.

Second, essay and short-answer responses also are often distorted by differences in students' writing abilities. Because students must write responses to essay questions in their own words, poor expression and errors in punctuation, spelling, and grammar often lower some students' scores. On the other hand, students who can express themselves well may be able to bluff their way through questions and inflate their scores.

Third, essay and short-answer items can be influenced by subjectivity during scoring. Not only are production items such as these difficult and time-consuming to score, but also consistency in scoring is hard to achieve. As the style and content of responses shift from paper to paper, grading standards also tend to shift. Even differences in the neatness of students' handwriting can affect scores (Sprouse & Webb, 1994; Sweedler-Brown, 1992).

Despite these shortcomings, essay and short-answer items can be used effectively to assess many kinds of learning. The best essay and short-answer items are those designed to measure only complex learning. In other words, they should not be used to assess students' knowledge of facts or principles, for other types of items do this much more efficiently. Their use should be restricted, therefore, to the assessment of higher levels of cognitive skills.

The question asked or the problem posed in an essay or short-answer item also should be focused and should present a clear and precise task. In addition, ample time must be provided for students to respond to each question or problem. This is particularly important because essay and short-answer items usually require time for thinking as well as for writing.

The scoring criteria, however, constitute the most crucial aspect of essay or short-answer items. These must be clear, precise, and easy for students to understand. In addition, they should be determined in advance and communicated to students. In most cases, this means that a "scoring rubric" for the item must be developed. A *rubric* identifies simply, clearly, and precisely the important dimensions of an appropriate response and how those will be determined. Students should be told, for example, whether grammar and spelling count and on what basis credit or points will be assigned. Scoring rubrics with precise scoring criteria are important both in gaining greater objectivity in scoring and in communicating to students how they might improve their marks.

The scoring criteria for judging the quality of students' responses to essay or short-answer items are determined primarily by the learning goal or objective measured by the item. For this reason, the table of specifications is a useful guide in establishing these criteria. Some teachers begin by developing a model response that clearly meets the learning objective they want to assess. They then determine the number of points to be assigned to the response and various parts within it. This is referred to as the "checklist approach." Other teachers establish criteria for judging the overall quality of a response and then use these criteria to establish four or five quality levels. Each response is then read and assigned to a level. This is called the "rating scale approach" (Stiggins, 1994a). Often a separate judgment of level is made for each of several criteria assessed in a response. This last procedure provides the most useful information for diagnosing and improving learning (Gronlund, 1993) and hence is preferred in mastery learning classes. An example of rating scale criteria is shown on the next page.

When scoring essay or short-answer items, the teacher should mark all students' responses to one item before proceeding to the next item. This process allows one to maintain more uniform standards when evaluating students' responses. Content and clarity (mastery of important concepts and skills) should be evaluated separately from form (grammar, punctuation, and writing proficiency), because different criteria will be applied for each. In addition, whenever possible, the teacher should score responses to essay or short-answer items without knowing the identity of the student. Undoubtedly, many teachers know their students by their handwriting, particularly at the elementary level where writing is a subject of instruction. However, by having students put their names on the back of papers or on a separate, attached sheet, the influence of possible bias can be controlled to some degree.

Additional suggestions for the development, scoring, and appropriate use of essay items are available in the books mentioned earlier, and also in the following works:

Coffman, W. E. (1971). Essay examinations. In R. L. Thorndike (Ed.), *Educational measurement* (2nd ed.). Washington, DC: American Council on Education.

Example of Rating Scale Scoring Criteria

Score	Description
5	The response is clear, accurate, and to the point. It includes relevant information and offers good support. Important connections are made, and insights important to the objective are included.
3	The response is clear and somewhat focused, but not particularly strong. Only limited support is offered for the points made, and the connections are remote. Few important insights are evident.
1	The response is off the mark. It does not show mastery of the important concepts or contains inaccurate information. No important connections are made, support is missing, or no important insights are included.

Mehrens, W. A., & Lehmann, I. J. (1991). *Measurement and evaluation in education and psychology* (4th ed.). New York: Holt, Rinehart & Winston.

Payne, D. A. (1992). *Measuring and evaluating educational outcomes.* New York: Merrill.

Thorndike, R. M., Cunningham, G. K., Thorndike, R. L., & Hagen, E. P. (1991). *Measurement and evaluation in psychology and education* (5th ed.). New York: Macmillan.

Alternative Assessments

Alternative assessment formats encompass a wide variety of assessment methodologies. Collectively, they are referred to as "performance" or "authentic" assessments because they are considered valuable activities in themselves and typically involve the performance of tasks that are directly related to real-world problems (Linn, Baker, & Dunbar, 1991). Alternative assessments engage students in activities that require the demonstration of certain skills or the creation of specified products. As such, they can assess many of the complex learning objectives that cannot be adequately addressed through more traditional assessment formats.

Alternative assessments are highly appropriate and widely used as formative assessments. Like completion and essay or short-answer items, they are considered a "supply or production response" format because all forms require students to construct or produce their responses. Also like essay or short-answer items, their use should be restricted to measures of higher levels of cognitive skills; that is, alternative assessments should be used primarily to assess learning objectives that involve applications, analyses, and syntheses. Although various forms of alternative assessments can be used to measure knowledge level objectives, traditional formats generally do so much more reliably and efficiently.

Alternative assessments include skill demonstrations, oral presentations, task performances and complex problems, compositions or writing samples, laboratory experiments, projects or reports, portfolios, and group tasks or activities. Each format requires teachers to observe students while they are performing or to examine the products that students create in order to judge the level of proficiency or mastery demonstrated. Mastery is determined by comparing each student's performance or product to preset criteria or standards.

The most challenging aspect in the use of alternative assessments, regardless of the form, is devising sound scoring criteria. To guide a teacher in developing and clarifying the appropriate criteria, Stiggins (1994a, p. 186) outlines the following six-step process.

Step 1. Begin by reflecting on the meaning of excellence in the performance arena of interest to you. Tap your own professional literature, texts, and curriculum materials for insights, too. And do not overlook the wisdom of your colleagues and associates as a resource. Talk with them! Include students as partners in this step, too. Brainstorm your own list of key elements. You do not have to list them all in one setting. Take some time to let the list grow.

Step 2. Categorize the many elements so that they reflect your highest priorities. Keep the list as short as possible while still capturing the essence of performance.

Step 3. Define each key dimension in clear and simple language.

Step 4. Find some actual performance to watch or examples of products to study. If this step can include the thoughtful analysis of one or more contrasting cases–an outstanding term paper and a weak one, a flowing and accurate jumpshot in basketball and a poor one, a student who functions effectively in a group and one who is repeatedly rejected, and so on–so much the better.

Step 5. Use your clearest language and best examples to spell out in words and pictures each point along the various continuums of performance you use to define the important dimensions of the achievement to be assessed.

Step 6. Try your performance criteria to see if they truly capture the essence of performance. Fine-tune them to state as precisely as possible what it means to succeed. Let this fine-tuning go on as needed for as long as you teach.

As these steps show, the process of devising sound scoring criteria is complex and ongoing. As we engage in the process, however, keep in mind our underlying purpose: to help students become better performers and more successful learners. Regardless of its format, a formative assessment is a learning tool, one that is designed to identify learning successes and point out where additional study and effort are needed.

Skill Demonstrations

In a skill demonstration, the teacher typically observes students as they display a particular skill and then judges their proficiency. Some skills are rather easy to judge and allow teachers to use a "checklist approach." This is especially common with skills taught in the early elementary grades. A kindergarten teacher, for instance, might watch children as they sort objects according to their shape and then draw inferences about students' abilities to recognize distinguishing features and make classifications.

Other skills, however, are far more complex and cannot be judged as easily. For example, a physical education teacher who is observing students' proficiency in dribbling a ball around a series of obstacles will find that making judgments is more difficult. When a more complex skill such as this is involved, demonstrations cannot be judged with a checklist that indicates either mastery or nonmastery. Instead, most teachers use a "rating scale approach." After observing students display the skill, they judge proficiency on a continuum of achievement levels ranging from very low to very high (Stiggins, 1994a). In either case, clear scoring criteria are essential so that students who do not perform the skill at a high level of proficiency can be offered specific guidance on how to improve.

Skill demonstrations are an appropriate assessment format at all levels of education. They offer teachers accurate evidence on students' competence and proficiency in a variety of important learning areas. Furthermore, skill demonstrations can be combined with more traditional assessment formats within the same formative assessment to tap a broader range of objectives. A technology and vocational skills teacher, for example, may want to assess students' knowledge of a particular piece of equipment, as well their ability to operate it safely and efficiently. To do so, the teacher would divide the formative assessment into two parts. The first part might be composed of matching and completion items that assess students' knowledge of the equipment and the steps necessary for its safe operation. The second part would involve having each student demonstrate correct operating procedures.

As with essay items, the most challenging aspect of skill demonstrations is developing the scoring criteria. These should be clear, concise, and communicated to students before the assessment. Many teachers distribute printed copies of the criteria to students when they teach a skill so that students know better what is expected and how to prepare for the assessment. Following the assessment, students are provided with a similar listing that indicates the teacher's judgment of their proficiency and the areas where improvement is needed.

The principal drawback of skill demonstrations as an assessment format is that they usually must be conducted or administered individually. Because of this, teachers should plan alternative learning activities for students who are not engaged in the assessment. Having students wait for long periods to demonstrate a particular skill is a waste of valuable time. Many teachers avoid this by coordinating assessment tasks with group activities or by making their observations in an unobtrusive way while students are engaged in skill-related work.

Oral Presentations

Although oral presentations are often thought of only as formal addresses or reports delivered to a large audience, they are actually a common assessment format at all levels of education. "Show and tell" activities in a kindergarten class are a form of oral presentation, as are "sound it out" activities and other word-recognition tasks in elementary language arts instruction. Oral reading by itself is a form of oral presentation. Foreign language and speech teachers both typically use oral activities in every unit of instruction. And teachers who include "class participation" as part of their grading criteria also are using oral presentations as part of their assessments of student learning.

In an oral presentation, the teacher listens to and interprets students' responses, evaluates quality, and draws inferences about the level of achievement. Oral presentations also allow the teacher to ask follow-up questions or prompt students to expand on their response. Furthermore, such a presentation can be a valuable learning experience for the presenter as well as the audience.

Like other alternative assessment formats, the use of oral presentations requires clear scoring criteria that are prepared in advance and communicated to students. Oral presentations also can be combined with other traditional assessment formats within a single formative assessment, much like skill demonstrations. In fact, this is a frequent practice in foreign language instruction.

Teachers often provide students with immediate feedback on their oral presentations in the form of oral comments or brief discussions of points for refinement. This kind of immediate feedback can be helpful to students so long as it is constructive and positive in tone. But students also should receive written feedback from the teacher, fellow students, or both to help them monitor and direct their improvement efforts.

Airasian (1994, p. 243) offers an example (page 74) of performance criteria for assessing students' oral reports. The general performance is first divided into three areas, and then specific criteria within each area are identified.

Example of Performance Criteria for Oral Reports

1. Physical Expression
   a. Stands straight and faces the audience
   b. Changes facial expression with changes in tone of the report
   c. Maintains eye contact with audience
2. Vocal Expression
   a. Speaks in a steady, clear voice
   b. Varies tone to emphasize points
   c. Speaks loudly enough to be heard by audience
   d. Paces words in an even flow
   e. Enunciates each word
3. Verbal Expression
   a. Chooses precise words to convey meaning
   b. Avoids unnecessary repetition
   c. States sentences with complete thoughts or ideas
   d. Organizes information logically
   e. Summarizes main points at conclusion

Task Performances and Complex Problems

Task performances and complex problems frame a challenge for students and set the conditions for meeting that challenge. In mathematics, they often take the form of structured exercises in which students must analyze the information provided and follow an appropriate sequence of steps to solve the problem. Many task performances are less structured, however, and are designed to present students with novel problems that may have more than one correct solution.

Szetela and Nicol (1992, p. 44) present an example (page 75) of a task performance or complex problem designed for elementary mathematics.

Like the other alternative assessment formats, task performances and complex problems are particularly useful in assessing more advanced cognitive skills such as applications, analyses, and syntheses. Many require that students not only generate a solution to the task or problem, but also explain the process they followed to reach their solution. Like other alternative assessment formats, task performances and complex problems can be combined with traditional assessment formats within a single formative to tap a broad range of learning objectives or goals. They are also appropriate at all levels of education.

A Mathematics Problem-Solving Task

A bowl contains 10 pieces of fruit (apples and oranges). Apples cost 5 cents each, and oranges cost 10 cents each. All together the fruit is worth 70 cents. We want to find how many apples are in the bowl. Kelly tried to solve the problem this way.

$$\begin{array}{r} 10 \times 5 = 50 \\ 2 \times 10 = \underline{20} \\ 70 \end{array} \qquad \begin{array}{r} 8 \times 5 = 40 \\ 3 \times 10 = \underline{30} \\ 70 \end{array}$$

$$\begin{array}{r} 4 \times 10 = 40 \\ 6 \times 5 = \underline{30} \\ 70 \end{array}$$

There are 30 apples in the bowl.

1. Is Kelly's way of solving the problem a good one?
   Tell why you think it is or is not a good way.
2. Did Kelly get the right answer?
   Explain why she did or did not.

Task performances and complex problems also have their shortcomings, however. They are generally time-consuming for students to complete but provide only a limited sample of their problem-solving skills. Some researchers suggest that approximately eight to twenty tasks may be needed to reliably estimate a student's capabilities in a particular subject area (Shavelson & Baxter, 1992). Task performances and complex problems also present unique scoring challenges, especially when many correct or appropriate responses are possible.

Guidelines for developing or evaluating task performances and complex problems are the same as those outlined for skill demonstrations and oral presentations. Clear and concise scoring criteria that can be understood by students are essential. An example of a rating scale for complex mathematics problems such as the one illustrated earlier is outlined on page 76 (Szetela & Nicol, 1992, p. 42).

Compositions and Writing Samples

Compositions and writing samples are undoubtedly the most common alternative assessment format used in classrooms today. They are introduced by

An Analytic Rating Scale for Complex Problems

1. Understanding the Problem
   - 0 No attempt
   - 1 Completely misinterprets the problem
   - 2 Misinterprets major part of the problem
   - 3 Misinterprets minor part of the problem
   - 4 Complete understanding of the problem
2. Solving the Problem
   - 0 No attempt
   - 1 Totally inappropriate plan
   - 2 Partially correct procedure but with major fault
   - 3 Substantially correct procedure with minor omission or procedural error
   - 4 A plan that could lead to a correct solution with no arithmetic errors
3. Answering the Problem
   - 0 No answer or wrong answer based on an inappropriate plan
   - 1 Copying error, computational error, partial answer for problem with multiple answers, no answer statement, or answer labeled incorrectly
   - 2 Correct solution

teachers in the early elementary grades and used in classes through graduate and professional school. Any time teachers ask their students to develop a brief written report on a particular topic or to compose an original composition about any subject or theme, they are using writing samples to assess students' learning.

Compositions and writing samples share many of the advantages of other alternative assessments. They are particularly useful in gauging students' abilities to analyze and synthesize what they know about a particular topic, and they should be used for this purpose exclusively. But, in addition, compositions and writing samples offer several advantages that are unique to this format. Specifically, they can be used to tap students' skills in language usage, their ability to present ideas in an organized and coherent way, and their extended use of appropriate detail or evidence in support of a particular point of view.

Furthermore, compositions and writing samples represent an excellent means of introducing students to the use of technology. Modern word-processing programs remove many of the laborious mechanical tasks that traditionally were part of the writing process. Without having to worry about line spacing, margins, pagination, and the like, students can concentrate on the substance and quality of their writing. Revision also becomes much easier because making changes no longer requires rewriting or retyping an entire work.

The procedures for developing and scoring compositions and writing samples are quite similar to the procedures described earlier in this chapter for essays and short-answer items. Because of the importance of organization and coherence in these longer samples of students' writing, however, additional scoring criteria are usually required. These criteria may be *holistic,* involving judgment of the overall quality of the work, or *analytic,* in which various aspects of the work are judged separately. Because analytic criteria are generally more prescriptive and offer students detailed feedback that can guide revisions, they are favored by most mastery learning teachers.

An example of a rating scale based on analytic criteria is shown on page 78 (Kentucky Department of Education, 1992). These criteria are part of the *Kentucky Instructional Results Information System,* a statewide assessment program.

As an assessment format, however, compositions and writing samples have three major drawbacks. First, they are difficult to score objectively and reliably. Many factors can influence teachers' judgments of students' compositions and writing samples. Although thoughtfully developed directions combined with clear scoring criteria help to limit the influence of subjectivity and bias, constant vigilance by teachers is necessary to ensure accuracy and fairness.

Second, the development and preparation of compositions and writing samples require a significant investment of time on the students' part. Gathering background information, analyzing its relevance, outlining, and preparing the response all require time. Although some theorists argue that these are useful learning experiences by themselves, which is probably true, they still take time away from other learning activities that may be equally valuable. One solution is to have students do most of the planning and development work outside of class as homework. Such homework can be highly effective if it includes specific directions to the task at hand, is checked regularly, and guides and directs students toward improvements in their work (Cooper, 1989, 1994).

Third, and probably most serious, compositions and writing samples are extremely time-consuming for teachers to read and score. Although specific scoring criteria make this process much more efficient, it still requires a lot of time. Consider, for example, the average high school teacher who may see 120 students in class each day. If each student completes a composition, and if the teacher spends just five minutes reading each composition and offering students individualized feedback, then the teacher would need ten hours!

Many mastery learning teachers resolve this dilemma by printing their writing or composition scoring criteria on separate scoring sheets. Each student

An Analytic Rating Scale for Student Compositions

Dimension	Description
Idea Development	The degree to which the writer • establishes and maintains a purpose • communicates with the audience
Organization	The degree to which the writer demonstrates • unity • coherence
Support	The degree to which the writer includes details that develop the main point(s)
Sentences	The degree to which the writer includes sentences that are • varied in structure and length • constructed effectively • complete and correct
Wording	The degree to which the writer exhibits correct and effective • vocabulary • word choice
Mechanics	The degree to which the writer demonstrates technically correct • spelling • punctuation • capitalization • usage

is then given two copies of this sheet and a brief explanation of how to use it. Because the scoring criteria were explained as part of the instructional unit, more detailed explanations are unnecessary. Students then exchange papers, read a classmate's work, and mark the scoring sheet accordingly. When all are finished, papers are exchanged again and a similar review is conducted. In this way, each student reads and evaluates the work of two different classmates. Finally, the papers are returned to their authors, with the scoring sheets prepared by the two classmates. Students then review the scoring sheets, confer with their classmates if there are discrepancies or further clarification is needed, and plan revisions accordingly. Their revised paper would be what we will later term formative assessment B.

This procedure offers significant benefits to both students and teachers. For students, reading the work of their classmates and using the scoring criteria can be valuable learning experiences. It gives them insights into how other students approach writing and how the scoring criteria apply to their own work. In addition, the feedback they receive is typically far more detailed than that provided by the teacher, who must read not two, but more than 100 papers. Teachers need to read each student's composition or writing only once, and the revised version they read is likely to be of much better quality.

Laboratory Experiments

Laboratory experiments are also a commonly used form of alternative assessment at every level of education. Although typically associated with science classes, laboratory experiments serve valuable instructional purposes in a wide variety of subject areas. Social studies teachers, for example, often engage students in experiments that involve the collection of survey data or polling information. In all cases, they are activities that permit students to pursue an experimental inquiry that focuses on process skills such as observing and inferring. In addition, they allow students to construct their own understanding of phenomena and relationships.

Like other alternative assessment formats, laboratory experiments are typically used to assess higher levels of cognitive skills. In most cases, they are combined with traditional formats within a single formative assessment. Because of their process orientation, laboratory experiments often require multifaceted assessment; that is, they may involve the demonstration of certain skills, lab notebooks in which students record their procedures and conclusions, and formal reports on findings and interpretations prepared by a team of students.

Creating good laboratory experiments that serve valuable instructional purposes can be challenging, however. The process is time-consuming and requires considerable scientific and technological know-how (Shavelson & Baxter, 1992). Developing scoring criteria for laboratory experiments is equally challenging, especially when a multifaceted approach is used. The procedures described earlier for skill demonstrations, task performances and complex problems, and compositions are useful guidelines in this process.

Projects and Reports

Projects and reports represent yet another common alternative assessment format that is used by teachers at all levels of education. They require students to produce a product that demonstrates not only their understanding of important concepts, but also their ability to organize and present that understanding in meaningful ways. Projects are the principal assessment format in visual and industrial arts, and they also are used extensively by science and social studies teachers. Reports, on the other hand, are used by teachers in every subject area and are especially common in integrated or thematic units of instruction.

Most projects and reports are extensive and often involve instruction over several units. For this reason, in most mastery learning classes they are used as a summative, rather than formative, assessment. They provide a culminating demonstration of what students have learned over a series of units that are all related to a particular topic or theme.

When used as a summative assessment, the project or report typically is divided into two or three parts. A science teacher, for example, may divide the preparation of a research report into three parts representing (1) a description of the problem and its significance, (2) methods and procedures for the investigation, and (3) results and conclusions. As each part is completed by students, the teacher offers specific feedback to guide their corrective efforts, much as is done with compositions and writing samples. Finally, the parts are assembled into a project or report and then submitted as a summative assessment of students' work.

As has been true with all alternative assessment formats, clear scoring criteria are crucial to the successful use of projects and reports as summative or formative assessments. These criteria must be understood by students and communicated to them well in advance of the assessment.

Portfolios

A *portfolio* is a collection of a student's work. The term is derived from artists' portfolios, which are collections of work put together by artists to show their style and range. Student portfolios have the same basic purpose: They are collections of students' products or performances that demonstrate their accomplishments or improvements over time. Portfolios are more than folders that hold all of a student's work, however. They are purposefully selected samples of students' work that are intended to show growth and development toward important learning goals (Airasian, 1994).

Because of their broad scope, multiple components, and cumulative nature, portfolios are more typically used in mastery learning classes for the purposes of summative, rather than formative, assessment. Like projects and reports, portfolios represent a culminating display of students' accomplishments. Although each entry in the portfolio may have been developed through a process that included a series of formative assessments, the portfolio itself is more appropriately used as a summative assessment device.

Group Tasks or Activities

Today, more and more teachers understand the important opportunities and benefits of cooperative learning (Johnson, Johnson, & Holubec, 1994). In most cooperative learning activities, students work together in small groups on collaborative projects or tasks to accomplish shared learning goals. These projects and task are designed to maximize the learning of all students in the group. Well-designed group tasks and activities require that students discuss the accuracy, quality, and quantity of their own and one another's work (Johnson & Johnson, 1989). As a result, students not only master academic goals but also develop important social skills.

For group tasks and activities to be beneficial to both the students themselves and all other group members, they must include components for individual accountability and positive interdependence (Johnson & Johnson, 1995); that is, the performance of each student must be assessed individually, and the results given back to the student and the group. In addition, students must recognize that they cannot succeed in the task or activity unless the other members of their group also succeed.

Like other forms of alternative assessment, group tasks or activities require clear and unambiguous scoring criteria. If the tasks or activities are highly complex, then separate criteria may be required for the group's overall work and each student's individual contribution. This is true, for example, when the "jigsaw" method of cooperative learning is used. In jigsaw activities, a different portion of the learning task is assigned to each of five or six members on a team, and task completion requires contingent and mutual cooperation (Aronson, Stephan, Sikes, Blaney, & Snapp, 1978).

The particular criteria that are specified will depend largely on the nature of the tasks or activities. Those criteria described earlier under laboratory experiments, projects, and reports should be especially helpful in this effort. If the task or activity involves both academic and social skill objectives, then separate criteria for each area will need to be identified and clearly communicated to students. Furthermore, if the task is highly complex or involves students for an extended period of time, then it may need to be divided into two or three subtasks. The assessment of each separate subtask can then serve as a formative assessment, while evaluation of the overall task or activity is a summative assessment.

Arranging Items on the Assessment

After developing items or prompts that address each important concept in a learning unit, we need to consider how these items and prompts can best be arranged in the formative assessment. This process is especially important if the assessment consists of multiple parts, as we discussed in the previous section. Generally, we must consider three aspects of assessment items to determine an appropriate arrangement. Although these aspects are usually interrelated, careful attention to each can enhance both the assessment's quality and validity.

The first aspect is *the level of learning measured by the item.* In most cases, items that measure the same level of learning should be grouped together in the assessment. For instance, items that measure students' knowledge should be grouped together and placed first in the assessment, items that measure students' abilities to make translations might come next, and so on.

Arranging items according to the level of learning enhances the formative assessment's use as an instructional tool. As students work through the assessment, they can make a more gradual shift in the cognitive processes required to answer each question or prompt. This type of arrangement also serves to order the complexity of items in the assessment. Items that measure knowledge-level skills are typically easier than those that measure higher level skills such as application or analysis. In addition, placing easier items early in the assessment can motivate students and prevent weaker students from becoming frustrated at the beginning of the assessment.

The second aspect to consider is *the type of item.* To simplify the assessment process and increase the efficiency of the formative assessment itself, all items of similar type are best grouped together; that is, matching items should be grouped in one section, multiple-choice items in another, alternative assessments in a third, and so forth. This arrangement allows the teacher to provide only one set of directions for each type of item, and it also allows students to maintain a uniform method of responding throughout each section. Sometimes differences in item type or format require dividing the formative assessment into multiple parts. The first part, for example, might be a paper-and-pencil instrument that includes sections with matching, multiple-choice, and completion items, while the second part might consist of a skill demonstration or laboratory experiment.

Generally, item types and levels of learning can be mutually accommodated with little difficulty, even if the formative assessment includes multiple parts. Items that measure a particular level of learning are usually of the same type. When conflicts do arise, the level of learning should probably be favored because of its instructional value.

The third and final aspect to consider in determining an appropriate arrangement of assessment items is the *content elements measured by the item.* A learning unit may cover a fairly wide range of content, depending on the subject and the level of instruction. The elements of content within a unit can usually be grouped in subtopics or "clusters." Often it is best to arrange the items in an assessment according to these clusters of content elements, especially if the clusters differ in their cognitive complexity. As a result, students need not shift back and forth from one content cluster to another as they proceed through the assessment.

In most cases, content element clusters easily accommodate both levels of learning and item types. Within most learning units, the clusters of content elements are usually hierarchically arranged. The simple and most basic elements are typically presented first, while more complex, higher level elements are presented later. Any departures from this general pattern should probably favor the level of learning when the items are arranged in an assessment, again because of this procedure's instructional value.

Relationships Among Assessment Items and Prompts

As we discussed earlier in this chapter, many mastery learning teachers find value in illustrating the direct association between the formative assessment and the table of specifications. This is usually done by placing the number of the assessment item that measures a particular objective beside that objective or content element on the table. This matching process guarantees that no important objectives or content elements are neglected on the assessment. It also clearly illustrates the relationship between the learning objectives outlined in the table of specifications and the assessment items.

Another practice that many teachers find quite useful is illustrating the relationships among the items in a formative assessment. Just as a learning unit's concepts and objectives have definite relationships, so do the assessment items and prompts that address those concepts and objectives (Airasian, 1969). For example, knowledge of particular terms in a unit often is essential to understanding a fact or process that incorporates those terms. Or knowledge of particular facts may be essential to determining the solution to a complex problem. If the formative assessment includes items that measure students' knowledge of those facts *and* their ability to solve such complex problems, then these items should be explicitly related.

Relationships such as these can be illustrated with a diagram similar to the one in Figure 3.1 (page 84). The circled numbers in the figure correspond to items in a formative assessment. These same numbers would be placed beside the important objectives or content elements that are identified in the unit's table of specifications.

The lines that connect the numbers show the relationships among the items. For instance, the figure shows that items 1 through 5 are designed to measure students' knowledge of particular terms. Item 6 measures students' knowledge

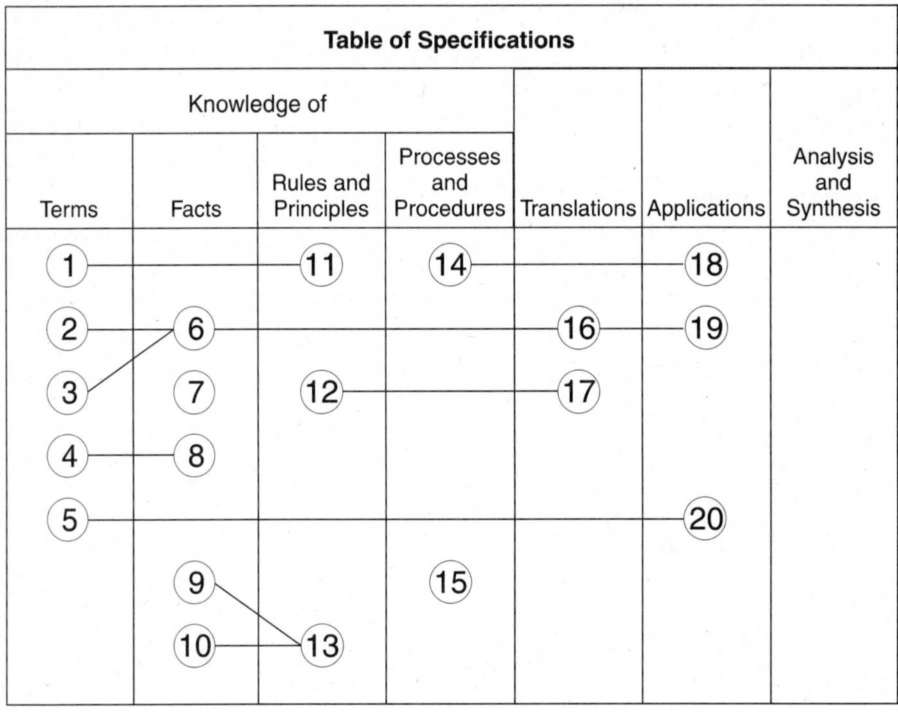

Figure 3.1 Relationships among items in a formative assessment

of a fact that incorporates the terms in items 2 and 3. Item 16, in turn, measures students' skill in translating the fact addressed in item 6. Students' ability to apply that fact in a new and different situation is measured in item 19. The lines that connect items 2, 3, 6, 16, and 19 clearly illustrate this relationship.

Such an extended relationship as this is rare in a formative assessment. In this case, these terms and facts must be especially important for students' learning. Most formative assessments generally contain several items that are not directly related to any other items, even though they also measure important objectives. This is true of items 7 and 15. Figure 3.1 also shows that the items are arranged in terms of the level of learning measured. Items placed later in the assessment measure higher level skills than those at the beginning.

Illustrating the relationships among items in a formative assessment is also useful when prescribing appropriate corrective activities. Obviously, a student who does not understand the definitions of important terms is unlikely to be able to translate or apply a fact that incorporates those terms. The corrective activity for this student would be returning to the basic definition of the terms. On the other hand, another student may understand the terms and facts but have difficulty with translation or application skills. This student requires correctives that provide additional practice in these specific kinds of skills.

Although the relationships among assessment items that measure different levels of cognitive skills hold for most subjects and most grade levels, there are many exceptions. For example, students learning elementary mathematics may be quite proficient with the facts and rules of subtraction, and they may be able to apply those facts and rules to solve complex problems. At the same time, those same students may have great difficulty recalling terms such as *subtrahend* and *minuend*. Even though exceptions such as these do exist, highlighting the relationships among assessment items can be helpful for both teaching and learning.

Characteristics of Good Formative Assessments

Many of the characteristics of good formative assessments are common to all good testing or assessment instruments, but others are unique to the formative process. The following list describes the principal characteristics of good formative assessments.

1. *A good formative assessment should be clear and legible to all students.* The major purpose of any formative assessment, regardless of its form, is to provide information to students on their learning progress. As such, all students must clearly understand the assessment and what they are required to do. If they cannot read and decipher the assessment, interpret words that are within it, or understand the scoring criteria, then they will be unable to gain prescriptive feedback and will not profit from the assessment experience.

2. *A good formative assessment should contain precise directions that are stated in clear and simple language.* Regardless of the format of the assessment–that is, whether it is a traditional paper-and-pencil instrument, a skill demonstration, or a composition or writing sample–clear and precise directions are critically important. The directions should indicate how students are to complete the assessment (How should answers be recorded? What should be the format of their response?), how the assessment will be evaluated or scored (Will partial credit be given? What are the dimensions of the rating scale? Does spelling count?), and how much time will be allowed for the assessment. In addition, the directions in a formative assessment should reemphasize that its primary purpose is to provide students with information on their learning progress. Generally, teachers orally review the directions to an assessment before administering it. But even when this is done, directions should also be included with the assessment itself. If questions arise during the assessment, students can consult these directions. Examples of useful directions can be found in Chapters 9 through 14.

3. *A good formative assessment requires a minimal amount of class time.* Although formative assessments serve many valuable instructional purposes, they should not take up an inordinate amount of class time. Students should be able to complete most formative assessments in twenty to thirty minutes; in other words, in about half a class period. In this way, the same class period can be used to administer the assessment, go over it, and give students immediate feedback on the results. Of course, this may not always be possible, especially when more time-consuming, alternative assessment formats are used. Keep in mind that a formative assessment should cover all of the learning unit's important concepts but not be so long that the time required to complete the assessment takes away from valuable instructional time.

More concepts and material can be covered on a formative assessment in less time by using the most efficient assessment format for measuring particular learning skills. Traditional assessments, especially matching and multiple-choice items, are highly efficient in measuring knowledge level skills. Their use can save a great deal of assessment and scoring time. Furthermore, they permit the option of having students quickly score their own assessments. Of course, some learning objectives require the free-response format of essay items or one of the alternative assessment formats. In most cases, though, traditional assessment items are most efficient for checking students' learning progress and identifying their learning difficulties when the instructional focus is on knowledge-level skills.

4. *Good formative assessments usually include "spiraling" items.* Spiraling items are assessment items that "refer back to" or build on concepts or material covered in previous learning units. For example, an assessment on the concepts from one learning unit might include two or three spiraling items that address objectives that were a part of earlier units. Spiraling items serve three important purposes. First, they reinforce previous learning and encourage retention of the concepts presented in earlier units. Second, they help to illustrate the transfer of concepts and generalizations from one unit to the next. And third, they offer students yet another chance to demonstrate their mastery of concepts that might have been difficult for them in earlier units. Although the number of spiraling items should be kept to a minimum in any formative assessment (no more than 10 to 20 percent of the items in the assessment), they are extremely useful in enhancing retention and improving learning.

5. *A good formative assessment should be well matched with the table of specifications.* As discussed earlier in this chapter, matching the formative assessment to the table of specifications ensures congruence between learning objectives and procedures for checking students' learning. Although using the table as a guide in developing or refining formative assessments helps to build this congruence, a follow-up check of the match between the table and the assessment provides additional assurance.

One technique for providing this additional check is to have a colleague review the formative assessment, asking two questions of each item or prompt: (1) What must a student know or understand to answer this item? (2) What must a student do to answer this item? The answers to these questions should locate each item or prompt precisely on the table of specifications. Any discrepancies between the colleague's and the assessment developer's judgments can be used to sort out or improve items that may be inappropriate or invalid. This additional check also strengthens the assessment's objectivity and reliability. A similar technique can be used to review and judge the adequacy of published assessments or assessments that a teacher may have developed previously.

Preparing a Parallel Form B Assessment

Using a second, parallel formative assessment in each learning unit is an essential element in the application of mastery learning. This assessment is often referred to as the *retake assessment* or as *formative assessment B* (the first one being *formative assessment A*). The second assessment is administered to students who did not attain mastery on the first one for the unit and thus were involved in individualized corrective activities. It serves as a check on the corrective activities to see if they were indeed successful in helping students overcome their learning difficulties. But, perhaps more important, the second formative assessment is a powerful motivational device that demonstrates to students that they can be successful in their learning and reach a high level of achievement.

Sometimes this second formative assessment is mistakenly labeled a "summative assessment," but it truly is not. Bloom (1968, 1976) drew clear distinctions between formative and summative assessments in terms of both their purpose and scope. Formative assessments are learning tools that are designed to diagnose student learning errors and prescribe corrective procedures in each unit of instruction. Summative assessments, on the other hand, are comprehensive evaluation devices that are used to certify competence and assign grades. The typical summative assessment covers concepts from two, three, or more instructional units. Hence formative assessments are more like quizzes, while summative assessments more closely resemble examinations. This distinction is further clarified in Chapter 5.

The second formative assessment in a mastery learning unit is referred to as *parallel* because it is designed to measure the same concepts and learning skills as the first formative assessment for that unit and is of comparable difficulty. In most cases, it is matched, item for item, with the first formative assessment, and both can be used interchangeably. This is not to say, however, that the items in each assessment are identical. Although the items in the second formative assessment measure the same concepts at the same cognitive level as those in

DIRECTIONS: Place a 1 to the left of the continent with the largest area and place a 3 to the left of the continent with the smallest area.

Assessment A item:

_____ Africa _____ Asia _____ Australia

Assessment B item:

_____ Antarctica _____ Europe _____ South America

Figure 3.2 An example of items that measure the same subject matter but vary in difficulty

the first, they ask questions in a somewhat different way or in a different format. Thus the use of the two assessments illustrates to students the importance of understanding the concept or objective rather than simply knowing the right answer to a specific question.

Of course, the parallel nature of formatives A and B depends largely on the assessment's format. If the assessment involves a skill demonstration, for example, then the performance criteria should be identical for formatives A and B, even if the task is somewhat altered. The scoring checklist or rating scale also should be the same. Comparing their scores on the checklists or scales from formatives A and B allows students to see precisely the improvements they have made. Likewise, if the formative assessment involves a composition or writing sample, then formative B would be simply the revised version of formative A and, again, the exact same scoring criteria would be used. When alternative assessment formats are used, therefore, keeping formatives A and B parallel requires consistency in the scoring criteria, even if the context is slightly altered.

Preparing a second formative assessment usually takes less time and effort than it did for the first. However, preparing a second assessment that is truly parallel to the first can be challenging. The general tendency in developing a second assessment is to create one that is more difficult. For instance, consider the two items in Figure 3.2 (adapted from Millman, 1981, p. 148). Both items were designed to measure the same content–that is, knowledge of the relative sizes of continents. But, invariably, students who can answer item A correctly find the second item, B, much more difficult because the second item requires them to make much finer discriminations.

Often, simply altering the format of an item can change its difficulty. A matching item that requires students to recognize the appropriate response is typically easier than a completion item that requires them to recall specific information. A multiple-choice item, on the other hand, is more likely to be comparable to the matching item because it too is a "selected response" type of item. Sometimes even subtle changes in the tasks students are asked to perform can drastically alter the difficulty. It is important to be aware of these possible discrepancies in difficulty when preparing the second formative assessment to assure students of a fair chance of success.

Again, colleague review is a good way to check a second formative assessment to see that it is both parallel and comparable in difficulty. In this review, questions should be raised about the concepts covered and cognitive level of the items or tasks, as well as the relative difficulty of each. In other words, the colleague should ask, "Are the items or prompts in this assessment of comparable difficulty to those in the first assessment?" A similar check can also be made in evaluating parallel assessments in published materials.

Setting the Standard for Mastery

A formative assessment should cover all of the important concepts in a learning unit. However, the assessment itself does not provide any indication of how well students are expected to learn those concepts. This is done by setting the standard for mastery for the assessment. The standard for mastery is the level of performance on the assessment that indicates that the concepts from the unit have been learned well. That level of performance is what we expect of all students. It is also the level that divides those who go on to enrichment activities from those who will be engaged in correctives.

Setting an appropriate standard for mastery is not as simple as it may seem. Several advanced statistical procedures are available to select an appropriate performance standard (see, for example, Angoff, 1971; Ebel, 1972), but these generally require greater time and statistical sophistication than are available to most classroom teachers. A simple percentage is the most typical standard employed by teachers who use mastery learning. The majority of mastery learning teachers choose the level at which a student would receive a high B or A grade, usually 85 percent correct on the assessment. Some teachers prefer a standard of 90 percent correct, while others are satisfied with 80 percent.

Setting the standard below 80 percent correct, however, is not a good idea. Below that level, students may not gain sufficient understanding of concepts that may be needed for more advanced work. The one exception to this general rule is when students are asked four questions addressing the same concept. Under these conditions, being able to answer three of the four questions correctly–that is, 75 percent–is probably sufficient.

Selecting a standard for mastery above 90 percent correct also should be avoided. Such a high standard places a great deal of importance on the assessment device itself, and rarely is an assessment or evaluation device perfect. All are likely to include one or more items that are ambiguous, inappropriate, or otherwise invalid. A standard of mastery above 90 percent correct may require students to do well on even these flawed items. In addition, Block's research on mastery assessment indicates that requiring perfect or nearly perfect performance on each unit can have marked negative consequences on students' interest and attitudes toward learning (Block, 1970, 1972). For these reasons, a standard for mastery on a formative assessment set between 80 and 90 percent correct is generally best.

This general rule has three addenda, however. First, it may be necessary to vary the standard for mastery, depending on the importance of a specific objective. Some objectives are so important and so critical for students' learning that they demand 100 percent mastery. Teaching children how to cross the street safely is one example. No one would be satisfied with only a 90 percent success rate on this objective. Similarly, the skills taught to prospective physicians or airline pilots must be perfectly mastered because of the serious consequences of any error. Therefore, while a mastery standard between 80 and 90 percent correct is applicable in most instructional situations, variations due to the importance of certain objectives are certainly acceptable.

Second, the mastery standard should never be set below the level of the B grade; that is, if the lowest B grade is given to the 85 percent level of performance, setting the mastery standard at 80 percent correct would be inappropriate. To do so indicates to students that they can attain "mastery" but still receive a grade of C. Most teachers find that even if the B performance level is set as the mastery standard, they must offer some provision within enrichment, such as extra credit, so that students can improve their mark from a B to an A. Options such as this are discussed in greater detail in the next chapter.

Third, there are distinct advantages for students if the teachers within a school reach consensus on the mastery standard to be employed. Doing so generally involves an open discussion of what each teacher feels is appropriate and what all can find acceptable. Having agreement on the mastery standard avoids the situation in which a student has one class where the standard is 85 percent correct, across the hall it is 80 percent, but further down the hall it is 90 percent.

Some teachers find the process of setting a mastery standard to be personally troublesome. They question, for example, what it really means to "master" something. Although this is an intriguing issue from a philosophical perspective, keep in mind that all teachers make decisions such as this every day. In the process of evaluating students' performance and assigning grades or marks to their work, teachers continually make judgments about various levels of "mastery." Although specifying the criteria for these judgments and clearly communicating those to students does not make the process any less arbitrary, it does make it less subjective. In addition, it offers students more specific guidance on what they must do to improve.

Formative Assessments and Grading

Grading practices and the use of formative assessments is an issue that is often raised in discussions on the implementation of mastery learning. As mentioned earlier, many teachers do not count formative assessment results as part of their students' grades. They believe that doing so takes away from the use of formatives as learning tools and that students would still see the formatives as grading and evaluation devices rather than as sources of information on their learning. These teachers use formative assessments only to provide students with feedback on their learning progress to guide the correction of learning errors.

Other teachers, however, need to use formative assessment results as one source of data in determining students' grades. Some of these teachers are required to record a certain number of grades for each student during a marking period and therefore feel compelled to include formative assessment results. Still others, particularly those who teach at the high school level, feel they need to give some credit to the formative assessments in order to enhance students' motivation to do well and formally recognize their learning successes.

Teachers who count formative assessment results as a part of students' grades use a variety of strategies. Although each strategy has advantages and disadvantages, some are clearly more beneficial to students' learning than others. Some are even detrimental to students' learning and should be avoided or discontinued.

The first strategy, and the earliest used by teachers implementing mastery learning, counts only the results from the second formative assessment. This strategy reinforces the use of formative assessments as learning tools and extends to students the "second chance" opportunity to demonstrate what they have learned. Students who attain the mastery standard on the first formative assessment simply receive that mastery score with the possibility of improving it by successfully completing enrichment activities. The one disadvantage of counting only the second assessment is that students may express concern about the possibility of their scores going down. Especially at the elementary level, some students become overly anxious about the second formative assessment because it is "the one that counts."

To avoid this dilemma, many teachers adopt the second strategy, which is to count the higher score from the two formative assessments. In other words, the student has no chance of doing worse because only improvement counts. This is undoubtedly the most commonly employed strategy in mastery learning classrooms today. If the correctives have been successful, then scores on the second formative assessment will always be better. The one exception occurs when the second formative assessment is unintentionally made more difficult than the first. This is an assessment problem, however, not a learning problem, and one that is easily remedied through adjustments in the assessment instrument.

A third strategy counts the second formative assessment but limits its value. In other words, even a score of 100 percent correct on the second formative assessment translates to only a B grade. To receive a grade of A, students must attain the mastery standard on the first formative assessment and engage in enrichment activities. This strategy was developed by teachers who had trouble motivating students to do well on the first formative assessment when they knew they would have a second chance.

Despite its logic, this strategy is counter to the philosophy of mastery learning and should not be used. It denies students the opportunity to use the formatives as learning tools, and it punishes those students for whom the mastery learning process works best. Furthermore, the practice of assigning a grade of B to students who demonstrate they have learned 100 percent of what the teacher counts as important is difficult, if not impossible, to defend. Some teachers counter that important learning objectives are gained through involvement in enrichment activities, and this strategy recognizes that achievement. But if this is the case, learning activities related to those objectives should be part of the instructional unit itself, and items assessing those objectives should be included on both formative assessments for the unit.

In a fourth strategy, teachers average students' scores from formative assessments A and B. This strategy was also developed by teachers who had difficulty in motivating students to do well on the first formative assessment. Even when rewarding enrichment opportunities were provided, these teachers found that some students simply took the first formative assessment without studying for it and then used that assessment to prepare for the second formative assessment because it was "the one that counts."

Like the strategy of limiting the value of the second formative assessment, however, averaging scores has negative consequences that make it inappropriate in mastery learning classes. In particular, this strategy overly penalizes students who have serious difficulties on the first assessment. Consider, for example, the student who attains only 50 percent correct on formative assessment A. After the assessment, this student works hard to correct her learning errors and attains 100 percent correct on formative assessment B. Although this student has evidently learned well what was expected in the unit, her averaged score is only 75 percent–a score that clearly does not reflect her level of learning. Students can be motivated to do well on the first formative assessment in better ways than punishing them with a low grade. Several effective and more positive techniques are discussed in Chapter 6.

A fifth strategy also was developed in an effort to motivate students to do well on the first formative assessment: Average the scores from formatives A and B, but give more weight to formative B. Teachers who use this strategy may give the second formative assessment three times the credit they give to the first assessment. In the case of the student who received a score of 50 percent on formative A and 100 percent on formative B, for example, the teacher would add 50 and 300 (3 × 100) and then divide by four to get an average score of 87.5 percent. Although this strategy is somewhat more defensible than using an unweighted average, it is still problematic and should be avoided.

A sixth strategy that is somewhat more complex but is becoming increasingly popular is to count formative assessment A but give add-on credit for formative B. Teachers who use this strategy typically give half "makeup" credit for both corrective work and the second formative. For example, suppose a student attains 40 percent correct on the first formative assessment, leaving 60 percent to make up. The corrective assignment for that student would be worth half the credit he needs to get 100 percent for the unit, or 30 percent (half the remaining 60 percent). If that student completes the corrective assignment, 30 percent is added to the first mark (40 + 30 = 70 percent). The second formative assessment is worth the other 30 percent needed. If the student attains 100 percent correct on formative assessment B, then his mark is raised from 70 percent to 100 percent for the unit. If the student attains 85 percent correct on formative assessment B, then his mark is raised to 85 percent for the unit. If on the second formative assessment the student attains only 70 percent correct or less, then his mark remains at 70 percent for the unit (avoiding taking away credit that already has been earned by students), but an individual conference is scheduled with the teacher to discuss why improvement was not greater. Under this strategy, additional credit (10 or 15 percent) can also be given for enrichment work, allowing students who attain the mastery standard on the first formative assessment to reach 100 percent or even more for the unit.

Strategies for Using Formative Assessments in Grading

1. Count only formative assessment B.
2. Count the higher score from A or B.
3. Count formative assessment B, but limit its value.
4. Average scores from formative assessments A and B.
5. Average, but give more weight to formative assessment B.
6. Count formative assessment A, and use add-ons for B.

Regardless of the strategy used, teachers must continually remind students that formative assessments are principally a source of information, showing students what is important to learn, how well they have learned those concepts and skills, and what they need to learn better. In other words, formative assessments are primarily learning tools. Even when formative assessment results are used in determining grades, it should be stressed that this is a secondary function of the assessment. Students should also be informed that the results from formative assessments are always given less weight in determining their grades than are the results from summative assessments and other culminating demonstrations of their learning. Additional considerations for grading and evaluating student learning are discussed in Chapters 5 and 6.

Technology and Formative Assessment

Computers are becoming widely available in schools throughout this country and around the world. Furthermore, today more and more students have computers in their homes. This increased availability of personal computers has led to the development of a growing number of highly creative software programs that offer individualized instruction on a multitude of topics. Many of these programs are on compact disks (CDs) or laser disks that include animation and color graphic displays that both amaze and delight students. The flexibility and ease of use of most modern computers–that is, their "friendliness"–also allows students to design their own programs and games with little programming knowledge. In addition, programs are now available that teachers can use to facilitate the process of formative assessment.

In many schools, teachers have recorded their formative assessments on computer disks (Haddock, 1982; Heikkinen & Dunkleberger, 1985). Generally, teachers have developed these assessments on their own, but some have simply entered assessment devices that are included in their instructional materials. Once on disk, teachers can decide whether they want students to receive feedback immediately after completing the assessment or item by item after students have entered their responses. Often the computer can then score the assessment, give students detailed analyses of their responses, and prescribe specific corrective or enrichment activities.

Computers offer teachers many advantages. Because of their information-processing speed, computers tremendously enhance the immediacy of the feedback that students receive from formative assessments (Christie & Savers, 1989). Computers also increase the efficiency and accuracy of the feedback information that teachers receive on students' learning progress (Farnsworth & Wilkinson, 1987). As mentioned earlier, computer word-processing programs allow teachers to use many alternative assessment formats that previously were impractical. Computers also facilitate sharing among teachers by making material available in a format that is easy to review and change. For example, a poorly worded formative assessment question found on a computer disk can be easily reworded, replaced, or simply eliminated. Before computers, making such a change would require cutting and pasting or retyping the entire assessment.

The use of computers for formative assessment will be limited to some degree by the available number of computers or computer terminals. Generally, only one student at a time can work at the computer when completing a formative assessment. But when they are available, computers can free teachers of many assessment and corrective management responsibilities and thus allow greater time for instructional planning.

Summary

Formative assessments are mastery learning's principal vehicle for providing students with feedback on their learning progress. These assessments help students identify what is important to learn and how well they have learned those concepts and skills. To develop a formative assessment, the teacher should take the following steps:

1. Identify the important objectives in the unit that are to be learned by all students. These objectives will include the concepts that students are expected to learn and the skills they are expected to develop in relation to those concepts. The table of specifications should serve as a guide in identifying the unit's most important content elements and learning objectives.
2. Review available assessment devices to ensure that all of the unit's important concepts and skills are addressed. Then develop items or tasks for any learning objectives that may have been missed or not fully measured. Keep in mind that both the content elements and the cognitive skills required of students must be considered and that the assessment format should match the skill level. If the assessment uses essay items or some form of alternative assessment, then clear and precise scoring criteria also must be developed.
3. Arrange the items and prompts in the formative assessment. Primary consideration should be given to the level of learning measured by the items and the instructional purposes of the assessment. Precise directions also must be included on the assessment so that students will know what they are expected to do and what criteria will be used to judge their performance.
4. Again, check the formative assessment against the table of specifications. This process ensures congruence between the unit objectives and the procedures for monitoring students' learning.
5. Develop a second, parallel formative assessment. The second formative assessment for a unit should measure the same objectives as the first, but it should ask questions in a different way or in a different format. If an

alternative assessment format is used, then the scoring criteria for judging students' performances or products should remain the same. The second formative assessment is used to check on the success of the corrective activities and also to illustrate to students that they can be successful in learning.

6. Check the two formative assessments for parallelism. To be optimally effective, the two formative assessments for a learning unit should measure the same objectives at the same cognitive levels and be of comparable difficulty.
7. Set the standard for mastery of performance on the formative assessments. A cutoff score should be established to indicate which students have appropriately mastered the unit and which should be encouraged to engage in corrective activities. In most cases, an ideal standard is 80 to 90 percent correct on the formative assessment.

Activities

1. Develop a table of specifications for a learning unit and identify those concepts and skills that are important for all students to learn well. (Use this chapter as the learning unit if another is not available.)
2. Prepare a group of assessment items or prompts that can be used to ascertain whether students have truly mastered each important content element or learning objective in the unit.
3. Arrange the items and prompts into a formative assessment, taking into account the level of learning measured, the type of item or prompt, and the content elements measured in each. Write directions for the assessment and develop the criteria to be used in scoring the assessment.
4. Prepare a second, parallel formative assessment that addresses the same important concepts and cognitive skills as the first but which asks questions in a different way or in a different format. Make appropriate adjustments if alternative assessment formats are used.
5. Have a friend or teaching colleague review both formative assessments, checking the parallelism of the assessments and their correspondence to the table of specifications. The friend or colleague should also estimate the time that students might need to complete each assessment. This ensures that the assessment process does not take up an inordinate amount of class time.
6. Discuss any discrepancies that arise in the review. This additional check enhances the validity of the formative assessments and ensures consistency between learning objectives and the procedures used to check students' learning.

4

Feedback, Correctives, and Enrichment

We are now ready to consider what takes place after students' learning progress has been checked: the feedback, correctives, and enrichment activities.

Nothing is more central or critical to the implementation of mastery learning than the feedback and corrective process. This is also the aspect of mastery learning that most clearly differentiates it from other, more traditional approaches to instruction. Although the feedback and corrective process typically requires no more than a single class period in a learning unit, it is the primary mechanism through which mastery learning becomes truly individualized. Through this process, each student receives precise information on his or her learning progress and is directed to specific corrective activities. The correctives are tailored to the unique learning styles and needs of individual learners. They are designed to help students overcome their learning errors so that they learn the unit concepts well and acquire the prerequisites for the next learning task. When the feedback and corrective process goes well, the improvements in student learning are often dramatic.

The Purpose of Feedback for Students

Providing feedback to students helps them identify what they have learned well or mastered, and what they need to spend more time learning. Most teachers offer informal feedback throughout the instructional process by questioning their students as they engage in learning activities and by monitoring classroom exercises and homework assignments. But students also need to receive more formal feedback on their learning progress that is both regular and specific. In mastery learning classrooms, this type of feedback is provided to students through the regular administration of formative assessments. As we discussed in Chapter 3, formative assessments typically are brief quizzes or skill demonstrations that are administered after each week or two of instructional time. They focus on the key concepts and skills from the unit and offer students specific information on their learning progress. As the result of a formative assessment, students should have clear ideas about how well they learned the unit's important concepts and what additional work is needed.

Formative assessments also offer students information on the adequacy of their preparations for class and whether their focus in studying meets the teacher's expectations. Suppose, for instance, that a teacher was interested in having students apply what they learned from a unit and solve complex problems, but that a student mistook the teacher's emphasis and concentrated on memorizing terms and facts. This disparity would become clear with the results of the formative assessment, which undoubtedly focused on applications and problem solving, not definitions and facts. In other words, the feedback provided by a formative assessment reinforces precisely what is most important for students to learn and be able to do in the unit, and it also communicates to students how well they have learned those concepts and mastered those skills.

The nature of the feedback provided will depend in part on the format of the formative assessment. For example, if the assessment is a short quiz composed of matching, multiple-choice, and completion items, then the feedback students receive may be simply a record of which items were answered correctly and which were missed. Knowing that each item is designed to assess a particular concept and skill, students can immediately turn to corrective activities that focus on those that they have not yet mastered. On the other hand, if the formative assessment includes essay items or involves one of the various forms of alternative assessment, then students will need a clear and precise description of what was lacking in their response and how it can be improved. To provide this description, specific criteria for evaluating students' responses should be developed, together with ways of communicating these criteria to students. If the formative assessment involves a skill demonstration, for example, then clear and explicit criteria for evaluating students' performance are essential if the feedback is to be prescriptive and useful.

The Purposes of Feedback for Teachers

The results from formative assessments also provide teachers with two critically important kinds of feedback. The first is an explicit description of each student's learning progress. With formative assessment results, teachers know which students are doing well, which are having problems, and exactly what problems those students are having. The formative assessment thus provides the teacher with precise information that can be used to guide corrective activities that focus on students' individual learning difficulties.

The second type of feedback that teachers receive is information about their original instruction's effectiveness. The results from formative assessments help teachers pinpoint what was taught well, which learning activities were successful, and which were not. The summary chart in Figure 4.1 (page 100) provides an example. Many teachers construct a chart like this as soon as they finish scoring a formative assessment. The marks beside each number indicate how many students answered the item incorrectly or failed to meet a particular criteria component.

Ideally, if the original instruction were effective and all instructional activities worked well, then few students would miss any particular item. However, look at items 7 and 12, and criterion 3 for the second essay item. Items 7 and 12 were answered incorrectly by more than half of the students in the class, and criterion 3 of the second essay item was missed by nearly all students. Clearly, either these are poor items and scoring criteria or the instruction on these concepts and skills was not effective. Perhaps these concepts were explained in a way that was vague or unclear to students. Perhaps the instructional activities that involved these concepts lacked focus, or the presentation in the textbook was confusing. Perhaps the questions or prompts in the formative assessment were inappropriate or ambiguous to most students. Or perhaps the scoring key had an error. Whatever the reason, this is important information to a teacher. A similar kind of summary can be prepared for skill demonstrations, compositions, or other alternative assessment formats by simply listing the criteria used for scoring and then indicating the number of students who did not meet each criterion. This procedure was followed for the essay items shown in Figure 4.1.

With the feedback from a formative assessment, teachers know where to concentrate their efforts in improving their teaching. They know where new approaches or different examples are needed, and where alternative materials or activities may be required. Certainly the concepts missed by a large number of students will need to be reexplained or retaught in a different way, and different learning activities will need to be planned. These improvements can then be carried over to future lessons and learning activities, enhancing the teacher's overall effectiveness.

Also note items 3 and 10 in Figure 4.1. These items were answered correctly by all students in the class. Perhaps these were two especially easy items, or perhaps their wording made the correct answer obvious. On the other hand, these items may have addressed concepts and skills that were taught exceptionally

Results from Formative Assessment Number 3.

Number of students in the class: 28.

Item	No. of Errors
1.	I
2.	III
3.	
4.	II
5.	卌
6.	I
7.	卌 卌 IIII
8.	卌
9.	II
10.	
11.	IIII
12.	卌 卌 卌 I
13.	III
14.	卌 II
15. Essay A	
Criterion 1	II
Criterion 2	IIII
Criterion 3	卌 II
16. Essay B	
Criterion 1	I
Criterion 2	卌 III
Criterion 3	卌 卌 卌 卌 III

Figure 4.1 A summary of incorrect responses on a formative assessment

well. The point is that a formative assessment not only identifies problems or difficulties, but also helps to identify successes and areas of strength.

Answer Sheet	
Name ______________________	Name ______________________
Formative No. ______________	Formative No. ______________
DIRECTIONS: Circle the letter of the correct answer or write the answer on the blank beside the number.	DIRECTIONS: Circle the letter of the correct answer or write the answer on the blank beside the number.
1. a b c d e ______	1. a b c d e ______
2. a b c d e ______	2. a b c d e ______
3. a b c d e ______	3. a b c d e ______
4. a b c d e ______	4. a b c d e ______
5. a b c d e ______	5. a b c d e ______
6. a b c d e ______	6. a b c d e ______
7. a b c d e ______	7. a b c d e ______
8. a b c d e ______	8. a b c d e ______
9. a b c d e ______	9. a b c d e ______
10. a b c d e ______	10. a b c d e ______
11. a b c d e ______	11. a b c d e ______
12. a b c d e ______	12. a b c d e ______
13. a b c d e ______	13. a b c d e ______
14. a b c d e ______	14. a b c d e ______
15. a b c d e ______	15. a b c d e ______
16. a b c d e ______	16. a b c d e ______
17. a b c d e ______	17. a b c d e ______
18. a b c d e ______	18. a b c d e ______
19. a b c d e ______	19. a b c d e ______
20. a b c d e ______	20. a b c d e ______

Figure 4.2 A general double answer sheet for formative assessments

Many teachers gather feedback on their teaching while at the same time providing feedback to students by using a double answer sheet with formative assessments similar to the one in Figure 4.2. This is an especially popular practice in early instructional units because it helps students become acclimated to the mastery learning process. Double answer sheets are appropriate for use with most traditional assessment formats. The one in the figure, for example, could be used with true/false items (a or b), matching items (up to five options), multiple-choice items, and completion items (write the word, name, symbol, or number on the blank). The use of double answer sheets with alternative assessment formats, however, requires certain adaptations. Teachers who use essays, short answers, or other writing samples as formative assessments, for instance, often use paper that includes "carbonless" copies for this purpose. Although multiple-copy paper may not be in great supply in most schools, many businesses have surpluses or unused old forms that they usually are willing to donate to teachers.

To use the double answer sheet, students simply record their answers twice, marking both halves of the answer sheet identically. When they complete the assessment, they tear the answer sheet in half, keeping one half and returning the other half to the teacher. In this way, both the student and the teacher have a record of responses to each formative assessment item. Some teachers have students correct both halves of the answer sheet before returning one. Other teachers ask students to return one half before scoring in the belief that correcting the assessment gives them a clearer picture of each student's progress. This procedure also minimizes the possibility of students changing answers while the assessment is being corrected.

Double answer sheets allow teachers to offer students immediate feedback on their performance. This is especially important because the effectiveness of such feedback is directly related to its immediacy (Kulik & Kulik, 1987). In other words, the sooner students receive feedback on their performance, the more likely that the feedback will be used to guide their improvement efforts.

Teachers who use double answer sheets generally go over the formative assessment as soon as students have completed it. In correcting the formative, students see precisely what items were missed and what concepts and skills they must concentrate on during their corrective work. As they review the assessment with their students, most teachers initiate corrective activities by again explaining those concepts that many students found difficult. When the scoring is completed, students can begin work immediately on correctives or enrichment activities. And all of this can be accomplished before the teachers correct and score their halves of the answer sheets.

When time permits, these teachers will correct their copies of the answer sheets, determine how well each student is doing, and make a summary chart similar to the one in Figure 4.1. They can then use this information to guide students in their corrective work. But equally important, the teachers can use the information to plan for improvements in their own teaching. Other examples of double answer sheets can be found in several of the mastery learning units in Part II.

Remember that whatever the formative assessment's format, it is a communication device for both students and teachers. The feedback it provides teachers is just as useful and as important as the feedback it provides students.

Essential Characteristics of Correctives

Obviously, gaining precise information about students' learning progress is vitally important, but if their learning is really to be improved, the information must be paired with specific activities to remedy any learning difficulties. In most mastery learning classes, these activities are referred to as *correctives.* In some programs, however, they are called *additional activities, additional practice, alternative activities,* or *second chance activities.* Regardless of the label, correctives serve a specific purpose in mastery learning: They help students correct the learning errors and remedy the learning problems they experienced during the original instruction.

To be successful, the correctives must be different from the original instruction. Simply having students go back and repeat a process that has already proven unsuccessful is unlikely to yield better results the second time. Above all else, corrective activities must offer instructional alternatives to students. In other words, they must provide students with an alternative pathway to learning success.

For the corrective activities to provide this different pathway, they must possess three essential characteristics.

First, they must present the concepts differently from their original presentation; that is, the content elements and skills must be explained in a different manner or from a different perspective and include different examples. If a deductive approach (that is, one that presents a general concept before moving to specific examples) was initially used, then an inductive approach (that is, one that presents a variety of specific examples before moving to the general concept) might work well as a corrective.

Suppose, for example, that a teacher explained how to compute the area of a rectangle by first explaining the rationale behind the formula–*Area* = *length* × *width*–and then moving to specific examples. A corrective approach might have students first cover different rectangles with unit squares, count how many squares are required to cover each rectangle, and then "derive" the formula. Whatever the approach, some change in format, style, or method of presentation is essential.

Second, corrective activities must involve students in learning in ways that are different from their original involvement. This means that the correctives must incorporate different learning styles or modalities (Carbo, Dunn, & Dunn,

1986; Gregorc, 1985; McCarthy, 1987; Renzulli & Smith, 1978) or different forms of intelligence (Armstrong, 1994). Learning styles are not abilities in themselves, but preferred ways of using one's abilities. Styles vary from student to student as well as within individual students depending on the task or situation (Sternberg, 1994). For example, a student may have a liberal style (that is, enjoys doing things in new ways) in science class but a conservative style (that is, prefers beginning with the familiar) in gym or mathematics classes. The theory of *multiple intelligences,* on the other hand, indicates that students have different inherent abilities and intellectual strengths, including the linguistic, logical-mathematical, spatial, musical, kinesthetic (or bodily), interpersonal, and intrapersonal (Gardner, 1983). According to multiple intelligences theory, teachers can help students learn better by linking instructional objectives to these different intellectual dimensions.

Variety and flexibility are the keys to using these ideas in corrective activities; that is, the full range of styles and intelligences must be considered. If students were originally taught through a visual demonstration, for example, then a more detailed auditory presentation or an individual opportunity to manipulate material tactually might be a useful corrective. If an individual learning kit was used initially, then working with the teacher or another student might serve well as the corrective activity. If a group activity was used initially, then an individual activity might be used as the corrective, perhaps one that uses computers or some other form of technology. Again, whatever the alternative, the student's involvement in the learning must be qualitatively different from the original instruction.

Essential Characteristics of Corrective Activities

1. Correctives must present the concepts differently from the way they were originally presented.
2. Correctives must involve students in learning in ways that are different from the way they were originally involved.
3. Correctives must provide students with a successful learning

Third, the corrective activity must provide students with a successful learning experience. This essential characteristic is just as important as the first two but often taken for granted. Regardless of its format or involvement, if a corrective activity does not help students overcome learning difficulties and experience learning success, then it is not an effective activity and should be discarded for another alternative. Correctives must provide students with the means to be successful in their learning, for that success enables them to be better prepared, more confident, and more motivated for future learning tasks.

Types of Corrective Activities

Planning for corrective activities is not easy. Most teachers naturally teach as they learn best, and that often is the way many of their students learn best. Because of the diversity among students, however, some probably learn best in other ways. Their primary learning style, modality, or intellectual strength is different from their teacher's. Many teachers consider these differences when they plan their original instruction and include activities that engage students through a variety of learning modalities. This typically makes the original instruction effective for a larger portion of students and reduces the number of students who must do corrective work. In mastery learning classes, however, we are interested in having *all* students learn well. Hence the corrective activities are specifically designed to offer a different, but equally valuable learning experience to students for whom the original instruction was not optimally effective.

Corrective activities can range from extremely simple to highly complex, depending on the resources available and the grade level of the students involved. The effectiveness of any particular corrective activity also varies with the grade level and, to some extent, the subject area. For example, at the high school level a simple and effective corrective activity in some subject areas is to have students carefully reread particular pages in the textbook where a specific concept is discussed. However, the same corrective activity is not effective for second- or third-grade students because of their more limited reading skills.

Many teachers find it useful to organize corrective activities into three groups: (1) activities to be done with the teacher, (2) activities to be done with a friend, and (3) activities to be done by oneself. Although any particular activity is likely to fall into more than one category, every activity should provide students with a difference in presentation and involvement. Furthermore, most mastery learning teachers plan several types of corrective activities for each unit. This not only allows students greater personal choice in their corrective work, but also accommodates a wider variety of learning modalities. An additional advantage of planning several corrective activities is that if a particular activity falls flat, then another can be immediately used without wasting valuable time.

Many mastery learning teachers find the following corrective activities effective: reteaching, individual tutoring, peer tutoring, cooperative teams, course textbooks, alternative textbooks, alternative materials, workbooks and study guides, academic games, learning kits, learning centers and laboratories, and computer activities.

Reteaching

Reteaching is one of the simplest and undoubtedly most commonly used corrective activities. Having the same teacher (or another teacher when team-teaching is employed) reexplain a difficult concept in a new way or with a different approach is often highly effective as a corrective. Even when other types of corrective activities are planned, most teachers use reteaching as they go over the formative assessment, explaining again concepts that many students misunderstood or found difficult. Reteaching also allows teachers to focus attention on those students who most need help.

The greatest challenge in reteaching is ensuring that it involves a different presentation and different level of student involvement. When reteaching a difficult concept, some teachers simply restate their original explanation louder and more slowly, perhaps believing that increased volume and a slower pace are what some students need. But this "louder and slower" approach is seldom effective. Reteaching requires the teacher to keep in mind the essential characteristics of an effective corrective activity.

When using reteaching, teachers generally bring together students with specific learning problems and then discuss, review, and reexamine their particular misunderstandings. In team-teaching, simply having another teacher explain a difficult concept often works well as a corrective. Reteaching can be done in small groups or on a one-to-one basis.

Individual Tutoring

Individual tutoring is one of the most effective of all corrective activities. Typically, a tutor simply goes through the formative assessment with an individual student, explaining those concepts that were missed in a new way or from a different perspective. During this process, the tutor constantly checks on the student's understanding. Even teachers who use other forms of correctives usually monitor the progress of their students with some form of individual tutoring, especially for those students who are having serious difficulties. Many teachers use students from advanced grades as tutors with excellent results. Others find that adults such as teacher's aides, parents, and elderly persons make excellent tutors. Regardless of who serves as the tutor, when individual tutoring is possible, it is one of the most efficient and most powerful types of corrective activity.

Peer Tutoring

Students who have already mastered the important concepts in the learning unit often make excellent tutors for their classmates. Like individual tutors, peer tutors typically can explain concepts from a different perspective or in ways that are different from the teacher's (Grossman, 1985). In addition, research evidence indicates that students who serve as peer tutors benefit as much or more from the experience as the students they help (Bargh & Schul, 1980; Webb, 1982). By helping a classmate understand a new concept, they deepen their own understanding.

When peer tutoring is used as a corrective activity, it is better if presented as one of several options and self-selected by both the student and the tutor. Requiring two students to work together can be counterproductive for both and detrimental to the mastery learning process. Furthermore, students who serve as peer tutors should not feel compelled to do so in every learning unit. They should be encouraged to take part in other forms of enrichment as well.

Cooperative Teams

In cooperative teams, three to five students meet to discuss their learning problems and help one another. The teams are heterogeneous, are typically assigned by the teacher, and can stay intact for several learning units. Although no particular grouping strategy is necessary in forming these teams, it is best if not all team members have the same learning problems.

During the typical corrective session, students go through the formative assessment item by item or point by point. A question or critical element missed by one or more students is explained by another team member who understands that concept or skill. If all members of the team are having difficulty, then they can work collaboratively to find a solution or call on the teacher for assistance. Most teachers find that students welcome these opportunities to work together and help one another. After each item is discussed and the difficulties are resolved, the group moves on to the next item, continuing through the assessment.

Course Textbooks

Having students reread explanations or discussions in the course textbook is a simple but highly effective corrective. When students return to the textbook and reexamine particularly important passages, they often are able to clarify issues that they missed in their first reading. By combining rereading with other activities–such as having students write a two- or three-sentence paragraph that explains a concept in their own words–teachers can help students improve their understanding and remedy their learning problems.

Teachers who use the course textbook as a resource during corrective activities simply indicate where a particular concept is explained or discussed in the textbook. Page numbers are often listed beside each item or problem on the formative assessment. These references also can be listed on the answer sheet for the formative. By carefully reviewing and rereading the relevant portion of the textbook, students often gain a better understanding of the concepts presented.

Although referring students to the course textbook may seem to be repeating "the same old thing" rather than using something new and different, students often do not read their textbooks carefully. And even those who do sometimes have difficulty identifying important concepts and the most critical information in the material as they read. Mastery learning programs at both the high school and college level have found correctives as simple as this to be effective in helping students overcome many learning problems (Guskey, Englehard, Tuttle, & Guida, 1978; Guskey & Monsaas, 1979).

Alternative Textbooks

When they are available, alternative textbooks often provide a different presentation or explanation of important ideas or concepts. Some teachers simply save their old textbooks when a new one is adopted to offer students an additional resource for information. Again, the page numbers in the alternative textbook where a particular concept is discussed can be listed beside each item or problem on the formative assessment or on the answer sheet. Alternative textbooks and materials also can provide additional practice exercises as well as enrichment or extension activities.

Alternative Materials

Alternative materials include movies, videotapes, audiotapes, videodisks, film-strips, models, and so forth. The variety of these materials makes them highly effective as corrective activities for a range of student learning styles. In addition, the variety of presentation formats allows the teacher to choose appropriate materials for student use with the teacher, with a friend, or working alone.

Workbooks and Study Guides

Workbook activities and study guides also can be useful correctives. Page numbers of particularly appropriate activities or exercises are easy to specify. In addition, the teacher usually can check activities or exercises directly. Workbook and study guide activities are usually different from activities in the course textbook and thus are an excellent alternative for presenting the unit material. In addition, unlike most textbook presentations of information, many of these activities extend students' learning by focusing on higher level cognitive skills such as application and analysis.

Academic Games

Academic games are usually group activities in which students work together to solve a particular problem or accomplish a task that relates to the learning unit. In essence, they are a variation on cooperative teams. The advantage of academic games is that most can be easily adapted or modified to suit particular learning objectives. In some cases, teachers even make up their own games when an appropriate one is not available. Teachers who use academic games as correctives generally find that, when carefully supervised, they help to involve students in learning and promote cooperation and collaboration among students.

Learning Kits

Learning kits usually present information and involve students in a different way than did the original instruction. Most kits are highly visual, and many involve the manipulation of materials. In addition, a kit can typically be used with the teacher, among a small group of students, or by a student working alone. Learning kits are widely available from commercial publishers, and many teachers even make their own.

Learning Centers and Laboratories

Directing students to a learning center or learning laboratory can often be a useful corrective activity. During the time they spend in these centers, students are given help on their specific learning problems, usually under the guidance of a learning supervisor or center aide. In addition, the activities in which they engage often are more hands-on and manipulative than might have been possible during the original instruction. Generally, the time spent in such a center is most effective when students are involved in a structured activity or are given a specific assignment to complete.

Computer Activities

Many teachers now use computers and other forms of technology as a primary resource for corrective activities. This includes not only computer-assisted instructional activities, but also CD-ROMs (which means "compact disk, read only memory"), videodisks, laser disks, interactive video, various forms of hypermedia, and a variety of powerful "on-line" resources. Some teachers have even begun to explore the use of CDIs (short for "compact disk interactive"), which deliver the best qualities of videodisks and the data and sound from CDs (Bortnick, 1995). Not only is this technology highly versatile, but also its "user-friendly" nature makes it appropriate at almost any grade level. In addition, research evidence indicates that it can be highly effective as an alternative instructional resource for many students in mastery learning classes (Christie & Sabers, 1989; Whiting, 1985).

Computer activities allow students to work alone at their own pace or in collaboration with a classmate. Many computerized tutorial programs also allow students to control the kind and amount of help they receive. In addition, helping interactions are more private and potentially less embarrassing. The only limiting factors are the quality of the software and the number of computers available. The use of computers and other forms of technology does require the teacher to spend class time explaining basic operating procedures and supervising students' initial involvement. When students become familiar with their operation and the software closely matches the objectives of the learning unit, however, computer activities can be a highly effective corrective (Schofield, Eurich-Fulcer, & Britt, 1994).

Corrective Activity	With the Teacher	With a Friend	By Oneself
Reteaching	✔		
Individual tutoring	✔	✔	
Peer tutoring		✔	
Cooperative teams		✔	
Course textbooks	✔	✔	✔
Alternative textbooks	✔	✔	✔
Alternative materials	✔	✔	✔
Workbooks and study guides	✔	✔	✔
Academic games	✔	✔	
Learning kits		✔	✔
Learning centers and laboratories		✔	✔
Computer activities		✔	✔

Table 4.1 The various types of corrective activities and how they might be used

Table 4.1 summarizes some corrective activities and how they might be used.

Specifying Correctives

One of the most important aspects of the corrective process is deciding the best way to specify the correctives–that is, deciding how to let students know what the correctives are and how they should be completed. In most instances, the sooner students become involved in corrective activities after the formative assessment, the better for their learning. Therefore students should be notified of their corrective activity options immediately following the formative assessment.

Generally, teachers use three methods to specify correctives to their students, and each has its own advantages and limitations. Some teachers even change their method of specifying correctives from one unit to the next to accommodate differences in assessment format. The techniques most commonly used are described below. Specific examples of each are also provided in the sample chapters in Part II.

Specifying Correctives on the Formative Assessment

The correctives that students should complete can be indicated right on the formative assessment itself. This is an especially popular method when the formative assessment is composed primarily of traditional types of items. In such instances, teachers simply list several sources of information on the concept or objective covered by an item beside that item on the formative. For example, the page numbers in the course textbook where that particular concept is discussed may be listed, together with page numbers from alternative textbooks, workbook activities, or study guides. At the high school or college level, many teachers also list the date of the class session in which the concept was explained. Typically, these resources are identified by adding a line after each item on the formative assessment such as:

(Text: pp. 56–57; Workbook: p. 21; Lesson: 4/13)

The directions to the assessment would explain that this means the concept that item addresses is discussed on pages 56 to 57 in the course textbook, on page 21 in the course workbook, and in the class notes from April 13. A student thus has three different sources of information on that particular concept. From this information, students may be asked to prepare a brief paragraph explaining the concept in their own words, answer several alternative questions, develop one or two new questions relating to the same concept, or complete any other activity that ensures their involvement in the corrective process.

Specifying correctives on the formative assessment works well when the correctives are fairly simple. Particularly for students in upper grades, having correctives paired with each item right on the assessment itself seems to facilitate involvement in the corrective process. It also helps students focus their efforts while working on correctives. When the correctives are more complex, however, including them on a formative assessment can complicate the assessment and make it unduly long. Furthermore, when the correctives are listed on the formative assessment, students must be allowed to keep their copy of the assessment.

Specifying Correctives on the Scoring Guide or Answer Sheet

Corrective activities also can be listed with each criterion on a scoring guide or beside each item number on an answer sheet. When this is done, however, the correctives must be explicit. Because students may not recall the details of their performance or skill demonstration, they need highly specific directions on what they must do to improve. In the case of a written assessment composed of traditional types of items, students need precise guidance on how to correct their errors. This is especially true if students are not permitted to keep the assessment as a reference to the concepts or skills to be learned.

A double answer sheet can be easily adapted to include a listing of corrective activities. Such an answer sheet would look somewhat different from the one in Figure 4.2. The half returned to the teacher would need to list only item responses, but the half kept by students would list item responses plus the designated corrective activities for each item. Again, these could be simply page numbers from textbooks or workbooks or more complex activities. In addition, while the answer sheet in Figure 4.2 can be used with any formative assessment that includes twenty or fewer items, listing the correctives on the answer sheet necessitates the use of a different answer sheet with each formative assessment.

Specifying Correctives on a Separate Sheet

A third way to specify corrective activities is on a sheet separate from both the formative assessment and the answer sheet. Using a separate "corrective sheet" also requires that the correctives be explicit, particularly if students do not keep a copy of the formative assessment.

There are two different types of separate corrective sheets. The first is distributed to students after the formative assessment, and it lists various corrective activities. The list might describe specific correctives for each item on the assessment, for item clusters, or for subsections of items. A single corrective activity might be designated for each, or several activities may be outlined from which students can choose.

The second type of corrective sheet is not distributed to students. Instead, it lists resources the teacher plans to use with students engaged in corrective work. This type of corrective sheet is most frequently used by teachers in the early elementary grades. At this level, formative assessments tend to be simple and typically cover only a few concepts or basic skills. Corrective activities at this level also tend to be simple and are generally directed by the teacher. This corrective sheet serves as a resource for the teacher. It lists activities and materials that are different from the ones used during the original instruction, but which address those same unit concepts and skills. Having such a list already prepared allows the teacher to move students quickly into corrective activities without losing time in transition.

Managing the Corrective Activities

In classes taught by most traditional methods, only the very best students engage in corrective work on a regular basis. These students review their quizzes and tests after the teacher has marked them, making sure that they understand the problems or concepts that they missed. The majority of their classmates, however, simply put the quiz or test in their notebook (or in the trash can) and proceed with work on the next unit. Involvement in corrective activities therefore is a new and unfamiliar experience for most students. Few are accustomed to getting information from assessments, to being shown by the teacher how to use that information, or to getting a second chance to demonstrate their learning. Because these activities are so new and different for most students, they must be carefully managed by the teacher, especially when mastery learning is being implemented for the first time.

Most mastery learning teachers administer a formative assessment after a week or two of instruction. Generally, the assessment is given at the beginning of a class period and usually requires no more than twenty or twenty-five minutes for students to complete. Some teachers, however, administer a formative assessment after only two or three days of instruction, while others may spend as long as three weeks on a particular unit before administering a formative. Furthermore, some formative assessments require only ten or fifteen minutes to complete, while others may take thirty or thirty-five minutes, depending on the material's complexity and the nature of the assessment. Although such differences may make some adjustments and modifications necessary, they usually can be accommodated with little difficulty.

In most cases, teachers correct the formative assessment in class after students have returned a record of their responses, usually on one-half of an answer sheet. While correcting the formative, the teacher goes over each item or assessment criterion, stopping occasionally to reexplain items or concepts that appear to be troublesome to a majority of students. After the correcting is complete, the mastery score is announced–usually between 80 and 90 percent correct. Most students will already know what the mastery score is because teachers generally explain the standard of mastery when orienting students to the new mastery learning procedures.

At this point, the class typically is divided into two groups: students who attained the mastery score or higher, and those who did not. Those who attained the mastery score are provided high quality enrichment activities, or they may volunteer to serve as peer tutors. Those who did not begin their corrective work. The exception occurs when cooperative teams are used, in which case students simply move together to begin working with their teammates.

The teacher must remember two important things if the class is divided into separate enrichment and corrective groups. First, students who attained the mastery standard must be recognized and praised. This can be done, for example, with simply a show of hands accompanied by verbal praise or congratulations from the teacher. Recognizing their achievement is reinforcing to these students, and it also helps to ensure their persistence in future learning units. Second, the teacher must express confidence in the skills of those students who have not yet attained mastery. These students should be assured that if they work to correct their difficulties, it is likely they will attain mastery on the second formative assessment for the unit. In addition, they will then have an excellent chance at mastery on the next unit's first assessment. Some teachers convey this confidence as an expectation of students' future performance, assuring students that with hard work, they can certainly reach mastery.

Once students who met the mastery standard begin work on their enrichment activities, the teacher turns his or her attention to the students involved in correctives. Especially in early learning units, the corrective activities must be fairly structured and teacher-directed because these procedures are new to the majority of students.

Most teachers begin the correctives with reteaching, or explaining the ideas and concepts that were difficult for students in a new and different way. With their explanations, they often pair alternative materials and examples in order to offer students another form of involvement. Typically, this is followed by guided practice activities in which students are helped through structured problems or exercises. Many teachers then turn to independent practice activities in which students work on their own to demonstrate their understanding. While students are working independently, the teacher generally moves from student to student, asking questions to ensure understanding and offering individualized assistance. At the same time, the teacher can check on those students engaged in enrichment, making sure they are on task and not having difficulties.

Keep in mind that correctives are not just one activity. In the example above, reteaching was combined with alternative materials, guided practice, independent practice, and individual tutoring. All of these activities can be monitored directly by the teacher. If students work on their own or with a friend to complete their correctives, then most teachers require completion of a specific assignment that is turned in to the teacher. This assignment may simply summarize the corrective work that was done, or it may be a more detailed exercise. Once students become accustomed to the corrective process, however, many teachers relax or eliminate this requirement.

Allocating Time for Correctives

The allocation of time is one of the most crucial aspects to the success of corrective activities. When mastery learning is first implemented, the correctives *must* be done in class under the teacher's direction. Teachers who begin implementation by allowing correctives to be done outside of class as homework or during a special study session before or after school are rarely successful. This is especially true when mastery learning is implemented in the middle grades or at the high school level. Such procedures do not work well initially because those students who most need and could most benefit from the correctives are typically the least likely to participate.

When the correctives are done under the teacher's direction in class, students see explicitly the benefits of mastery learning to them. They gain direct evidence on how the process works, what the teacher is trying to do, and what the payoff is for them. Once they have this evidence, they are much more likely to engage in corrective activities on their own. Although mastery learning does not make learning easier, it provides a strategy that these students can use to become more successful and more confident as learners.

After students become accustomed to the mastery learning process and realize its personal benefits, the teacher can drastically reduce the amount of class time allocated to correctives. The correctives also can be less structured and less teacher-directed. More corrective work can be handled as a homework assignment or in special study sessions before or after school. In addition, as students catch on to mastery learning, more of them typically do well on the first formative assessment. As a result, more students are involved in enrichment and fewer in corrective activities. The amount of corrective work that students need to reach the mastery standard also diminishes (Whiting, Van Burgh, & Render, 1995). These developments allow for still further reductions in the amount of class time spent on correctives.

Most teachers begin their implementation of mastery learning by allocating one to one and one-half class periods to corrective and enrichment activities in the first learning unit. In one class session, they administer, review, and correct the formative assessment and begin correctives and enrichment. The second session may be devoted entirely to corrective and enrichment activities. In the third session, they administer the second formative assessment to students in the corrective group while the other students continue their enrichment work. The second part of the class is then devoted to introducing the next learning unit.

After three or four units, this format is altered so that corrective work not completed during the first class period is assigned as homework. In the next class session, correctives are reviewed, any additional problems are discussed, and the second formative assessment is administered. After several more units, most teachers find that they can further reduce the class time allocated to correctives. When this is done, however, the first and second formative assessments are still best administered on different days to allow time outside of school for corrective work and review.

Few mastery learning teachers allow more than one or two class periods for correctives between the first and second formative assessments because of the demand for content coverage. Few teachers can afford to spend more than a day or two on corrective work when they are required to cover a given portion of the curriculum within a certain time. Taking extra time during early units to familiarize students with the corrective process, however, helps to ensure that students will continue these activities when the amount of class time allotted for correctives is reduced. In addition, by ensuring that students learn early units well, instruction in later units can proceed more rapidly. Students are better prepared to learn new concepts, and less time must be spent in review activities. Thus the time lost to correctives in early units is made up through a faster instructional pace in later ones.

Motivating Students to Do Correctives

Getting students to become involved in the corrective process and to complete their corrective work is a major challenge. Although we cannot guarantee that all students will actively engage in corrective activities, there are several ways to encourage and to maintain their involvement.

First, having the correctives be teacher-directed activities done in class virtually guarantees that students will complete their work, at least in these early learning units. When corrective activities are fairly structured and teacher-directed, students are more likely to take them seriously and put forth the effort necessary to complete them. Once they see firsthand how the process benefits them, they are much more likely to complete subsequent corrective assignments on their own.

Second, explaining mastery learning to students in some detail at the beginning of the term or school year also motivates students to do corrective work. Although the mastery learning process is new and different and requires extra work for the vast majority of students, most will cooperate if they understand the reasons for each step in the process and how it can help them learn.

Third, some teachers explain to students that the corrective process is actually a way to take the guesswork out of learning. They point out that a formative assessment shows precisely what is important for students to learn and whether or not their preparations for the class have been adequate. The corrective activities simply represent the additional things that must be done to attain mastery on the unit. They have no tricks, secrets, or surprises. Most teachers find that students are less apprehensive and more willing to take risks when they know what is expected of them.

Fourth, some teachers stress to students that the corrective process is simply "the one extra step it takes to be successful." Most students see quizzes and tests as their one and only chance to be successful–and many are not. Corrective activities, however, can be viewed as the extra step that allows all students the opportunity to reach success. In most cases, if students are initially involved in some form of corrective activity and, as a result, see improvement in their scores from the first formative assessment to the second, then motivational problems disappear. Many teachers report that students are eager to begin their corrective assignments in order to have a "second chance" at success. And, as mentioned earlier, the experience of success is one of the most powerful of all motivational devices.

Finally, some mastery learning teachers use still other motivational techniques. Many acquaint parents with the mastery learning process and encourage them to assist their children in doing corrective work. Parents generally appreciate these opportunities to help their children with specific learning problems. Other teachers count completed corrective assignments as the ticket to the second formative assessment; that is, to qualify for the second formative and the second chance to demonstrate what they have learned, students must first complete their corrective work. These teachers stress that they are doing special things to help their students learn well, but students also have responsibilities in the process–the major one being to complete their correctives.

Regardless of the technique employed, it is crucial that students become actively engaged in corrective activities, especially during early units. If mastery learning is to improve students' learning and result in higher levels of achievement for all, then they must be involved in the corrective process. (Additional suggestions on motivation are discussed in Chapter 6.)

Essential Characteristics of Enrichment

Within any group of students, there are likely to be several fast learners. These are students who have developed highly effective learning strategies or for whom the original instruction was especially effective. These students do well on the first formative assessment and score at or above the mastery level. Having demonstrated their mastery of the unit's concepts and skills, there is no need for them to take part in review, reteaching, or corrective activities. They should not, however, sit around biding their time while the other students are involved in correctives. Instead, these students should be given opportunities to extend and enrich their learning. This is the primary purpose of enrichment activities in mastery learning.

Enrichment activities provide students with opportunities to broaden and expand their learning. Often enrichment goes beyond the established curriculum and allows students to become involved in topics or areas of their choice. Suppose, for example, that a student is keenly interested in some aspect of a subject that was just touched on in class but not thoroughly explored. Enrichment activities might allow the student to investigate that topic in greater depth. In this way, mastery learning is different from most "continuous progress" approaches to instruction, in which a student's only option after mastering a unit is to move on to the next sequential unit.

As we discussed in Chapter 1, effective enrichment activities have two essential characteristics. First, they must be rewarding to students and offer exciting learning opportunities. If enrichment is only busywork or repeats earlier classroom activities, then it presents no reward for doing well on the formative assessment. Similarly, if enrichment only provides more and harder problems for students to solve, then doing well on the formative assessment simply means these students have to do more. Enrichment activities, therefore, must be involving enough that students will want to take part. Furthermore, when enrichment activities are rewarding and exciting, students become more highly motivated to attain mastery on the first formative assessment.

Second, effective enrichment activities must be challenging and provide students with a valuable learning experience. Enrichment activities represent an excellent opportunity to involve students in higher level cognitive skills and tasks such as analysis, synthesis, evaluation, and critical thinking. Although these higher level tasks are usually more difficult for students, they are precisely the kind of activities that fast learners find most stimulating and challenging.

In addition, teachers should remember that enrichment activities need not be directly related to the content of the learning unit. Although enrichments usually should relate to the subject being taught, these opportunities do not have to be restricted to a specific unit's content. Some learning units do not lend themselves to enrichment. This is especially true of early units in an instructional sequence that typically focus on basic skills or review material presented in previous years. Teachers who relate enrichment activities directly to the content of such units quickly find themselves perplexed and frustrated. Every subject area, however, has a broad range of exciting and challenging enrichment opportunities. So long as these do not require an inordinate amount of time and offer students valuable learning experiences, they can be considered appropriate enrichment activities.

Essential Characteristics of Enrichment Activities

1. Enrichment must be rewarding to students and offer exciting learning opportunities.
2. Enrichment must be challenging to students and provide a valuable learning experience.
   - Enrichment need not be directly related to the content or objectives of the unit.

Planning Enrichment Activities

Some teachers are exceptionally creative and able to develop many different types of enrichment activities for their students. Most teachers, however, find the development of high quality enrichments to be one of the most challenging aspects of implementing mastery learning. Because these activities typically go beyond the regular curriculum, planning for them requires teachers to go beyond their usual classroom practices and consider entirely new areas of learning. Enrichments also require teachers to extend their own thinking in ways that are exciting but often difficult at first.

For these reasons, teachers sometimes neglect the development of high quality enrichment activities when they first implement mastery learning, concentrating instead on the corrective process. From their perspective, those students involved in correctives have greater learning needs. As a result, the students engaged in enrichment spend their time doing busywork that may have little educational value. The frequent use of "word-search" puzzles and other simple skill games are examples. This neglect of enrichments undoubtedly accounts for the results from some studies of mastery learning that show the process to be more effective for slow learners than for students who learn more quickly (Chan & Cole, 1986).

We must recognize that students involved in enrichment activities also have special learning needs. Furthermore, involving these fast learners in busywork just to keep them occupied is detrimental to their learning progress. High quality enrichment activities are essential to these students's learning and to the mastery learning process.

At the same time, although teachers must plan for enrichment activities, they do not have to develop these activities on their own. Many resources are available from which teachers can draw high quality enrichment activities. Among the best are materials and activities that are designed for gifted and talented students. More and more publishers today are turning their attention to developing materials for these students, and they are an excellent resource for enrichment activities.

The following are several publishers who offer materials, activities, or computer software that is specifically designed for use with gifted and talented students. Most of these materials are accompanied by recommendations about the grade level or age of students for which they are most appropriate. These publishers also offer flyers and catalogs describing their materials, many of which include sample activities.

Critical Thinking Press & Software, P.O. Box 448, Pacific Grove, CA 93950-0448

Dale Seymour Publications, P.O. Box 10888, Palo Alto, CA 94303-0879

Thinking Works, P.O. Box 468, St. Augustine, FL 32085-0468

In addition, several individual publications and periodicals offer lots of useful ideas for high quality enrichment activities. Some that mastery learning teachers have found to be particularly useful include:

Games magazine, published by Games Publishing Group, 19 West 21st Street, New York, NY 10010

Handbook of Instructional Resources and References for Teaching the Gifted, by F. A. Karnes and E. C. Collings (1980), published by Allyn & Bacon, A Division of Simon & Schuster, Inc., 160 Gould Street, Needham Heights, MA 02194

Mind Joggers! by S. S. Petreshene (1993), published by the Center for Applied Research in Education, Inc., Route 59 at Brookhill Drive, West Nyack, NY 10995-9901

Teaching Gifted Kids in the Regular Classroom, by S. Winebrenner (1992), published by Free Spirit Publishing, 400 1st Avenue North, Suite 616, Minneapolis, MN 55401

The Schoolwide Enrichment Model: A Comprehensive Plan for Educational Excellence, by J. S. Renzulli and S. Reis (1985), published by Creative Learning Press, P.O. Box 320, Mansfield Center, CT 06250

ZigZag magazine, published by Games Publishing Group, 19 West 21st Street, New York, NY 10010

Zillions magazine, published by Consumers Union of the U. S. Inc., 101 Truman Avenue, Yonkers, NY 10703-1057

These resources offer materials, activities, and software for students from kindergarten to college level. They range from relatively simple to extremely complex. An example of a simple but challenging enrichment exercise is the following problem:

> DIRECTIONS: This is an addition problem. Each letter represents a unique numeral. Exactly ten different letters are involved, so every numeral from 0 through 9 will be used. To solve the problem, simply determine what numeral each letter represents.

```
  DONALD
 +GERALD
 -------
  ROBERT
```

Hint: D = 5*

Solving this problem requires only addition and subtraction skills. In fact, because every numeral will be used, the problem may be solved through a process of elimination. As simple as this problem appears, however, it is challenging to even sophisticated college students. Stimulating and challenging problems such as these make excellent enrichment activities for a broad range of students.

Many school districts and educational systems have directors or coordinators of gifted education who can recommend a variety of these types of activities. Librarians, media specialists, and counselors may have their own suggestions and recommendations not only on materials and activities, but also on ways to

*Solution:

```
  526,485
 +197,485
 --------
  723,970
```

adapt available resources to the needs of particular students and specific classroom situations.

Types of Enrichment Activities

The fast learners who do well on the first formative assessment and qualify for involvement in enrichment activities are usually more self-directed in their work. For this reason, enrichment activities typically do not require as much structure as corrective activities. And just as providing options for students involved in corrective work is a good idea, so is making several different types of enrichment activities available to students. Allowing students some degree of choice and flexibility in these activities enhances their rewarding characteristics.

Master learning teachers have found the following enrichment activities to be particularly successful: peer tutoring; cooperative teams; students developing practice exercises for fellow students; skill-related media materials; special projects and reports; challenging games, problems, and contests; and advanced computer activities. Each activity involves students in higher level cognitive skills and, if well planned, can be both rewarding and challenging to fast learners. Keep in mind that enrichment activities should be related to the general subject of a learning unit, but they need not relate directly to that unit's specific content. What is important is that they offer students a valuable learning experience and be activities in which they will want to participate.

Peer Tutoring

Helping another student to understand the material in a learning unit can be an enriching experience for fast learners. As they try to find ways to explain an idea or concept to a classmate, most students discover that they gain a better understanding of the concept themselves. Research studies on peer tutoring indicate, in fact, that the benefits for the tutor may be even greater than for the student being tutored (Bloom, S., 1976; Cohen & Kulik, 1981; Goodlad & Hirst, 1989). Peer tutoring also encourages involvement in higher level cognitive skills, such as viewing the idea or concept from several different perspectives, thinking of new applications or examples, and analyzing its various components (Gartner & Riessman, 1994).

Despite its many positive benefits, however, peer tutoring should not be the only option available to students involved in enrichment. And although teachers can actively encourage fast learners to become involved in peer tutoring, they should not demand participation. Requiring students to serve as peer tutors can be detrimental to social interactions among students within the class. A better practice is to begin with a group activity, such as cooperative teams, and then extend this to individual peer tutoring in later units.

Cooperative Teams

As discussed earlier in this chapter, cooperative teams involve three to five students working together to discuss their learning problems and help one another. These heterogeneous teams are assigned by the teacher and usually stay intact for several learning units. In early learning units, the fast learners typically serve as team leaders, directing the discussion of the formative assessment and helping teammates who may be having difficulties. In later units, leadership roles are usually shared. The goal of the team is to have every member reach the mastery standard. If they do, then the team may qualify for extra credit (see discussion below) or some other form of special recognition.

Most teachers find that fast learners welcome these opportunities to work with their classmates. Sharing their understanding allows them to extend their learning in new and creative ways. Cooperative teams also help students develop important social skills that will be essential in later work and professional endeavors (Guskey, 1990a).

Developing Practice Exercises for Fellow Students

Instead of working directly with other students, fast learners can help to create new practice exercises for a particular learning unit. The challenge of trying to come up with new ways of presenting particular concepts or introducing new skills can be exciting. As they struggle with making the concepts easier to understand and determining which kind of exercises would be most beneficial, these fast learners also use a variety of higher level cognitive skills. In addition, the process helps students recognize more clearly the challenges their teachers face on a daily basis.

Developing Skill-Related Media Materials

Constructing models, filmstrips, slide shows, audiotapes, videotapes, and other types of audiovisual materials are especially exciting activities to many students. These materials can be in the form of learning kits, academic games, or other alternative learning resources. They are often useful to slower learners as corrective activities and, like practice exercises, their development usually involves higher level cognitive skills. When resources are available to allow students these opportunities, they make excellent enrichment activities.

Special Projects and Reports

Working on a special project or preparing a special report is a highly rewarding enrichment activity for many fast learners. This project or report should be on an idea that is particularly interesting to the student and related to the subject. In some cases, the project may be extended as an enrichment over two or more learning units. This enhances the student's motivation to do well on the first formative assessment in the next unit in order to return to the project.

Specific guidance and direction from the teacher are usually necessary when students first begin a special project or report, especially with regard to project specifications, limits, and time lines. Therefore it is best to reserve this enrichment option until after students have become accustomed to the mastery learning process. Once familiar with it, however, fast learners generally welcome these opportunities to work more or less on their own. In addition, such projects give students the chance to develop their own special talents and explore new areas of interest.

Remember, however, that special projects and reports can be frustrating to fast learners if research materials on the topic they select are not available in the classroom or even the school library. The use of modern technology, especially online sources of information and data, has enabled many teachers to avoid this problem. But even when students have access to such technology, teachers still must check regularly on students' progress and offer specific feedback to ensure the project or report stays on track.

More Challenging Games, Problems, and Contests

Many teachers find that fast learners are intrigued by more challenging games or problems related to the subject. For instance, mathematics teachers find that many students are fascinated by problems related to geometric reasoning, complex functions, and topography. Logic problems and exercises in inductive or deductive reasoning are also fascinating to many. For example, consider the following problem:

> DIRECTIONS: A cat, a small dog, a goat, and a horse are named Angel, Beauty, King, and Rover. Read the clues below to find each animal's name.*
>
> a. King is smaller than either the dog or Rover.
> b. The horse is younger than Angel.
> c. Beauty is the oldest and is a good friend of the dog.

	A	B	K	R
C				
D				
G				
H				

* From Harnadek (1978)

Fast learners in upper elementary and middle grades not only are challenged to find solutions to these types of problems and games, but also learn from one another as they compare their problem-solving strategies. Again, books, workbooks, and activities for gifted and talented students are particularly useful resources for these types of games and problems.

Advanced Computer Activities

Computers and other forms of technology are an excellent resource for enrichment activities. The many programs available today through CD-ROMs, videodisks, laser disks, interactive video, various forms of hypermedia (including CDIs), and numerous online resources present teachers and students with a wide variety of enrichment options. And, as we discussed earlier, this technology is highly versatile, "user-friendly," and appropriate at almost any grade level. In some cases, students can even become involved in developing their own computer programs to solve problems or create new games. Although some direction and planning on the part of teachers are essential for these kinds of activities, they offer fast learners a variety of exciting challenges.

Similar to their use in correctives, computers allow fast learners involved in enrichment to work alone at their own pace or in collaboration with classmates. Again, the software and number of computers available are limiting factors. Because many software programs also retain a record of each student's accomplishments, teachers have ready access to detailed information on how well students have done and how far they have progressed. When students become familiar with the use of computers and the software has definite educational purposes, computer activities can be highly effective as enrichments.

The material in the box below provides a brief summary of these enrichment activities. The list is not comprehensive, and many other options are available for involving fast learners in challenging tasks that require higher level cognitive skills. Note that these kinds of activities can provide exciting and valuable

Types of Enrichment Activities Used in Mastery Learning Classes

Peer tutoring
Cooperative teams
Developing practice exercises for fellow students
Developing skill-related media materials
Special projects and reports
More challenging games, problems, and contests
Advanced computer activities

learning experiences to all students and should be offered as learning opportunities for all whenever possible.

Providing for the special needs of fast learners will always be a challenge to teachers. In addition, monetary, physical, and staff limitations often seriously restrict the enrichment activities that teachers can make available to their students. Still, fast learners in mastery learning classes *must* be challenged and have opportunities to extend their learning.

Managing the Enrichment Activities

Even though the students involved in enrichment activities are typically self-directed learners, the newness and difference of the mastery learning process requires some adaptation on their part. To help students become accustomed to enrichment and to understand its purposes, the teacher should begin with activities that are well defined and fairly structured, especially in early elementary grades where students may be used to receiving specific directions from their teachers. Therefore, in addition to the characteristics of reward and challenge, the enrichment activities used in early learning units should have three other characteristics.

First, these early enrichments should be activities that students can work on *independently.* Because the procedures of mastery learning are different from what most students have experienced previously, they may have difficulty combining the academic aspects of an enrichment activity with the social aspects of group work and staying on task. Independent activities, on the other hand, help students gain a clear understanding of what enrichment is and the special benefits they gain from being involved in it.

Second, early enrichment activities should be *self-directional;* that is, they should require neither a lot of direction or explanation from the teacher nor constant monitoring. Most teachers want to get the fast learners quickly involved in enrichment activities and turn their attention to directing and monitoring the work of students engaged in correctives. To do this, these initial enrichment activities must be self-directional.

Third, early enrichments should be activities that students *can complete within the time allotted for the units;* that is, within one or two class periods. This is the amount of time the other students will spend working on correctives and taking the second formative assessment. By having students complete the enrichments within this time frame, they not only learn about the enrichment process but also are ready to begin the next learning unit with the other students.

After three or four units, students will be much more accustomed to the mastery learning process and how it works. They also will have a better understanding of their responsibilities in the process and precisely what is expected of them. At this point, teachers generally find they can lessen the structure imposed on both the correctives and enrichments. Most discover that they can offer students more options and greater choice in selecting enrichment activities. Group work and learning teams become more practical and can operate more efficiently. Students also can be engaged in activities that extend over several learning units, such as special projects or reports. Some teachers allow students to come up with their own enrichment ideas. The number of possible activities that can be made available to students is endless, so long as they offer students valuable learning experiences.

Additional Characteristics of Enrichment Activities in Early Learning Units

1. They should be activities on which students can work independently.
2. They should be fairly self-directional.
3. Students should be able to complete them within the time allotted for the unit.

Engaging All Students in Enrichment

In early learning units, many teachers take some class time to engage *all* students in enrichment activities after the second formative assessment. They select an activity that students are likely to find exciting but which they can complete within a relatively short period of time. Engaging all students in enrichment permits everyone to experience firsthand the reward and excitement offered by these types of activities. As a result, students are more highly motivated to do well on the first formative assessment in the next unit so they can take part in enrichments.

Teachers often find that the benefits of this option carry over to later units. When the class time allotted to enrichment activities is reduced in later units, students involved in correctives frequently ask if they can work on the enrichment activities on their own time. In this way, enrichment activities continue to be a valuable learning experience for all students throughout the instructional sequence.

Enrichment and Extra Credit

If enrichment offers the opportunity to engage in activities that are truly rewarding and challenging to students, then most will be eager to take part.

Occasionally, however, teachers find students who are reluctant to participate. Especially at the secondary level, some students have no interest in enrichment because, from their perspective, they have already reached "mastery" and qualify for the high grade they want. To encourage these students to participate in enrichment activities, some teachers require all students to complete enrichment in order to receive a high grade. But as we discussed in the previous chapter, this practice is counter to the mastery learning philosophy and detrimental to the process.

Some teachers also offer extra credit for enrichment; that is, successful completion of the enrichment activity adds extra points to a student's unit score or grade. When this is done, clear scoring criteria that relate to specific standards of quality must be established for the enrichment activity. A student should not receive credit simply for taking part in the activity; credit should be rewarded for a specific product or other demonstrable outcome.

Although some educators believe that the use of extra credit diminishes the excitement students might derive from an activity, current evidence indicates that it has no effect on students' intrinsic motivation (Cameron & Pierce, 1994). Furthermore, this minor adaptation is often all that is needed to get reluctant students to participate in enrichments. Allowing extra credit also makes enrichment more appealing to students who see participation in correctives and the second formative as the only way they can improve already high marks. This and other aspects of grading are discussed more thoroughly in Chapter 6.

Special Education and Gifted Education

When they first encounter the ideas of mastery learning, some educators assume that its widespread use could result in the elimination of all special education and gifted education classes. However, this is not the case.

In his earliest descriptions of mastery learning, Bloom (1976) emphasized that no matter how students are grouped for learning, some students will always have learning problems that are so severe that they will require special programs. He believed that this might include the lowest ranked 5 to 10 percent of students. Similarly, some especially talented and bright students–perhaps the top-ranked 5 to 10 percent–also should have special programs. Mastery learning was designed as a way for teachers to provide higher quality instruction for the 80 to 90 percent of students who fall between these extremes.

Special education and gifted education programs are essential to providing for these students' unique learning needs, even if mastery learning is widely used. Their special learning requirements often make regular classroom instruction inappropriate, regardless of its quality. Determining appropriate entrance criteria for these special programs, however, is one of the most pressing dilemmas that educators face in structuring special education and gifted education classes. No matter how much care and precision go into setting these criteria, they always remain arbitrary to a large degree. This is not to say that students placed in these programs should not be. Rather, it simply implies that there are many students who would undoubtedly benefit from the special services provided in these programs yet never have the opportunity to participate.

One of the great advantages of mastery learning as an instructional process is that in every learning unit, students who could benefit from extra time or an alternative approach to learning receive these through the correctives. Likewise, students who could benefit from involvement in learning activities designed for gifted and talented students are provided that opportunity through enrichment. Best of all, the particular students involved in correctives or enrichments vary from unit to unit. One student might be engaged in correctives during one unit and enrichments in the following unit, or vice versa. Grouping remains flexible throughout the instructional sequence, because involvement in correctives or enrichment activities is contingent on each student's performance and learning needs at that time. Furthermore, mastery learning is an excellent and highly efficient means for teachers to provide high quality instruction to students with special learning needs who are placed in their classrooms through "inclusion" programs (Guskey, Passaro, & Wheeler, 1995; Passaro, Guskey, & Zahn, 1994). Although mastery learning may not solve all of the problems teachers face in their efforts to provide effective instruction for increasingly diverse groups of students, it is a practical tool that helps many teachers be more successful with their students.

Summary

Regular and specific feedback on learning progress can help students improve the effectiveness of their learning and help teachers improve the effectiveness of their teaching. With mastery learning, this feedback is provided to both students and teachers through the results of formative assessments. Students who do not attain the standard of mastery on the formative assessment are directed to individualized corrective activities. Correctives provide these students with alternative approaches to learning a particular unit's important concepts and skills. They present the concepts in a different format, involve students in a different way, and help students remedy their learning difficulties.

Those students who attain the standard of mastery on the formative assessment are provided with opportunities to extend their learning through enrichment activities that are rewarding and challenging and that involve higher level cognitive skills. Although enrichment activities are typically related to the subject being studied, they need not be related directly to that unit's content.

Enrichment thus allows teachers to engage fast learners in a wide variety of exciting learning experiences.

Teachers vary greatly in the way they implement the elements of feedback, correctives, and enrichment. Most are also flexible in their implementation practices over a series of learning units, generally beginning with activities that are more structured and then moving to activities that offer students greater variety and individual choice. Regardless of the format, however, feedback, correctives, and enrichment remain crucial elements in the mastery learning process.

Activities

1. Develop a list of possible corrective activities for each item, group of items, or scoring criteria included on the formative assessment constructed in Chapter 3. Make sure these correctives involve different learning styles or types of intelligence, and include a variety of ways for students to become actively engaged in the corrective process.
2. From the list of corrective activities in Table 4.1, select two or three that you believe would be particularly appropriate for the students you teach or plan to teach. Indicate why these activities would be appropriate, what changes or adaptations might be necessary, and what additional correctives might be especially useful with your students.
3. For the formative assessment developed in Chapter 3, determine how corrective activities might best be specified for students. Prepare the correctives for the method you have chosen.
4. Develop a list of possible enrichment activities for students who attain mastery on the formative assessment. Remember that these activities must be rewarding and challenging and should involve higher level cognitive skills.
5. Discuss possibilities for corrective and enrichment activities with a friend or teaching colleague. Often the resources that one teacher uses will differ from those used by another. Sharing information in this way can offer valuable alternatives for both participants.

5

Summative Examinations and Assessments

The use of assessments for formative purposes is an essential characteristic of mastery learning. Giving students regular and precise feedback on their learning progress is crucial in our efforts to help them become more effective learners. But in most school situations, learning progress eventually must be evaluated. Marks must be reported, grades must be assigned, and summaries of those reports must be sent to parents and school administrators. Although several criteria can and should be used in reporting on students' learning progress and assigning grades, students' scores on major examinations, projects, and reports constitute a principal source of evaluation information. These culminating demonstrations of student learning are generally referred to as *summative examinations* and *assessments.*

The Purpose of Summative Examinations and Assessments

The primary purpose of a summative examination or assessment is to gather cumulative information on students' learning so grades can be assigned or competence in a particular skill or task can be determined. Obviously, the purpose of a summative assessment is different from that of a formative assessment. A formative assessment is used primarily to check students' learning progress and pinpoint any learning difficulties they may be experiencing. It is designed to help both the student and teacher focus on the learning that is essential in moving toward mastery. A summative examination or assessment, on the other hand, is much more general. It is used primarily to evaluate how well larger goals or objectives have been attained over all or a substantial part of a course.

In addition to this difference in purpose, two other features distinguish summative examinations and assessments from formative assessments. The first is the portion of the course covered by the assessment. A formative assessment measures students' learning of the important concepts and skills from a single learning unit, which usually involves a week or two of instructional time. Everything that is important for students to learn in that unit is included in the formative assessment. A summative examination or assessment, however, is much broader in scope and covers a much larger portion of the course. For example, a summative assessment might cover the material presented in three, four, or even more learning units. As such, summative examinations and assessments are usually longer than formative assessments and require more time to administer. A summative assessment may require a full class period for students to complete, while formative assessments can usually be administered in twenty-five minutes or less. Summative assessments therefore are administered less frequently than formative assessments.

The level of generalization is the second feature that distinguishes summative examinations and assessments from formative assessments. Because of limited assessment time, a single summative assessment cannot include all of the important elements from each learning unit. Therefore summative examinations and assessments are usually designed to focus on broad abilities and larger course outcomes than on each learning unit's specific details. The level of generalization in a summative assessment will depend, of course, on the subject, the grade level, and the desired learning goals for the course. But, in most cases, summative examinations and assessments are more general in focus than are formative assessments.

The Relationship Between Formative and Summative Assessments

Despite their differences, formative and summative assessments have a strong and definite relationship. This relationship is best seen in the concepts and skills assessed. Figure 5.1 (page 132) illustrates this relationship.

The largest oval in the figure represents all of the new information, concepts, and skills that may be presented to students as part of a learning unit. This includes examples used in presentations, stories told to help students make connections

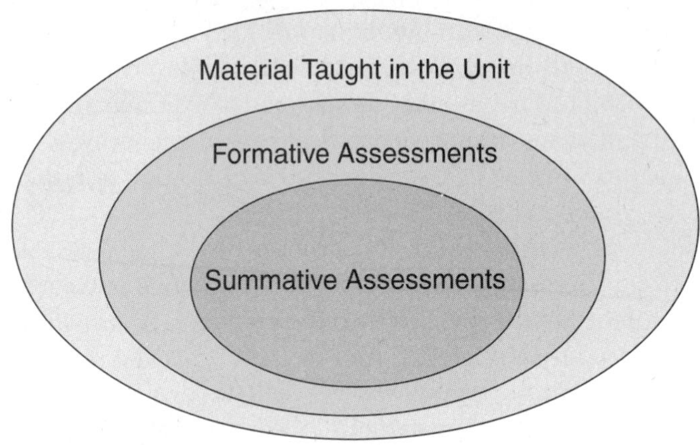

Figure 5.1 The relationship between the concepts and skills measured on formative assessments and summative examinations and assessments in mastery learning

to previous learning, and the variety of details a teacher mentions when discussing a particular topic. The next oval represents that portion of the presented material assessed by the formative assessments. This oval includes those elements judged by the teacher as important for all students to learn. In Chapter 2, we referred to the process of making these judgments as *valuing*. Note, however, that no portion of this oval rests outside the larger oval. In other words, if a particular concept or skill is considered important enough to include on a formative assessment, then students should have opportunities to learn about that concept and actively engage in that skill as part of the learning unit.

The smallest oval represents those concepts and skills that are included in a summative examination or assessment. These are the content elements judged by the teacher to be most central to the course and most important to students' understanding. Making this distinction requires another level of valuing by the teacher. Note, however, that no portion of this oval rests outside the formative assessment oval. This means that everything on a summative examination or assessment has already been encountered by students in an earlier formative experience.

In mastery learning, these ovals always share the same center. In other words, content elements not important enough to cover in the formative assessments are not included in a summative examination or assessment. Summative examinations and assessments focus on those concepts that are most central to learning in the course or term of instruction.

Because of the direct relationship between summative examinations and assessments and the formative assessments, the same tables of specifications used in developing the formative assessments can also serve as excellent guides in preparing a summative assessment. In addition, using the tables of specifications in this way further ensures consistency between instructional objectives and goals, and procedures for evaluating students' learning.

Differences Between Summative and Formative Assessments

1. *Purpose:* Summative assessments are used to evaluate students' learning on broad course goals in order to assign grades or certify competence. Formative assessments are used to check students' learning progress and diagnose learning errors.
2. *Scope:* Summative assessments are cumulative demonstrations of learning that cover concepts from several learning units. Formative assessments focus on a single unit's important concepts and skills.
3. *Level of generalization:* Summative assessments focus on broad abilities and overall course goals. Formative assessments address a unit's important learning objectives.

Criterion-Referenced Versus Norm-Referenced Standards

Another similarity shared by summative assessments and formative assessments is that they both are criterion-referenced measures; that is, results from both are judged in terms of specific learning criteria. Both provide information about how well students have learned or mastered particular learning objectives. On a criterion-referenced assessment, it is possible for all students to receive an A grade, if they demonstrate that they have learned the material well. In other words, each student's performance on the assessment is judged in reference to well-defined learning standards.

Norm-referenced measures, on the other hand, judge each student's performance in relation to how well other students in the same class or at the same grade level did on the assessment. Norm-referenced standards are employed, for example, when teachers grade students on a curve. By this method, students are first rank-ordered according to their performance or proficiency. The top percentage is then assigned a grade of A, the next percentage receives a B, and so on. Norm-referenced standards also are used in reporting the results from most standardized achievement tests. For example, percentile rankings, stanines, grade equivalents, and normal curve equivalents (NCEs) are all norm-referenced scales.

Norm-referenced measures can provide useful information. They are particularly helpful in making large-scale comparisons (for example, in comparing the relative achievement levels of students in different states). In addition, because norm-referenced measures are generally designed to maximize the variation in students' scores, they are useful in distinguishing among students for the purposes of selection (for example, selecting students for college admission). But knowing how a student compares with classmates tells us nothing about what that student has learned or is able to do. In addition, grading on a curve has several negative aspects that make the practice inappropriate in classrooms at any level.

Grading on a curve accentuates the differences among students based on what are often ill-defined criteria. Differences between grades or marks, therefore, are difficult to interpret at best, and meaningless at worst (Bracey, 1994). Furthermore, grading on a curve makes learning a highly competitive activity with students competing against one another for the few scarce rewards (high grades) distributed by the teacher. Under these conditions, students readily see that helping others become successful threatens their own chances for success (Johnson, Johnson, & Tauer, 1979; Johnson, Skon, & Johnson, 1980). As a result, learning becomes a game of winners and losers, and, because the number of rewards is kept arbitrarily small, most students are forced to be losers (Johnson & Johnson, 1989).

Teachers who grade on a curve often do so believing that it ensures fairness and equity in grading. It is certainly easier than defining specific learning criteria and judging students' performance in relation to those criteria. Even though grading on a curve typically yields greater consistency in grade distributions from one teacher to the next, the practice's fairness and equity are more myth than reality (Guskey, 1994e). It has profound negative consequences for teachers, students, and the relationship they share, and it should never be used in a mastery learning class.

Developing Summative Assessment Items and Prompts

The challenges involved in developing good items or performance prompts for a summative assessment are essentially the same as those involved in developing them for the formative assessments. Questions must be carefully constructed so that they measure the concepts or objectives identified as important for students' learning. Furthermore, they should measure students' understanding of those concepts or objectives at the appropriate cognitive level. An additional challenge is that they also must measure a fairly broad range of learning objectives within the limited amount of time available for the assessment. For this reason, most teachers include a combination of several types of items and prompts in each summative assessment. Many also combine traditional assessment formats with one or more alternative assessments. Again, however, the level of the learning objective largely determines the most appropriate type of item for gathering information about students' mastery of that objective.

Generally, the guidelines and suggestions outlined in Chapter 3 for developing different types of items and prompts for formative assessments also apply to summative assessments. In fact, many teachers develop items simultaneously for both assessments. These items are then arranged to form the summative assessment using the same guidelines followed for the formative assessments. If an alternative assessment format is used, then similar scoring criteria should be employed. This is especially important when task performances, compositions, projects, reports, or portfolios are used as summative assessments.

After a summative assessment is developed, it is a good idea to have a colleague review it in the same way that the formative assessments were reviewed. The colleague should consider whether the items and prompts truly measure the course's important learning objectives and goals and whether any important concepts or skills have been neglected. A review such as this identifies item flaws, ambiguous scoring criteria, and other errors in the assessment. Furthermore, it enhances the assessment's validity.

Analyzing Summative Assessment Results

After a summative examination or assessment is administered, most teachers check it carefully, make notes to students where appropriate, and record students' scores. But the assessment also provides a host of other kinds of information that can be useful in evaluating the overall effectiveness of one's teaching as well as in planning revisions in a course or instructional sequence.

Item or Criterion Difficulty

Analyzing students' responses to individual examination items or assessment criteria produces one of the most useful types of information available from summative assessment results. Many teachers first tally the number of students who answered each item incorrectly or failed to meet a particular criterion. (This is similar to the process we described in Chapter 4 in constructing a summary chart of formative assessment results.) They then divide this number by the total number of students who took the assessment and subtract this fraction from 1; that is:

$$\text{Item / criterion difficulty} = 1 - \frac{\text{No. incorrect responses}}{\text{No. examinees}}$$

The result is an index known among measurement specialists as *item* or *criterion difficulty.* The "difficulty" of an item or specific criterion can range from 0 to 1. A difficulty of .25 means that 75 percent of the students responded to the item incorrectly or failed to meet the criterion. Such an item or criterion would be considered fairly difficult. On the other hand, an item or criterion with a difficulty of .90 would be one that only 10 percent of the students responded to incorrectly. This item would be judged as fairly easy, at least for this group of students.

Unfortunately, because of the way the item or criterion difficulty index is computed, it is often misinterpreted. For example, we might assume that a criterion with a difficulty of .80 would be more difficult than a criterion with a difficulty of .40, but actually the opposite is true. The criterion with .80 difficulty was responded to appropriately by only 20 percent of the students, while the criterion with .40 difficulty was met by 60 percent of the students. Because misinterpretations such as this are so common, some theorists have suggested that the index might be more appropriately labeled *item* or *criterion easiness,* because higher values actually indicate easier items or criteria (Henrysson, 1971). Even though this suggestion is sensible, it seems unlikely to catch on.

Once a difficulty index is calculated for each item or criterion on a summative assessment, teachers can quickly survey the assessment and get a fairly accurate picture of their teaching effectiveness. Assuming that all assessment items and criteria are valid and reliable, those missed by only a small number of students (with a difficulty of .80 or greater) cover concepts or skills that apparently were taught well. Conversely, items or criteria missed by a large portion of students (with a difficulty of .50 or less) were more difficult for students and seemingly were less successfully taught. The procedures, techniques, or learning activities used to teach these concepts or skills were less effective, for the majority of students at least, and probably ought to be altered or revised.

Remember, however, that these judgments assume that all items and criteria in the assessment are valid and reliable. This may not be the case. For instance, an item answered correctly by nearly all students may have been one for which the correct answer was obvious, even to students who were uninformed. Similarly, an item missed by a large number of students may have been ambiguous, misleading, or particularly confusing. The possibility of these types of flaws should be kept in mind when the teacher reviews the difficulty of summative assessment items and prompts, especially when an item or particular criterion appears more difficult than expected for students.

Item or Criterion Discrimination

Item or *criterion discrimination* is another common type of index used by measurement specialists to describe how examination items and assessment criteria are functioning. This index describes how well an individual item or criterion distinguishes between students who do well and those who do poorly. For example, if those students who responded appropriately to a particular criterion also attained the highest overall assessment scores, and those who responded inappropriately attained the lowest overall scores, then that criterion would be said to be "discriminating."

The item or criterion discrimination index is usually derived by computing a "point biserial correlation coefficient" (Glass & Stanley, 1970, pp. 163–164). This statistic is a measure of the relation between students' responses to the item (right = 1, wrong = 0) and their scores on the assessment, less that particular item. An item or criterion that is perfectly discriminating, like the one described above, would have a discrimination index of +1. An item or criterion that approximately equal numbers of high-and low-scoring students answered correctly (and incorrectly) would have a discrimination index equal to 0. Under certain circumstances, high-scoring students might answer a particular item incorrectly or respond inappropriately, while low-scoring students might get it right. An item or criterion such as this would have a discrimination index of –1.

In most cases, calculating item or criterion discrimination indexes requires time and computer facilities that are unavailable to most classroom teachers. But even if these resources are available, the teacher should remember that a high level of discrimination in items or criteria is incongruous with the purpose of summative assessments.

Item or criterion discrimination indexes are especially useful in evaluating assessments that accentuate the differences among students. As discussed earlier, many standardized achievement tests, particularly those used for selection purposes, are designed with this aim. The purpose of summative assessments, however, is not to accentuate individual student differences, but to gather cumulative evidence on students' learning in order to report on progress, certify competence, and assign grades. A summative assessment is thus a culminating demonstration of what students have learned. If the teaching and learning are effective, then the vast majority of students should do well on a summative assessment. In fact, the application of mastery learning is successful to the degree that almost all students do uniformly well on summative assessments and attain high grades. Thus the computation of item or criterion discrimination indexes for summative assessments in mastery learning is generally considered invalid and inappropriate.

When to Construct Summative Assessments

There are two points of view regarding the best time to construct summative assessments. Each approach offers distinct advantages, and teachers generally use the procedure that best suits the way they organize and conduct their classes.

The first and probably most popular point of view holds that summative assessments are best constructed before the course or term begins. By doing so, teachers gain a clearer picture of the final learning goals and what students should be able to do when they reach those goals (Block & Anderson, 1975). In other words, the destination is clearly in mind before the journey begins. Furthermore, with the procedures for evaluating student learning and certifying competence already specified, teachers can better focus their attention on planning instruction and organizing learning activities to help students attain those goals and objectives.

The second point of view is that summative assessments should be constructed near the end of the course or term. Preparing assessments then allows teachers to tailor them more closely to the particular emphases in the course–emphases that may vary from year to year or class to class. Especially in courses where students are given options in selecting topics of interest or courses involving current events, appropriate summative assessments can only be prepared at the end of the course or term.

In most cases, however, when a summative assessment is constructed makes little difference in its content or format. If a course is well organized, then those elements identified at the beginning of the course as important for students to learn will be the same as those identified at the end of the course. The time at which a summative assessment is prepared is often simply a matter of convenience for the teacher. The first time a course or subject is taught, the teacher usually constructs the summative assessments during the term, primarily because there was no time to develop them earlier. The vast amount of time and energy required in preparing to teach–gathering materials, planning instructional activities, collecting alternative resources, and so on–often does not allow time to develop summative assessments before the course begins. However, the second time a course is taught or in the second year, the teacher has a version of the summative assessments and thus can refine these if necessary before the second round of teaching begins. Similarly, if standardized assessments or examinations are used, or if assessments are provided with the teaching materials used in the course, then these also should be reviewed and refined to ensure that they are aligned with the course's overall goals and objectives. In this way, the teacher can ensure congruence between the instructional objectives and procedures for evaluating students' learning.

Grading Summative Assessments

The purpose of summative assessments is to provide an overall evaluation of students' learning. As such, it is usually necessary to assign marks or grades to students' assessment scores. In most cases, especially at the secondary level, grades of A, B, C, D, and F are used. At the elementary level, more descriptive labels are typically employed, such as *beginning, developing, proficient,* and *advanced.* With the increased use of alternative forms of assessment, still other marking or classification systems are becoming popular. In the state of Kentucky, for example, portfolios of students' work in language arts and mathematics, as well as students' level of performance on various performance tasks, are rated as *novice, apprentice, proficient,* or *distinguished* (Guskey, 1994f).

The most common technique used in grading summative assessments is to assign a letter grade or performance classification to a certain range of correct responses on the assessment–typically an A for 90 to 100 percent correct, a B for 80 to 89 percent correct, and so on. This can be done for the assessment as a whole or for separate subsections, each relating to a different course goal. Strict percentage standards such as these are appropriate for most classes, provided that the summative assessment is both valid and reliable. In addition, like the standard for mastery, percentage standards are criterion-referenced, easily communicated to students, and easy for students to understand.

Under certain circumstances, however, departures from these strict percentage standards may be necessary. For example, some teachers believe that if they use a mastery standard of 85 percent correct for the formative assessments, then it would be unfair to students to use a different standard, such as 90 percent correct, for assigning an A grade on a summative assessment. Therefore those who use a mastery standard of 85 percent correct on formative assessments often assign an A grade to summative assessment scores between 85 and 100 percent correct, a B grade to scores from 75 to 84 percent correct, and so on. Other teachers simply indicate to students that mastery is attained by an A or B grade, both of which indicate a high level of achievement. These teachers may use a mastery standard of 80 percent correct on the formative assessments, and then the 90 to 100 percent correct criterion for an A grade on the summative assessment, 80 to 89 percent correct for the B grade, and so forth.

The strict percent correct standards on a summative assessment also might be altered to take into account inappropriate or invalid items on the assessment. This often occurs when a newly developed assessment is being used. No matter how carefully an assessment is prepared, it is likely to include a few items that are ambiguous or misleading to many students. To avoid penalizing students for answering these items incorrectly, their responses should not be counted in tabulating students' scores and marks. If the assessment is to be used again with other students or in future classes, then these items should be revised or rewritten.

Teachers who introduce mastery learning in their classes generally find that students who do well on the formative assessments also do well on summative assessments. This is because the regular use of formative assessments compels all students to pace their studying and to meet high learning standards at regular intervals throughout the instructional sequence. Furthermore, the corrective process after each formative assessment presses students to correct any errors in their learning in order to meet that high standard. Students who engage in correctives and remedy their learning difficulties typically find they have little to do the night before a summative assessment, other than review the formative assessments and their corrective work. This situation is quite different from students in most traditional classes, who do the largest part of their studying and learning only one or two nights before a major examination. Although some of these students may then be able to recall the material they studied for the exam, much of what they "learned" will be forgotten soon afterward. Students in mastery learning classes, on the other hand, view summative assessments with less anxiety. Having paced their learning, they are prepared and confident in what they can do.

Some teachers further reduce grading and assessment anxiety by offering students some options with respect to their summative assessment scores. For example, some mastery learning teachers give students the choice of counting either the score they receive on their summative assessment *or* their average score on the first formative assessment from each unit in determining their grade. This policy serves two important purposes. First, it helps to alleviate some of the tension that students often bring to assessment and evaluation situations, particularly when they know the results of that assessment determine in large part the grades they receive. Second, it provides students with an additional incentive to do well on the first formative assessment in each unit. When offered this option, students know that having a high average score on their first formative assessments can guarantee a good grade. Nevertheless, the vast majority of students still do better on the summative assessment and improve their marks.

Whatever grading standards a teacher decides to use for summative assessments, they must be clearly communicated to students before the assessment is administered. In this way, students know precisely what is expected of them and what they must do to attain a high grade or mark. These standards can be altered, of course, to allow for poor items or other assessment flaws, but clear and unambiguous grading standards are an important part of all summative assessment forms.

Grading in Mastery Learning Classes

Although summative assessment results should be used as a primary source of information in assigning students' marks or grades, it is usually unwise to use the score from a single summative assessment as the *only* grading criterion. Most mastery learning teachers administer at least two or three summative assessments during a marking period or term and count the results from each assessment. These assessments often vary in format. For example, one might be an examination composed of multiple-choice and essay items, another a special project, and the third an evaluation of students' portfolio entries. Some teachers vary the weight they attach to each summative assessment, depending on how comprehensive it is or how much work it requires. To use only the results from a single summative assessment unduly emphasizes a rather limited source of information about students' learning progress.

In addition, mastery learning does not require that *only* summative assessment results be counted in determining students' marks or grades. Certainly these assessment results are important and usually weighed heavily (Cangelosi, 1990), but many mastery learning teachers also include a variety of other criteria in assigning grades. Some consider "process" criteria in addition to the "products" of summative assessments (Guskey, 1994e). Teachers who count daily work, homework assignments, class participation, or formative assessment results, for example, are using these process criteria. No matter which criteria are employed, however, clear performance standards must be specified for each, and these standards must be clearly communicated to students. Furthermore, students must be given explicit feedback and guidance as they work to attain these standards. This again reflects the feedback and corrective process that is essential to mastery learning.

Actually, the use of mastery learning does not require teachers to make any significant changes in their grading standards. The only change that would be necessary is if a teacher previously graded students on a curve or by some other norm-referenced standard. Students in a mastery learning class always should be graded with respect to what they have learned and are able to do, never in terms of their relative standing among classmates.

General Guidelines

Mastery learning teachers use a variety of different grading practices, each developed to fit their context and to be fair to students. Currently, no evidence indicates that any one method of grading is best under all conditions or in all circumstances. Still, teachers should follow two guidelines in developing their grading policies and practices (see Guskey, 1996).

First, regardless of the method or form used, *grading and reporting should provide accurate, quality information about what students have learned, what they can do, and whether their learning status is in line with expectations for that level.* This means the criteria on which a mark or grade is based must be clearly defined. In addition, this information must be understood by those for whom it is intended–typically, students and their parents. Grading and reporting should be seen, therefore, more as a challenge in clear thinking and effective communication than as an exercise in quantifying achievement (Stiggins, 1994b).

Second, *grading and reporting methods should enhance, not hinder, teaching and learning.* Although grading is not essential to teaching or learning, it can enhance instructional processes. Clear, easily understood reporting forms facilitate communication between teachers and parents. And when both parties speak the same language, joint efforts to help students are more likely to succeed. Better communication also ensures that parents' efforts to assist their children are in concert with those of the teacher.

Following these two guidelines requires careful planning, excellent communication skills, and an overriding concern for students. The result will be high quality information on student learning.

Guidelines for Developing Grading and Reporting Practices

1. Grading and reporting should provide accurate, quality information about what students have learned, what they can do, and whether their learning is in line with expectations for that level.
2. Grading and reporting methods should enhance, not hinder, teaching and learning.

Implications

Although the development of grading policies that comply with these guidelines may appear easy, their use challenges several long-time grading practices. Two of the most common are (1) the practice of averaging to obtain a student's mark or grade and (2) assigning a score of zero to work that is late, missed, or neglected.

Averaging falls far short of accurately describing what students have learned. For example, students often say, "I have to get a B on the final examination to pass this course." Such a comment illustrates the inappropriateness of averaging. If a final examination or summative assessment is truly comprehensive and students' scores accurately reflect what they have learned, then should a B level of performance translate to a D for the course grade? If the purpose of grading and reporting is to provide an accurate description of what students have learned, then averaging scores from past assessments with measures of current performance must be considered inadequate and inappropriate.

As mentioned earlier, any single measure of learning can be unreliable. Consequently, most researchers recommend using several indicators in determining students' grades or marks–and most teachers concur (Natriello, 1987).

Nevertheless, the key question is, "What information provides the most accurate depiction of students' learning at this time?" In nearly all cases, the answer is "the most current information." If students demonstrate that past assessment information no longer accurately reflects their learning, then that information must be dropped and replaced by the new information. Continuing to rely on past assessment data miscommunicates students' learning (Stiggins, 1994b).

Similarly, assigning a score of zero to work that is late, missed, or neglected does not accurately depict students' learning (Raebeck, 1993). Is the teacher certain the student has learned absolutely nothing, or is the zero assigned to punish students for not displaying appropriate responsibility (Canady & Hotchkiss, 1989; Stiggins & Duke, 1991)?

Furthermore, a zero has a profound effect when combined with the practice of averaging. Students who receive a single zero have little chance of success because such an extreme score skews the average. This is why, for example, in scoring Olympic events such as gymnastics or ice skating, the highest and lowest scores are always eliminated. If they were not, one judge could control the entire competition simply by giving extreme scores. An alternative is to use the median score rather than the average or arithmetic mean (Wright, 1994), but using the most current information remains the most defensible option.

Whatever grading standards are used, the grade or mark must accurately reflect what the student has learned. This is, after all, the major reason that we grade students' work and performances. When this principle guides all grading decisions, those decisions are more likely to be seen as fair and equitable to all concerned.

Limiting Grades to A, B, and I

In some schools, the introduction of mastery learning is combined with a revised grading policy that allows the assignment of only three possible grades to students' work or performance: A, B, or I (Incomplete). The rationale behind this policy is that it communicates clearly to students and their parents that substandard work will no longer be accepted. In other words, if the work is not done well, it's not done! The major advantage of such a grading policy is that it makes clear the intention of teachers to have all students perform at a high level. However, this policy has several major drawbacks that make it extremely difficult to execute, especially during the early stages of implementing mastery learning.

First, such a policy often creates inordinate management problems for teachers. In particular, what is the teacher to do with students who accumulate many I's or incompletes over the course of the school year? To resolve this problem, most schools find it necessary to implement a required summer school program that provides students with structured opportunities to complete their work at the A or B level. Although such a program can be beneficial, it is costly and requires a substantial increase in resources.

Second, most schools that initiate the A, B, or I grading policy include a contingency policy that converts an I grade to an F or failing grade if it is not made up within a limited amount of time (usually one school term or school year). This is done to compel students to put serious effort in completing their work. Such a policy typically draws strong criticism from parents, however, who see it as inherently unfair. They consider such a policy equivalent to firing (failing) every baseball player who does not have a .300 batting average.

Third, reducing the number of grade categories or getting rid of grades altogether confuses helpful evaluation with the disincentive of isolated, ill-defined grades. Any reporting system should be complete. It should place students' performance on a continuum (Wiggins, 1994). Simply eliminating the lower levels of that continuum does little to help mastery learning teachers in their efforts to help all students perform at the highest levels.

For these reasons, implementing an A, B, or I grading policy probably should be avoided in the early stages of mastery learning. Teachers can accomplish a great deal by improving the quality of their instruction without altering current grading policies and practices, so long as those practices relate to clear performance criteria.

Teaching and Assessment

Occasionally, the use of summative assessments has led to criticism of mastery learning as simply a procedure for "teaching to the test." As we discussed in Chapter 1, however, this is not the case. The important issue is what forms the basis for teaching. In mastery learning classes, the learning goals and objectives are the basis for teaching, not a specific test or assessment device. Summative assessments are developed to assess students' mastery of those goals and objectives. So, in mastery learning, rather than "teaching to the test," we are more accurately "testing or assessing what is taught."

Similarly, some teachers argue that assessments of student learning should go "beyond" the concepts and skills that are taught; that is, we should use summative assessments to find out what students have learned "in addition" to the concepts and skills that are part of their instruction. Undoubtedly, many students, perhaps even most, learn far more than we set out to teach them. But to assess, evaluate, and grade students' learning in terms of things they were not taught is inherently unfair.

Learning goals and objectives typically do go beyond the level of basic knowledge or recall of information. Most teachers want their students to be able to apply what they have learned in new or different situations, to be able to reason and solve complex problems, and to synthesize what they have learned with other knowledge and understanding. These higher level cognitive skills are particularly important learning goals. But if students are to be evaluated in terms of these skills, they should be given opportunities to practice and use them as a part of their learning. They also should receive feedback on their progress in developing these skills, and guidance when they encounter difficulties. Although some students will probably develop these skills on their own, the summative assessment should not serve as the initial experience most students have with these higher level processes, especially if they are used as a basis for evaluation and grading.

Summary

The primary purpose of a summative examination or assessment is to gather cumulative information on students' learning so grades can be assigned or competence in a particular skill or task can be determined. Summative assessments typically cover a larger portion of the course and are more general than individual formative assessments. Like formative assessments, however, summative assessments cover the concepts and skills that are most central to learning in the course. In addition, they are designed to be congruent with overall course goals and objectives, as well as with class instructional activities. For these reasons, the tables of specifications are useful guides in preparing summative assessments.

Generally, procedures for assigning marks or grades to the scores students attain on a summative assessment are based on simple percentage correct standards, with some flexibility to take into account test imperfections and class differences. Marks may be assigned to the assessment as a whole or to separate subsections of the assessment. These procedures are always criterion-referenced, however, and never norm-referenced. Although summative assessments are a principal source of information about students' learning, additional criteria also can be used in assigning grades to students, so long as these criteria are made explicit and clearly communicated to students. Whatever grading standards are used, the grade or mark must accurately reflect what the student has learned.

Activities

1. Develop a series of items or prompts for a summative assessment, based on the same learning units for which formative assessments and correctives were developed in Chapters 3 and 4. For each item or prompt, also indicate the cognitive level it is designed to assess.

2. Obtain a copy of a published examination or assessment device used with the subject or grade level you teach or plan to teach. Then classify the items or prompts in this assessment according to the categories used in constructing the table of specifications. Finally, consider the following questions:
   a. How closely does this examination or assessment match the objectives you defined as important for the course?
   b. Does this assessment include items or prompts that you would *not* include in a summative assessment on this material?
   c. Has this assessment failed to address any ideas, concepts, or skills that you believe are important?

6

Applying Mastery Learning

Up to this point, our discussion has focused on planning for mastery learning. We have considered the organization and development activities that generally take place outside the classroom. Now we are ready to move into the classroom–to apply all that we have planned and to manage the mastery learning process within the classroom environment.

Approaches to Program Implementation

As mentioned earlier, individual applications of mastery learning vary widely. But approaches to its large-scale implementation usually can be assigned to one of two categories: *professional development* and *curriculum materials* (Guskey, 1980b). Each approach has proven quite successful when combined with careful planning and high quality follow-up support. However, both approaches require different kinds of resources and different kinds of support.

Professional Development

When the professional development approach is used, groups of teachers, administrators, and other staff members meet in workshops or seminars to learn about and discuss mastery learning and its application. Then in teams, or sometimes individually, they organize or develop the materials they will need to implement mastery learning in their classrooms. These materials usually consist of three components for each learning unit. The first is a systematic outline of the important concepts and skills students are to learn in the unit. This is typically referred to as a table of specifications (discussed in Chapter 2). The second is a pair of parallel formative assessments that measure students' mastery of those important concepts and skills (discussed in Chapter 3). The third is a set of specific feedback and corrective activities that are matched to the formative assessments and designed to help students remedy their individual learning difficulties. Also included are suggestions for enrichment activities that extend the learning of the fast learners in the class (discussed in Chapter 4). In some cases, the materials also include a collection of assessment items and prompts that can be used to construct summative assessments (discussed in Chapter 5).

When teachers have the opportunity to work in teams, they usually share the materials they organize and develop. This reduces drastically the amount of work required of individual teachers. Suppose, for example, that five teachers who teach the same course or at the same grade level work together on a team. If each teacher develops materials for two or three different units, then all can leave the seminar with materials prepared for ten or fifteen units. With these materials in hand and their firm understanding of the mastery learning process, they are ready to begin applications in their classrooms.

Curriculum Materials

The curriculum materials approach seeks the same results but through different means. When this approach is employed, a team of curriculum specialists, writers, artists, teachers, and mastery learning experts develop packages of materials for teachers to use in adapting their instruction to the mastery learning format. These packages of materials typically contain the same components as those developed in the professional development approach, but they are usually more detailed. In addition, they often are directly linked to a school system's established curriculum and, in some cases, represent a complete instructional package.

Under the curriculum materials approach, teachers, administrators, and other staff members are first involved in a relatively short training session on mastery learning. The packages of mastery learning materials are then distributed, along with directions on their use. In most cases, demonstrations are given that include a sample unit of instruction, assessments, correctives, and enrichment. Typically, teachers also are offered follow-up assistance once they begin their implementation efforts.

Comparing Approaches

The professional development approach is more widely used among school systems in the United States. Its major advantages include its involvement of teachers in the development process, its reliance on their classroom expertise, and its built-in mechanisms for individual adaptation. Furthermore, when teachers are involved in planning and development procedures, they have a stronger sense of ownership and pride in the materials they develop and in the mastery learning process. They also tend to feel more confident in making changes in the materials when problems are encountered or errors are identified. However, this approach does require extra work from teachers, which can be a burden when combined with all of their other responsibilities. For this reason, many school systems organize summer workshops in which teachers work together and share responsibility for developing materials.

The major advantage of the curriculum materials approach is its ability to effect rapid large-scale implementation. When packages of materials are available for teachers to apply mastery learning in a subject at a particular grade level, most find it relatively easy to incorporate the materials with their regular teaching activities. However, when teachers are not familiar with or are not involved in the planning and development procedures, they typically have more difficulty altering or revising the materials. Furthermore, they often do not have the necessary skills to apply mastery learning in other subjects or courses for which materials are not available (Cooper & Leiter, 1981). Although the curriculum materials approach has been used in some school systems in the United States (e.g., Katims & Jones, 1985), its most successful applications have been in other countries (e.g., Hau-sut, 1990; Reezigt & Weide, 1990). Table 6.1 (page 150) summarizes the advantages and disadvantages of both the professional development and curriculum materials approaches.

Combining Approaches

Implementing mastery learning on a large scale does not, however, require choosing one or the other approach. Increasingly, school systems and educational institutions combine elements of both approaches to use the advantages of each. In these instances, teachers first meet in brief workshops or seminars to learn about the theory of mastery learning and prepare materials for a single learning unit. Then packages of materials organized in a mastery learning format are distributed. In some cases, these materials were prepared by previously trained teachers. In other cases, the materials were developed by a central curriculum staff or purchased from a particular publisher. The newly trained teachers are encouraged to make any revisions or additions to these materials that they believe are necessary to make them appropriate for their classes. Most teachers find revising, altering, and adding to the materials relatively easy. It allows them to ensure that the materials more closely match their personal instructional objectives and meet the needs of particular students. Making revisions and additions to a set of materials is also easier and less time-consuming than devising entirely new materials. So the combination of the two approaches

Approaches to Implementation	Advantages	Disadvantages
Professional Development	Personal ownership and pride	Slow in achieving large-scale implementation
	Fosters individual adaptation	Extra work for teachers
	Builds on the professional skills of teachers	Costly in terms of teacher time
	Enhances cooperation and sharing among teachers	Skills lost when teachers move or retire
	Promotes better understanding of mastery learning processes	
	Greater teacher enthusiasm	
	Fosters expansion into other subjects or courses taught by the same teachers	
Curriculum Materials	Rapid large-scale implementation	No personal ownership or pride
	Little extra work for teachers	Applications are more mechanical
	Less costly, after materials aredeveloped or purchased	Little expansion into other subjects or courses, unless materials are available
	Greater standardization in implementation	Materials must be constantly updated
	Unaffected by changes in the teaching staff	

Table 6.1 Advantages and disadvantages of two approaches to implementing mastery learning programs

enhances the rate of program expansion while allowing teachers to feel personal pride in the program and confidence in adapting the materials.

Evaluating Mastery Learning Units

Regardless of the approach taken to implementing mastery learning, teachers must evaluate the materials they plan to use. If they take the professional development approach, teachers will need to review the materials they and their colleagues have prepared to ensure quality and precision. If teachers use the curriculum materials approach or if materials are available from a commercial

Evaluation Criteria for Mastery Learning Unit

1. Title Page
   A. Does the unit include a title page?
   B. Does the title page include the following information:
      1. Subject area for which the unit was prepared?
      2. Topic of the unit?
      3. Grade level of the unit?
      4. Instructional time required for the unit (from Introduction to completion of formative assessment B)?
      5. Name and address of the unit developer?
2. Table of Specifications
   A. Does the table address the two central questions:
      1. What do I want students *to learn* in this unit?
      2. What do I want students *to do* with what they learn?
   B. Is there evidence of *valuing* in the table?
   C. Is there evidence of a *match* between the table and the formatives?
3. Formative Assessments
   A. Does the assessment match what was valued on the table?
   B. Do the items in the assessment match the cognitive level desired on the table?
   C. Are directions clear and concise?
   D. Is the assessment of reasonable length?
   E. Does the assessment display appropriate measurement properties (i.e., reliability and validity)?
   F. Are formative assessments A and B parallel?
      1. Do they address the same concepts and content?
      2. Are they of comparable difficulty?
4. Correctives and Enrichments
   A. Are the correctives qualitatively different from the original instruction?
      1. Do they *present* the concepts in a different way?
      2. Do they *involve* students in a different way (i.e., tap different learning styles, modalities, or intelligence)?
   B. Are the enrichments activities things students will want to do?
      1. Are they *rewarding* to students?
      2. Are they *challenging* to students?
      3. Do they offer students a *valuable learning experience*?

Table 6.2 Evaluation criteria for mastery learning units

publisher, then these must be checked and possibly revised to ensure that they match each teacher's instructional goals.

Table 6.2 shows the criteria for evaluating mastery learning units. They are stated as brief questions that teachers should ask as they organize or develop their own units or review mastery learning units developed by others. Following criteria for a title page, the questions address each of the three major unit components discussed earlier. The title page offers a brief description of each unit for use in planning an appropriate instructional sequence. It is especially helpful if units developed by different teachers are exchanged for everyone to use.

Although these criteria are general, most teachers find them useful in quickly analyzing each unit. When units are prepared as part of a mastery learning course (often the case in the professional development approach), these criteria are the basis for offering teachers feedback on the units they develop for course credit. In many mastery learning courses, these criteria are extended to offer more descriptive indicators of quality and to help guide unit development.

Orienting Students

The success of any mastery learning program depends largely on the quality of individual classroom applications. Orienting students to the mastery learning process is an important part of each application. Generally, students are unaccustomed to assessments as part of the instructional process and their use as learning tools. Most students are unfamiliar with procedures for correcting their learning errors and the possibility of a second chance to demonstrate their competence. The teacher therefore must set aside time at the beginning of a course or school term to familiarize students with these new ideas and the procedures involved in mastery learning.

Teachers who use mastery learning have developed a variety of creative ways to orient their students. Some use games or short mastery learning lessons in which the entire mastery learning sequence–teaching, formative A, feedback and correctives, formative B–is completed in a single class period. This helps students understand the process and how it will benefit them. Others hold an open discussion of mastery learning in which they explain the process, describe what the teachers' and students' responsibilities are in the process, and answer students' questions.

Most teachers begin their orientation by stressing their confidence that all students can do well in the class–and probably better than they have ever done before. The teachers explain that there are definite standards for learning in the class and that they expect everyone to be able to meet these standards. They also emphasize that grading and evaluation are based on what is learned, not on how classmates compare with one another. As a result, everyone in the class could get an A grade, and helping someone else does not hurt anyone's chances for success.

As they explain the sequence of events in the mastery learning process, many teachers mention that these activities have always been done by the very best students. Most students are simply unaware of how useful these activities can be. The teachers point out that the regular learning checks or quizzes administered in the class, called formative assessments, are really learning tools. These short assessments are designed to help students find out whether their studying and class preparations have been adequate. If not, then students get specific information on where they need to improve. In this way, learning errors and difficulties can be corrected before they accumulate.

Most teachers also stress that they want to work *with* their students, to help them all learn well and really master the subject. The teachers emphasize that there are no tricks on any quiz or assessment. What is tested and evaluated is what is important for students to learn. The path to success, therefore, is explicit, and *all* can be successful if they supply the necessary effort.

To further clarify the mastery learning process, some teachers hand out a short letter on the first day of class in which they outline procedures for assessment, correctives, and enrichment activities. The criteria used to assign marks or grades also are sometimes mentioned. Figure 6.1 (page 154) shows an example of this type of letter.

Because the mastery learning process is different from most students' classroom experiences, some may not catch on at first. Students are generally accustomed to quizzes and other assessment devices being used solely for evaluation and to having only one chance at a successful mark. Using assessments as learning tools and restudying after the assessment (and not just studying before) to improve one's mark are new and different experiences for the vast majority, especially high school and college students. Thus teachers often must periodically reorient their students, emphasizing again and again the important aspects of the process and the teachers' expectations for learning success. After a relatively short time, however, most teachers discover that even their slowest students develop more positive attitudes about learning, the class, and their ability to succeed.

Orienting Parents

To take advantage of the powerful influence that the home can have on students' learning, many teachers enlist parents' support as they implement mastery learning. Research shows that parents will become more involved and give more help to students if they get frequent reports on what is being taught in school and how they can support the teachers' efforts (Owac, 1981; Moles, 1982, Williams & Chavkin, 1989). The formative assessments and correctives used in mastery learning are an excellent way to inform parents about what is being taught, the difficulties their children are having, and how the parents might help.

Many teachers tell parents about mastery learning in a letter they send home at the beginning of the term or school year. Teachers at the elementary level find

INTRODUCING MASTERY LEARNING

This class is part of an exciting new program called:

MASTERY LEARNING.

In MASTERY LEARNING the class will spend about two weeks on each new learning unit. At the end of the unit, every student will complete a short assessment called ASSESSMENT A. If you get 90 percent or more correct on this assessment, you have achieved MASTERY. If you get less than 90 percent correct, there are a few more things you must do. The results from the assessment will tell you exactly what you did not understand in the unit. These are the things you need to review and restudy.

Following the assessment there will be a special CORRECTIVE AND ENRICHMENT period. Students who got 90 percent or more correct on the assessment will work on special ENRICHMENT activities or projects designed to extend their learning in exciting ways. Students who got less than 90 percent correct will study and practice the things they did not understand or were mistaken about. These activities are called CORRECTIVES.

On the following day, the students who worked on CORRECTIVES will take a second assessment called ASSESSMENT B. If you study and correct your errors, the mark on ASSESSMENT B will be much better than the mark on ASSESSMENT A because you now have learned everything very well. The same procedure of:

ASSESSMENT A → CORRECTIVES & ENRICHMENT → ASSESSMENT B

will be repeated in each unit.

As you can see, in MASTERY LEARNING no one is permitted to fall behind and everyone can reach MASTERY. The regular assessments and correctives will help you do your very best.

Figure 6.1 An example of a letter to students explaining mastery learning

this to be a particularly effective way to gain parental support. The letter explains the basic aspects of mastery learning, why the teachers are using it, and how parents can help. It also explains the idea of correcting any learning errors identified on the formative assessments and the procedures for checking on improvement between formative assessments A and B. Figure 6.2 provides an example of this type of letter.

Dear Parent:

This term your child will be involved in a new program called MASTERY LEARNING. It is a teaching process designed to help all students improve their learning.

With MASTERY LEARNING, the class will spend about two weeks on each learning unit, engaged in a variety of learning activities. At the end of each unit there will be a short assessment that is considered part of the instructional process. It is designed to show each child what was learned well and what was not. Special CORRECTIVE activities are then provided to help children overcome whatever learning difficulties they may be experiencing. These should be worked on in school ***and at home.***

For children who do not get 90 percent correct on the assessment, a second assessment will be given after they have completed their CORRECTIVE activities. Ninety percent correct is the MASTERY standard on all assessments. This second assessment gives children a second chance to show that they have learned the unit very well. Children who do well on the first assessment and achieve MASTERY will be given special ENRICHMENT activities that provide exciting opportunities for them to extend their learning.

Through the MASTERY LEARNING process, we believe that every child can learn very well and truly master each unit. Your support in this process is very important, however, particularly when your child is working on CORRECTIVE activities.

If you have any questions, I would be happy to discuss MASTERY LEARNING with you.

Sincerely,

Mr. Yeksug

Figure 6.2 An example of a letter to parents explaining mastery learning

Most teachers find that informing parents about mastery learning and involving them in the process serves several useful purposes. First, it facilitates communication between teachers and parents. In particular, the formative assessments provide an excellent vehicle for letting parents know what is being taught and what skills are being emphasized. Second, when parents understand the teacher's specific expectations and instructional procedures, then the consistency between home and school supports for learning are greatly enhanced. And third, parents are usually willing to offer their support if they know precisely what help their children need and how they can assist. Enlisting their help through involvement in mastery learning can be especially effective in this effort. In many schools, parents are among the strongest supporters of mastery learning.

Teaching for Mastery

One of mastery learning's most appealing aspects is its basic neutrality with regard to curriculum and instruction. Nothing in the theory or practice of mastery learning specifies what should be taught or how it should be taught. Those decisions are left to the teacher. The key to successful implementation, therefore, is not for teachers to change what or how they teach to fit mastery learning, but to find ways of adapting mastery learning's essential elements to fit their curriculum and specific instructional methods.

At the same time, a growing body of research on the elements of effective classroom instruction has found four general categories: *cues, participation, reinforcement and reward,* and *feedback and correctives* (see Bloom, 1976; Dollard & Miller, 1950; Lysakowski & Walberg, 1981, 1982). Elements in each category are important to instructional quality regardless of whether one takes a constructivist (Prawat, 1992a), direct (Carnine, Grossen, & Silbert, 1995) reciprocal (Rosenshine & Meister, 1994), or wholistic (Goodman, 1987), approach to instruction.

Cues

Cues are the explanations that teachers offer during instruction. They often highlight the organizational and structural patterns of the new material presented and indicate how it relates to other, already learned material. They also convey what is expected of students and what is most important for them to learn. Examples of cues are *advance organizers* and *guided practice.* In the latter, a teacher gradually introduces a skill while assisting students as they practice the skill (Good and Grouws, 1979; Hunter, 1982; and Rosenshine & Stevens, 1986).

Cues are generally enhanced if a teacher is well organized, has an appropriate sequence of lessons, offers suggestions to students for organizing their learning, ensures that all important material is covered, and engages students in work that is of appropriate difficulty. Although these ideas might seem like common sense for most teachers, occasionally reevaluating one's teaching in view of these elements can be useful.

Participation

Participation is the degree to which students are engaged or involved in learning during class. Research studies that measure participation in terms of "time-on-task" (Anderson, 1976, 198la) or "academic engaged time" (Denham & Lieberman,

1980; Rosenshine, 1979; Walberg, 1988a) show it to be extremely important to student learning. Teachers can encourage participation by conveying enthusiasm and interest in the subject they teach, illustrating relevant examples, using practices that are appropriate for their students' developmental levels, and frequently monitoring students' progress. Participation is also encouraged by planning for a variety of activities during class sessions, appropriately pacing the instruction, frequently asking questions, and reducing the time spent beginning a lesson or in transition between lessons or topics.

Remember that great variation is typically found among students' levels of participation. Studies indicate this difference may be as great as one to ten; that is, during a fifty-minute class session, some students may spend as many as forty minutes actively engaged in learning while other students spend as few as four minutes (Anderson, 1975a, 1976). Adding more hours to the school day or extending the school year will do little to reduce this variation. However, learning will be greatly enhanced if students can be encouraged to become involved in learning for a larger portion of their class time.

Reinforcement and Reward

Reinforcement and reward are the motivational incentives that teachers offer students. Appropriate praise and encouragement from teachers, for example, can strongly influence students' motivation for learning (Deci, 1971). Usually, the teacher must make a conscious effort to ensure that praise and encouragement are not limited to just the top students in the class. In addition, praise can lose its effectiveness if offered too often or for behaviors that are simply appropriate or expected (Brophy, 1981).

Mastery learning offers many opportunities to reinforce and reward students for their efforts and achievements, particularly through the formative assessment process. Identifying and praising students for their specific improvements from the first to the second formative assessment and from one unit to the next is easy. Undoubtedly, learning success is one of the most powerful motivational incentives. Furthermore, the opportunity to engage in exciting and stimulating enrichment activities offers students one more type of reward.

Feedback and Correctives

Feedback and correctives are, of course, an integral component of the mastery learning process. The best feedback to students is immediate, specific, and direct, and it offers explicit directions for improvement. However, it must occur at regular intervals throughout any course of instruction. Feedback to students should also convey the teacher's expectations for success and confidence that all students can attain that success.

More ideas on effective classroom instruction are available in the following references:

Anderson, L. W., & Burns, R. B. (1989). *Research in classrooms: The study of teachers, teaching and instruction.* New York: Pergamon Press.

Baron, J. B., & Sternberg, R. J. (Eds.) (1987). *Teaching thinking skills: Theory and practice.* New York: W. H. Freeman.

Doyle, W., & Good, T. L. (Eds.) (1982). *Focus on teaching.* Chicago: University of Chicago Press.

Harmin, M. (1994). *Inspiring active learning: A handbook for teachers.* Alexandria, VA: Association for Supervision and Curriculum Development.

Madaus, G. F., Kellaghan, T., & Schwab, R. L. (1989). *Teach them well.* New York: Harper & Row.

Marzano, R. J. (1992). *A different kind of classroom: Teaching with dimensions of learning.* Alexandria VA: Association for Supervision and Curriculum Development.

Orlich, D. C., Harder, R. J., Callahan, R. C., Kauchak, D. P., Pendergrass, R. A., Keogh, A. J., & Gibson, H. (1990). *Teaching strategies: A guide to better instruction.* Lexington, MA: Heath.

Ornstein, A. C. (1995). *Strategies for effective teaching* (2nd ed.). Dubuque, IA: Brown & Benchmark.

Checking Unit Mastery

When a unit's initial instructional activities are completed in a mastery learning class, the teacher must check students' learning by administering a formative assessment. Students are then given feedback on what they have learned well and what they need to work on. Next comes the most crucial part of the mastery learning process: the corrective and enrichment phase.

Because correcting learning difficulties is so important to students' learning success, most teachers begin with a fairly structured procedure to ensure that students become involved with and complete their corrective work. For example, in early units teachers generally have all corrective work done in class under their direction. In later units, they generally ask students to complete a written assignment that can be checked or turned in before formative assessment B is administered. This assignment guides students' corrective work, particularly when they are working individually or in small groups without the teacher's direct supervision. Some teachers offer additional incentive by giving a small amount of credit to corrective assignments in determining grades, just as they might do with homework assignments. Students not involved in correctives are, of course, engaged in enrichment activities that are designed to extend their learning.

When their corrective work is done, these students take formative assessment B. Because many teachers divide the assessment into sections and set a specific mastery level of performance for each section, students may be asked to address only those sections for which they did not achieve the mastery standard. Other teachers have students answer only those items on formative assessment B that they missed on assessment A. Both procedures reduce the time required for formative B, although they do make record keeping a bit more complicated. Still other teachers have students complete formative assessment B in its entirety. This requires more time to administer the assessment, but it does simplify record keeping. Those students involved in enrichment activities continue their work while the other students are completing formative assessment B.

Occasionally, teachers find that students who attain mastery on formative assessment A also want to take formative B to improve their mark; that is, a student who received 90 percent on formative A may want to take formative B to raise his or her mark to 100 percent. Teachers vary in their policies on this matter. Some allow these students to take formative B, particularly if its results are counted as a part of the grade. But other teachers feel these fast learners might better spend their time in challenging enrichment activities rather than in overlearning the material in a unit. By attaching some small amount of extra credit to the enrichment activities, these teachers are usually able to persuade such students that continuing the enrichment activities is more to their advantage.

After the Second Formative Assessment

Ideally, the corrective activities will be successful, all students will remedy their learning difficulties, and all will attain mastery on formative assessment B. But, unfortunately, it is not unusual to find a few students who do not reach the mastery standard even on formative B. What can or should we do for them?

Some mastery learning teachers are able to provide these students with more assistance and then offer a third or fourth parallel formative assessment. However, the practical constraints of classroom instruction often make this impossible. The demand for curriculum coverage and the limited amount of class time available frequently prevent teachers from going back a third or fourth time. In most cases, the teachers must move on and begin instruction on the next unit. But this does not mean that the teacher forgets about these students or the concepts they still find difficult. Teachers simply must be flexible in helping all students learn well. Even though they may move on, most teachers try to provide these students with another review of difficult concepts. Some teachers suggest more alternative resources relating to those concepts, while others offer more practice exercises. Although these activities are typically completed by students outside of class, teachers stress their willingness to check or correct them whenever completed.

The use of *spiraling items* on formative assessments is another excellent way to check again on the concepts that students found particularly difficult. Spiraling items or prompts are those that refer back to concepts or skills from previous units (Martin, 1978). Their use in formative assessments serves two important purposes. First, they provide students with yet another chance to demonstrate their learning. Second, they are a simple yet highly effective way to enhance learning retention. Spiraling items help students understand important linkages across learning units and enhance students' performance on the cumulative summative assessments. To achieve these important benefits, from 10 to 20 percent of the items on a formative assessment should be spiraling items.

For students who do not reach the mastery standard on formative assessment B, the teacher must express confidence that they probably will attain mastery in future units if they continue to make a strong effort. Most teachers point out that the improvements that students made from formative A to formative B illustrate how the mastery learning process is working. Many also stress that students will have other chances to demonstrate their mastery of the current unit's concepts on future formative and summative assessments. This is what is meant by "extended opportunities to learn."

Teachers also must keep in mind that students learn things in different ways and *in different order.* In other words, no perfect learning sequence exists for any topic or subject area that is appropriate for all learners. Some students who struggle with basic skills, for example, are very sophisticated in problem solving. When these students engage in problem-solving activities, those basic skills begin to make sense to them. Other students need to master certain basic skills before they can be successful in solving problems that involve applying those skills. Because of these differences, rigidly adhering to a single learning sequence for all learners will be detrimental to the learning progress of some, perhaps many, students. Through the regular use of formative assessments with spiraling items and cumulative summative assessments, however, teachers can better accommodate these individual learning order differences. In this way, teachers allow students the flexibility to take different but equally effective and successful paths to established learning goals.

On the other hand, if a fairly large number of students do not attain mastery on formative assessment B, then moving on to the next unit would be foolish. When this occurs, most teachers carefully review what was done in the unit to determine what might account for these results. They typically give special attention to the correctives and the second formative assessment. Perhaps the corrective activities were inappropriate for students or not significantly different from the original instruction. Perhaps formative assessment B was not parallel to formative A. As discussed earlier, sometimes second formative assessments are made more difficult than the first assessments. Often teachers ask students, individually or as a group, what changes could be made in the instruction or in their studying to improve these results. Discussions such as these are often beneficial for both teachers and students.

Remember, however, that mastery learning is not a perfect teaching and learning process. It is not an educational panacea, and it may not be completely appropriate for every student. The learning problems of some students are so severe that specialized learning programs are required. But mastery learning does offer the vast majority of students the opportunity to make great progress in their learning and have many more successful learning experiences.

Motivational Schemes

Motivating students is a problem that all teachers face, regardless of their situation. But the special conditions of mastery learning present teachers with unique opportunities to enhance students' motivation and improve their involvement in learning activities. In particular, mastery learning gives teachers a way to capitalize on the powerful motivational value of learning success. Students like to do the things they do well, and they enjoy the sense of competence that success brings. Thus if a teacher can help more students achieve success in learning, then fewer are likely to have motivation problems.

Students typically define learning success in terms of *praise from the teacher, learning progress,* and *getting good grades* (Smith & Woody, 1981).

Praise from the Teacher

Being told they are doing a good job is important to students, regardless of their age (Brophy, 1981). In a mastery learning class, praise is particularly important for students who have done well on the formative assessments. Some teachers add to this by having those students who attain mastery on the assessment stand and be recognized by the class, perhaps through applause. Other teachers put special marks or stamps on formative assessment papers or scoring sheets to signify that the student has achieved mastery. Whatever the method, recognizing students' hard work and success is essential.

Learning Progress

Recognizing students' learning progress is also important to motivation. Most teachers make a point of praising students for their improvement from formative assessment A to formative B, even if the mastery standard was not attained. They also stress their confidence and expectation that all students will reach mastery in the next unit.

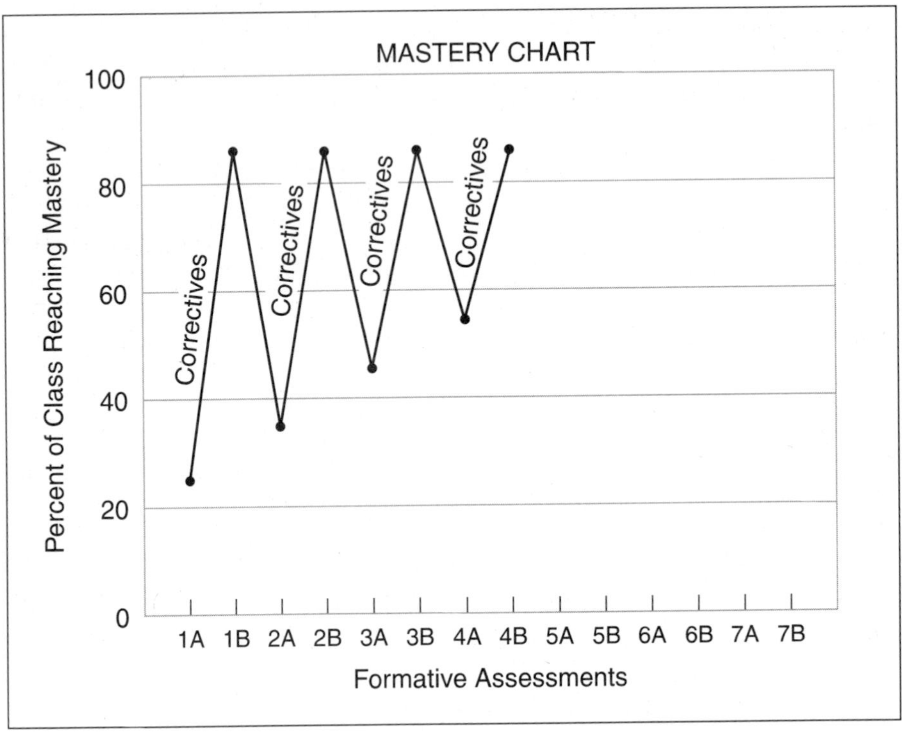

Figure 6.3 An example of a classroom mastery chart

To further recognize students' learning progress, many teachers post a *mastery chart* in their classrooms, similar to the one in Figure 6.3. This chart plots the class's progress from unit to unit throughout the term. As the figure shows, only a small percentage of students may attain mastery on formative assessment A in the early units. If the corrective activities are successful, however, most students should reach mastery on formative assessment B.

As the term goes on and more students catch on to the mastery learning process, a larger percentage should begin to attain the mastery standard on formative A. Gradually, more students become involved in enrichment activities while fewer are involved in correctives. Furthermore, those involved in corrective work typically have fewer learning errors to correct and can proceed through the corrective phase more rapidly.

A mastery chart serves several useful purposes. First, it enhances cooperation among students and fosters general class spirit. Many teachers find that peer tutoring occurs spontaneously in mastery learning classes as students urge one another to do well. Some teachers even report that peer pressure develops to attain the mastery standard. High school teachers who post a mastery chart for each of their classes, for example, often find that competition develops between classes to attain a higher mastery percentage.

Second, a class mastery chart is better than the typical "progress chart" that lists individual students' names followed by colored bars or stars. Such a chart invites comparison and competition among students, discourages cooperation, and is detrimental to most students' learning. A mastery chart, on the other hand, invites cooperation by illustrating progress toward shared learning goals.

Third, the mastery chart becomes a valuable feedback device for the teacher. Specifically, the chart can help teachers identify implementation problems. For example, if the percentage of students who attain mastery between formative assessments A and B does not increase significantly, then something is wrong. Perhaps the correctives were ineffective, students did not understand the process, or formative assessment B was more difficult than assessment A. Whatever the reason, this is a sure sign of problems and a clear indication of the need for change. Likewise, if the percentage of students who attain mastery on formative assessment A does not increase from unit to unit, then something is wrong. Students may not be preparing adequately for formative assessment A, the enrichment activities may not be appealing to students, or incentives for students to do well may be missing. Again, this clearly indicates a need for change.

In addition to a class chart, some teachers have students keep individual mastery charts on which they plot their own progress. An example is shown in Figure 6.4 (page 164). These individual charts allow students to see their progress from formative assessments A to B, as well as from one unit to the next.

Getting Good Grades

Getting good grades is another extremely important incentive for most students. It is so important, in fact, that any mention to students of an assessment, test, or assignment inevitably brings such questions as, "How much does it count?" and "What do I need to do to get an A?" Most students readily see the mastery learning process as an aid in helping them learn better and get higher grades. But sometimes the importance that students attach to getting a good grade makes it difficult for teachers to entice them to do well on formative assessment A. If formative assessment results are not counted as a part of the grade, then some students feel they are unimportant. Similarly, if only formative assessment B is counted as a part of the grade, some students may postpone studying until after assessment A and then study it in order to do well on assessment B (see the discussion of this problem in Chapter 3).

The easiest and best way to stimulate students to do well on formative assessment A is to have enrichment activities that are truly rewarding and challenging. Another technique that some teachers use is to offer students *mastery certificates* as tangible recognition of their success. These certificates of mastery

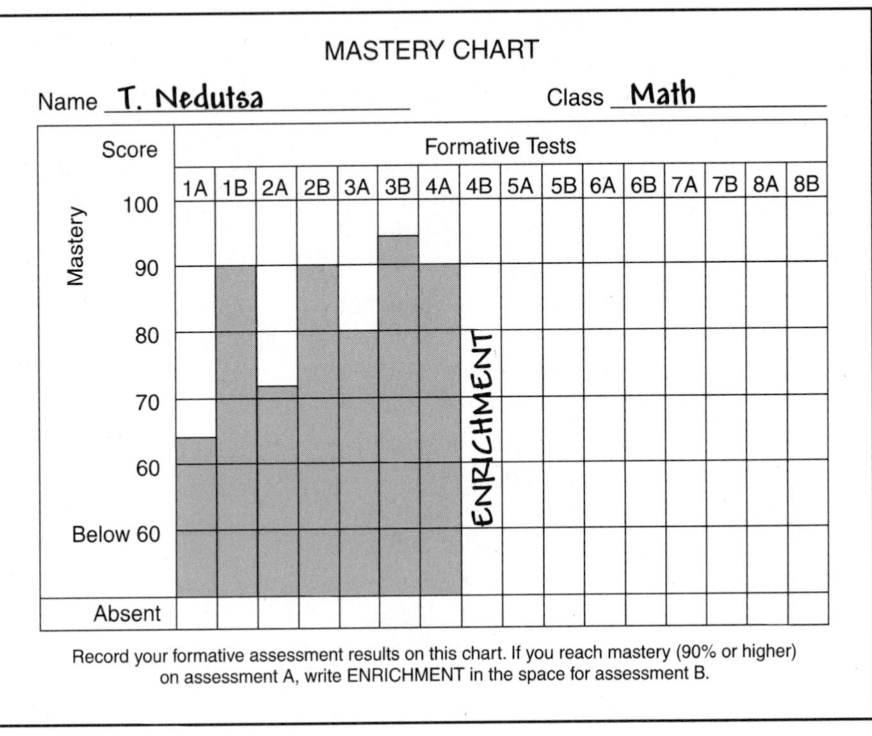

Figure 6.4 An example of a student's individual mastery chart

are presented to students for attaining the mastery standard on a formative assessment. In some classes, students who attain mastery on formative assessment A receive a large certificate, while those who attain mastery on assessment B receive a smaller version. In other classes, teachers use certificates of different color: yellow (gold) for mastery on formative assessment A and white (silver) for assessment B. Figure 6.5 shows an example of such a certificate. Although teachers are sometimes discouraged from using these symbols of learning success, they are generally appreciated by students at all levels. In addition, research evidence indicates that such recognition can be a powerful incentive to students without being a detriment to students' intrinsic motivation (Cameron & Pierce, 1994).

Mastery Learning and the Inclusive Classroom

Many modern educational improvement initiatives contain provisions for including a broad range of students who are eligible for special education. Although "inclusion" is interpreted in many different ways, it often means

WESTMONT HIGH SCHOOL

Johnstown, Pennsylvania

This is to certify that

____

has achieved MASTERY *in the Social Studies unit on*

____

__________________	__________________
Principal	Social Studies Teacher

Figure 6.5 An example of a mastery certificate

placing students with mild disabilities, and those who are at risk of failure, in regular education classrooms for all or part of the school day. Although generally supportive of such efforts, teachers are also keenly aware of the special instructional challenges presented by these students (Lombardi, Nuzzo, Kennedy, & Foshay, 1994).

Growing evidence shows that mastery learning can help teachers better meet the special learning needs of students with disabilities while maintaining a high quality instructional program (Mortimer, Van Wingerden, Zahn, Meyers, & Passaro, 1995). In some schools, teachers use the formative assessment and corrective process of mastery learning to help these students identify and correct their specific learning difficulties. Peer tutoring and cooperative learning activities are sometimes used to encourage involvement of students with disabilities with their classmates. In other cases, special education teachers come into the classroom and help the regular teacher with assessments, correctives, and enrichment activities. This team-teaching model provides individual assistance for students who need additional time and support, and it also facilitates cooperation between regular and special education teachers. Furthermore, it provides the regular classroom teacher with a model for specific methods for correcting learning difficulties that, in turn, improve the overall quality of their teaching (Guskey, Passaro, & Wheeler, 1995).

Common Teacher Concerns

The concerns that teachers express about implementing mastery learning vary, of course, but some are common to almost all applications. In particular, teachers are typically concerned about *time constraints, the fairness of a second chance, fast learners,* and *higher level cognitive skills.* Although these are serious and pressing concerns, in most cases they can be resolved with little difficulty.

Time Constraints

When they first implement mastery learning, teachers often worry about the constraint of class time. With only a limited amount of time available, many teachers fear that introducing feedback, corrective, and enrichment procedures will reduce the amount of material they will be able to cover. As a result, they will have to sacrifice coverage for the sake of mastery.

It is true that the first few units in which mastery learning is implemented require more time than usual. Because the process is so different from the classroom experiences of most students, extra time is needed to orient them to the mastery learning procedures, help them see assessments as learning tools, and help them use assessment results in a systematic way to correct learning difficulties. As a result, a mastery learning class may be somewhat behind a more traditional class during the first two or three units.

After students become familiar with the mastery learning process, however, most teachers find that they can pick up their instructional pace. Students in a mastery learning class tend to be engaged in learning activities for a larger percent of the time they spend in class, so they learn more and learn faster in later units than do students in more traditional classes (Arlin, 1973; Fitzpatrick, 1985). As students catch on to mastery learning, they also tend to do better on the first formative assessment in each unit. With fewer students involved in correctives and an accompanying reduction in the amount of corrective work required, the amount of class time allocated to correctives in later units can be drastically reduced. In addition, because students in mastery classes have learned the concepts and skills from early units quite well, they are better prepared for later, more advanced units. Less time needs to be spent in review activities. Thus most teachers find that with slight changes in the pacing of their instruction (slightly more time in early units but less time in later ones), they are able to cover just as much if not more material as when they used more traditional approaches to instruction (Block, 1983; Guskey, 1983; Guskey, Englehard, Tuttle, & Guida, 1978). Despite contentions to the contrary (Slavin, 1987), currently no evidence shows that coverage must be sacrificed for the sake of mastery in mastery learning (Guskey, 1987b).

The following suggestions also will help to ensure that the necessary concepts and skills are covered within the time available.

1. *Carefully plan the pace of instruction for the entire term.* Generally, by the third or fourth unit, most mastery learning teachers pick up their instructional pace. A gradual increase is always easier for students to handle than a rapid increase later in the term. With clear ideas about the final course goals, the instructional pace for meeting those goals can be more flexible.

2. *Reduce the amount of time spent in reviewing material.* Mastery learning compels students to pace their learning. Therefore general reviews are required less frequently, and the time previously used for review can be used for correctives, enrichment, or further instruction.

3. *Gradually reduce the amount of class time spent on corrective activities.* After students become accustomed to the corrective process, it usually requires substantially less class time. As discussed earlier, as students catch on to the mastery learning process and begin to do better on the first formative assessment, fewer of them are involved in corrective activities, and those who are involved usually have fewer difficulties to correct. In fact, many teachers find that after four or five units, most correctives can be completed by students outside of class as a homework assignment. Of course, this depends to some degree on the unit's difficulty. But, in general, once the corrective pattern is established and students see its utility in helping them succeed at learning, less class time is needed for corrective work.

The Debate Over Time Needed

Over the years there has been a debate among researchers about the amount of time needed in mastery learning classes. Interest in this variable stems from early writings on mastery learning and specifically Bloom's (1971a) notion that under more appropriate instructional conditions, students become more similar in their level of achievement and *in their learning rate;* that is, the difference between the time needed for the fastest and slowest learners to learn certain concepts to a specified level begins to diminish. Bloom further suggested that mastery learning might offer students these more appropriate instructional conditions. Two early studies by Anderson (1975a, 1976) supported Bloom's ideas.

Later studies and reviews by Arlin (1982, 1984a, 1984b), however, challenged this notion and argued that learning rate is a fairly stable and unalterable student characteristic. Arlin suggested that the positive gains evidenced in most mastery learning programs come mainly from continually providing greater amounts of learning time for students who are experiencing problems or difficulties. Because this time must come from somewhere, Arlin argued that it is gained either by involving students in additional corrective instruction outside of class or by sacrificing time for learning in other areas or other subjects. Therefore, according to Arlin, the higher levels of achievement attained by mastery students come not so much from the mastery learning procedures as from simply greater allocations of time.

However, in a reanalysis of Arlin's evidence (Arlin & Webster, 1983; Arlin, 1984a), Guskey and Pigott (1988) showed that these results had been misinterpreted. In fact, Arlin's own evidence showed that over a series of instructional units the differences between fast and slow learners *decreased* under mastery learning. Arlin's results thus were actually quite similar to Anderson's (1975a, 1976) and supported Bloom's (1971) original contentions.

Certainly, the introduction of mastery learning compels many, perhaps most, students to spend additional time in learning activities. But this time need not come from that allocated to learning in other subjects, as some have suggested (Arlin, 1984b; Slavin & Karweit, 1984). It comes instead from improvements in the *quality* of the time spent, rather than increases in quantity (Anderson & Burns, 1987; Guskey, 1983). Studies show, for example, that under mastery learning students spend a greater portion of their time in school actively engaged in learning (Anderson, 1976), and they make better use of learning time outside of school (Block & Tierney, 1974). In addition, instructional time in mastery learning classes is used more purposefully by both teachers and students, the time spent in transitions between instructional events and in nonacademic interactions is decreased, and the rate of student off-task behavior is drastically reduced (Fitzpatrick, 1985; Tennyson, Park, & Christenson, 1985). Evidence also indicates that the need for additional time diminishes over a series of instructional units (Block, 1974; Guskey & Pigott, 1988). Still others have argued that the costs associated with providing additional time are relatively modest and that the benefits far outweigh those costs (Block, 1983). Thus mastery learning appears to improve both the quantity and quality of students' learning time.

The Fairness of a "Second Chance"

When they first learn of mastery learning, some teachers express concern about the fairness of giving students a "second chance." From their perspective, it is unfair to offer the same privileges (and high grades) to students who require a second chance to demonstrate mastery as are offered to students who achieve the mastery standard on the first formative assessment. According to these teachers, such students probably did not adequately prepare for the first assessment or did not show appropriate responsibility.

The students who achieve mastery on the first formative assessment certainly deserve special privileges and will be rewarded by the opportunity to engage in enrichment activities. But those students who attain the mastery standard on the second assessment have also learned the unit concepts and skills quite well. More important, they may not be at fault for failing to achieve mastery on the first formative assessment. Perhaps the fault lies with the teacher. Maybe the teaching strategies used during the initial instruction were inappropriate for these students, and the correctives proved more effective. If privileges (and grades) are determined on the basis of performance, and these students have performed at the same high level, then they certainly deserve the same privileges (and grades).

A comparable example is a driver's license examination. Many individuals do not pass the examination on their first attempt. On the second or the third try, however, they reach the same high level of performance as others did on their first. Should these drivers be penalized for not being adequately prepared or for not showing appropriate responsibility? Should they, for instance, be restricted to driving in fair weather only? In inclement weather, should they be required to park until the weather clears? Of course not! Because they eventually met the same high performance standards as those who passed on their initial attempt, they are granted the same privileges. The same should hold true for students who show that they, too, have learned well.

Other teachers raise the issue of the absence of a "second chance" in many professions. A surgeon does not get a second chance to perform an operation successfully, and a pilot does not get a second chances to land a jumbo jet safely. Because of the high stakes involved, both are required to perform their jobs correctly the first time.

But we must remember in each case how these professionals were trained. The first operation performed by the surgeon was on a cadaver, which allows considerable latitude for mistakes. Similarly, the pilot was required to spend many hours in a flight simulator before ever attempting a landing from the cockpit. In both instances, mistakes are recognized to be an inherent part of the learning process. Experiences such as these allowed these professionals to learn from their mistakes and improve their performance. Similar training techniques are used in nearly every professional endeavor. Only in schools do students face the prospects of "one shot, do-or-die," with no chance to demonstrate what they learned from previous mistakes.

Fast Learners

Many teachers also worry about the special demands of fast learners. While most teachers see the value of the mastery learning process for slower students and for the broad middle range of students, some initially believe that it may restrict the progress of top students. Furthermore, some teachers feel that even occasionally using fast learners to tutor slower learners may limit their "potential."

One of mastery learning's most promising aspects, however, is that it actually allows fast learners greater flexibility than they typically have in more traditional classes (Guskey, 1982a). A formative assessment readily identifies the fast learners and frees them from unnecessary review and reteaching exercises. In addition, well-planned enrichment activities offer these students the chance to explore a wide variety of alternative learning experiences. As a result, fast learners have the opportunity to extend their learning into new and exciting areas that interest them, and their overall experience in school becomes much more positive (Anania, 1981; Dillashaw & Okey, 1983; Nordin, 1979).

On those occasions when the teacher structures peer tutoring within a class, faster students experience valuable interactions that are usually unavailable in most traditional or individualized instructional programs. Working with other students to attain common learning goals not only enhances cooperation and sharing among students, but also strengthens and broadens the tutor's original learning (Bargh & Schul, 1980; Webb, 1982). Cooperative social interactions such as these can play an important part in the educational experience of all students (Johnson & Johnson, 1989, 1994).

Higher Level Cognitive Skills

Many teachers also express concern about teaching for higher level cognitive skills. Most teachers readily see the utility of mastery learning for teaching elementary or basic skills, but some have difficulty comprehending its application for more complex student behaviors.

The focus of many mastery learning teachers' instruction, however, is specifically on higher level cognitive skills. These teachers have devised a variety of ways to teach such skills and have matched their assessment and corrective procedures to these objectives. In fact, some of the most successful applications of mastery learning have been in programs designed to teach students the higher level skills associated with writing (Knight, 1981), reading comprehension (Jones & Monsaas, 1979; Katims & Jones, 1985), and mathematics problem solving (Mevarech, 1989). Other successful applications have focused on drawing inferences, deductive reasoning, and various thinking skills (Arredondo & Block, 1990; Kozlovsky, 1990; Soled, 1987). Mastery learning has also been used at the college level to teach medical problem solving (Mevarech & Werner, 1985), legal research (Feinman & Feldman, 1985), business education (Whiting

& Render, 1987), and English composition and counseling (Guskey & Monsaas, 1979). Research studies of students' achievement of higher cognitive skills under mastery learning instruction also illustrate its direct applicability (Denton & Seymour, 1978; Mevarech, 1981, 1985; Seymour, 1977). So even though mastery learning works well with instruction on basic skills, it is equally effective when applied to instruction in higher level cognitive skills.

Administrative Support

It is impossible to overemphasize the importance of administrative support for a mastery learning program. Although teachers can certainly implement mastery learning on their own, the support of administrators at all levels is crucial for the growth and maintenance of a program (Barber, 1979; Cunningham, 1991; Ryan, 1985).

One of the most important tasks of administrators is to recognize that mastery learning requires most teachers to make changes. Undoubtedly, some teachers already use many of the elements of mastery learning in their teaching, but most find that its use requires adaptations in the way they plan or revisions in their instructional format. Changes such as these take time. Furthermore, they can only occur in an environment that is conducive to experimentation. The best administrative support, therefore, is based on collaborative planning, collegial exchange, and mutual adaptation (Fullan, 1991; Little, 1982; McLaughlin, 1978).

Many administrators show their interest and support for mastery learning by attending workshops and participating in development activities with teachers. This helps them to become more familiar with the process and also gives them a better understanding of the work involved (Del Seni, 1981). Some administrators further facilitate collegial exchange by scheduling a common planning period at least once a week for those teachers who use mastery learning. Most administrators also schedule monthly follow-up meetings for teachers to discuss problems and collaboratively devise solutions. Other administrators establish a central school location (e.g., a desk and file cabinet) where mastery learning teachers can meet, collect materials, and review materials developed by others. Most important, they openly express their appreciation for the extra work and professional dedication of the teachers involved (Stahman, 1981).

Furthermore, although the decision to implement mastery learning is generally left to the teacher, most administrators actively encourage teachers to try mastery learning, at least on a small scale. Once the early implementers see that mastery learning works well for them and their students, their commitment to the process grows and their enthusiasm becomes contagious (Guskey, 1986; Huberman & Miles, 1984). Because the ideas have gained credibility, more and more teachers choose to become involved. The teachers who are experienced with mastery learning can then serve as models and peer coaches for their less experienced colleagues, helping them overcome any initial implementation problems. Evidence of success can also be used to persuade, and perhaps challenge, those who may resist change and new ideas.

Admittedly, a voluntary approach probably will result in slower and more gradual change. But the changes that do occur typically endure because the teachers come to "own" the new educational ideology and technique and are committed to it (Joyce & Showers, 1988). On the other hand, mandated change or top-down models of program implementation are seldom successful and seldom remain once the mandate has been removed (Purkey & Smith, 1982).

Rewards for the Teacher

Implementing mastery learning usually means extra work for a teacher. At a minimum, it requires preparing two assessments for each unit and planning alternative corrective activities. Why, then, would anyone want to use this process when it adds extra time and effort to the already heavy workload of teaching?

Most teachers first try mastery learning because it directly addresses some of their most pressing problems. Many struggle to find a way to provide appropriate instruction for the wide variety of students in their classes. They would like to offer their students more individualized help. They also would like to have their students feel better about themselves and be more motivated to learn. To these teachers, mastery learning is a tool they can use to solve these problems. Unlike many other innovations, using mastery learning does not require drastic changes in the way they teach. Most can implement the process with relatively minor alterations in classroom procedures. And mastery learning fits within the time limitations, curriculum demands, and constraints of the classroom environment. Although it may not make teaching any easier, it does offer teachers a way to be more effective in what they do.

At the same time, research evidence indicates that mastery learning affects teachers in definite ways. Teachers who successfully implement mastery learning, for example, typically alter their expectations for students' achievement and have difficulty predicting which students will do well and which will experience learning difficulties (Guskey, 1982b). After using mastery learning, most teachers also change their explanations as to why they are effective in the classroom, giving less importance to personality factors and far more to teaching practices and behaviors (Guskey, 1985c). In addition, teachers who use mastery learning and see improvement in student learning generally feel better about teaching and their roles as teachers, accept more personal responsibility for their students' learning and failures, and are more open to other opportunities for improvement (Guskey, 1984, 1988a).

The most important rewards for teachers that come from mastery learning, however, are undoubtedly the changes in the students. Teachers typically find that students in mastery learning classes are more involved in the learning process and more interested in learning. Sometimes student attendance rates increase, and classroom disruptions and discipline problems decrease. In general, as students become more successful in their learning and gain increased confidence in themselves, their teachers feel more purposeful and fulfilled.

In addition, teachers frequently report that mastery learning also brings a welcome change to their role in the classroom. In more traditional classrooms, learning is often highly competitive. Students compete among themselves for the few rewards (high grades) awarded by the teacher. Under these conditions, a teacher becomes a rule maker and the director of competition who is responsible for judging and classifying students. With mastery learning, however, learning becomes more cooperative than competitive. Students generally see themselves as on the same side as the teacher and out to master what is to be learned. The teacher thus becomes an instructional leader and learning facilitator working with students (Guskey, 198la, 1985b).

Finally, many teachers say that mastery learning renews the enthusiasm they once had for teaching (Guskey, 1980a). As mentioned earlier, the zest with which most teachers first enter the classroom is often lost because of the harsh difficulties they encounter in their first year or two of teaching. Mastery learning provides a way for many teachers to deal effectively with those problems. In using mastery learning, they feel better about being teachers and often express increased professional pride (Guskey, 1985d).

Teaching is, and undoubtedly will remain, one of the most difficult and challenging professions. It taxes even the most dedicated individuals. With mastery learning, however, many teachers discover newfound vigor and excitement about their challenges and increased enthusiasm about their chances of being remarkably successful.

Summary

The two major models for the large-scale application of mastery learning are the *professional development approach* and the *curriculum materials approach.* The first approach focuses on staff development and individual adaptation, while the second concentrates on high-quality materials and standardized applications. Elements of each can be combined to take advantage of their most positive qualities.

Orienting students and parents to the mastery learning process is extremely important in classroom applications. Careful planning, clearly communicated standards, and procedures for rewarding success in learning are essential. Although many teachers are first concerned about time, the fairness of a "second chance," fast learners, and teaching higher level cognitive skills, these worries are usually resolved with thoughtful discussion, reflection, and planned adaptations.

Administrative support, although not essential in individual classroom applications, is crucial to program expansion and maintenance. Furthermore, it guarantees higher quality implementation and continuation.

Even though implementing mastery learning requires extra work for teachers, the rewards in terms of enhanced student learning outcomes, increased effectiveness, and a renewed sense of excitement about teaching make it worthwhile for most.

Questions for Discussion

1. What problems do you think teachers are likely to face when they first implement mastery learning? What could be done to make implementation easier? How could we reduce the work required of individual teachers?
2. What additional types of administrative support might teachers need when they first implement mastery learning? What types of support might be required later in the process? What administrative problems might arise at the school or district level when a mastery learning program is first implemented?
3. What different types of resources or support would be needed to implement mastery learning at the elementary level? the middle school level? the secondary or college level?
4. How do the issues involved with implementing mastery learning compare to those of other programs or other aspects of school curricula?

7

Evaluating Mastery Learning

In the preceding chapters, we covered the major elements of planning and procedures for managing the classroom application of mastery learning. Now we are ready to consider evaluation procedures.

To determine whether mastery learning has led to meaningful change and positive results, we need some form of evaluation. We must gather information that will let us know whether intended improvements were made. We also need to determine if there were any unintended consequences. The collection and use of this kind of information is the focus of this chapter.

The Purposes of Evaluation

Evaluation in education takes place on many levels and typically serves a different purpose at each level. The major purpose in evaluating students' learning progress, for example, is to determine the degree of change that has taken place in individual students (Airasian, 1971; Bloom, Madaus, & Hastings, 1981; Hopkins & Antes, 1990). But teachers, administrators, schools, materials, curricula, policies, and programs are also evaluated, and the purpose of evaluation is quite different for each (Worthen & Sanders, 1987).

In addition to the differences in levels, evaluation at a single level also can serve a variety of purposes. Evaluations of teachers, for instance, can serve formative purposes by providing data and suggestions that have implications for improving instruction. On the other hand, teacher evaluations can also serve summative decision-making purposes in regard to promotion, tenure, assignments, and salary (Millman & Darling-Hammond, 1990).

This chapter's primary concern is evaluating mastery learning at the classroom and school level. The purpose of evaluation at this level is to gain information about the relative value or worth of the mastery learning process in a particular setting. In essence, we want to determine (1) whether the introduction of mastery learning has made any difference, (2) what intended or unintended changes have occurred, and (3) how application of the process might be improved. To do so, we must decide what information will best address these issues, systematically collect that information, and then analyze it in a meaningful and purposeful way. Assuming the information we gather is both valid and reliable, we then will be able to make reasonable judgments about relative value and worth. In addition, we will be able to make better decisions about continuation, maintenance, alterations, and further applications.

The types of questions that could be raised about the application of mastery learning are undoubtedly limitless. Our focus in this chapter, however, is only on questions that relate to student learning. Regardless of the scope or magnitude of the evaluation, results in terms of student learning are crucial. They are the central element in evaluating any instructional improvement effort. Student learning outcomes are also the principal criteria by which most teachers judge their effectiveness. This is not to imply that questions about program planning and implementation, cost-effectiveness, teachers' attitudes and perceptions, or administrative involvement and support are insignificant. These important areas relate directly to program success, but are beyond the scope of our discussion here.

Student learning is broadly defined in this context to include a wide range of outcomes. It is not confined to a single standardized measure of student achievement, but includes a variety of achievement indexes. It also can include student affective measures such as attitude toward school, attitude toward particular subjects, and academic self-concept. In addition, student learning can include school-based measures such as enrollment in higher level classes, attendance, dropout rates, and administrative disciplinary actions.

Much of what we know about the application of mastery learning has come from evaluation studies. Unfortunately, generalizations from their results have sometimes been limited because these studies did not use rigorous experimental designs (Block & Burns, 1976; Guskey & Gates, 1986). At the same time, however, nearly all of these studies were conducted in actual classroom settings and within the constraints of actual classroom environments. As such, they offer valuable insights into how well mastery learning can work, the conditions under which it is likely to work best, and when adaptations are needed for it to attain the desired results.

Gathering Data on Student Achievement

The mastery learning process was designed as a way for teachers to enhance their students' learning outcomes. Certainly one of the most important is student achievement. To determine whether mastery learning has truly helped more students learn well, teachers must gather evidence on their level of achievement.

Three different types of achievement data can be collected at different times during an instructional sequence. Each point provides different information and is used to address different questions. The first type is data gathered before instruction begins (preinstruction or pretest data), the second is gathered while instruction is progressing (formative data), and the third when the instruction sequence is completed (summative data).

Preinstruction Data

Most teachers like to get some idea of their students' entry level knowledge and skills. With this information, they can alter their teaching to make it more appropriate or revise their instructional format to accommodate students' special needs. In addition, if they teach more than one section of a course, they may want to know whether the students in each section are fairly similar or quite different. To gain this information, many teachers administer a preinstruction assessment or pretest at the beginning of the term or school year.

Preinstruction assessments are typically of two types. The first is an instrument that assesses knowledge and skills that are required for the current course or area of study. These prerequisites are the basic understandings that a teacher might expect students to have gained from previous work in the subject. Information gathered from this type of assessment helps the teacher determine whether students are generally well prepared and ready to move ahead or whether they need review or remediation.

The second type of preinstruction assessment measures students' knowledge of the concepts and skills the teacher plans to teach. This information helps the teacher identify segments of the material that students have already learned well so they need not be repeated. This kind of preinstruction assessment is also useful in establishing a baseline from which achievement gains can be calculated.

Keep in mind, however, that preinstruction assessments can be overused. Some teachers, for example, begin every learning unit with a formal pretest. This practice not only requires a great deal of time that could be used for instruction, but also only confirms what the teacher already knows: Students don't know things they haven't yet been taught. In addition, because students generally perform poorly on such pretests, the practice compels the majority of students to begin each learning unit with a negative, failing experience. Therefore an appropriate balance in the use of preinstruction assessments must be sought. A variety of other, less formal ways are available for teachers to gather information about students for use in planning instruction (Cartwright & Cartwright, 1984; Guerin & Maier, 1983).

Formative Data

Formative assessment results can be useful in regularly evaluating the mastery learning process. As we discussed in the previous chapter, by plotting formative assessment results in a mastery chart (see Figure 6.3), a teacher can readily assess progress and identify problems. If only a few students do better on formative assessment B than they did on assessment A, then the correctives may be ineffective, the students may not have done the correctives, or formative assessment B may be more difficult than assessment A. Similarly, if the number of students attaining mastery on formative assessment A does not increase in later units, then a reorientation may be needed or more exciting enrichment activities may need to be devised.

Obviously, formative assessment results offer an efficient and readily available source of data for evaluating how well the mastery learning process is working. In addition, because this information is gathered while the program is ongoing, it can be used to guide immediate revisions and alterations that might help to improve final summative results (Beyer, 1995).

Summative Data

Undoubtedly, summative assessment or examination results are among the most important sources of achievement information for evaluating mastery learning. In fact, for many applications, these results represent the bottom line. Generally, the scores that students attain on the major assessments or examinations developed by the teacher represent the principal source of summative data. However, course examinations, department examinations, district or statewide assessments, or any standardized achievement examination also can be used for evaluation. But when these devices are used, steps must be taken to ensure that the assessed concepts and skills are closely aligned with the instructional objectives of the course of study. If they are not well aligned and the assessment device measures things other than what were taught, then it is an inappropriate and invalid indicator of the success of an instructional strategy designed to improve student learning (Leinhardt & Seewald, 1981).

Results From Studies on Student Achievement

Few instructional strategies have been evaluated as thoroughly as mastery learning. In fact, a search of the ERIC system, a data base on education publications and materials from the Educational Resources Information Center, yields nearly 2,000 articles related to the topic of mastery learning. Among these are hundreds of articles describing research and evaluation studies. This massive research base has been summarized in five major research syntheses, all of which focused on mastery learning's effects on student achievement:

Block, J. H., & Burns, R. B. (1976). Mastery learning. In L. S. Shulman (Ed.), *Review of research in education* (Vol. 4, pp. 3–49). Itasca, IL: Peacock.

Burns, R. B. (1986). Accumulating the accumulated evidence on mastery learning. *Outcomes, 5*(2), 4–10.

Guskey, T. R., & Gates, S. (1986). Synthesis of research on the effects of mastery learning in elementary and secondary classrooms. *Educational Leadership, 45*(8), 73–80.

Guskey, T. R., & Pigott, T. D. (1988). Research on group-based mastery learning programs: A meta-analysis. *Journal of Educational Research, 81*(4), 197–216.

Kulik, C. C., Kulik, J. A., & Bangert-Drowns, R. L. (1990a). Effectiveness of mastery learning programs: A meta-analysis. *Review of Educational Research, 60* (2), 265–299.

Although these syntheses were conducted at different times, used somewhat different criteria in choosing the studies to review, and sometimes used different review methodologies, they yielded strikingly similar results. Each synthesis concluded that mastery learning had strong and positive effects on student achievement. Even though the magnitude of the effect varied from study to study, it was consistently positive. In fact, the most recent comprehensive review of the research on mastery learning (Kulik, Kulik, & Bangert-Drowns, 1990a, p. 292) concludes:

> We recently reviewed meta-analyses in nearly 40 different areas of educational research (J. Kulik & Kulik, 1989). Few educational treatments of any sort were consistently associated with achievement effects as large as those produced by mastery learning. . . . In evaluation after evaluation, mastery programs have produced impressive gains.

Mastery learning is regularly identified as one of the most effective instructional strategies that teachers can employ at any level of education (Walberg, 1984). Some researchers have even suggested that the superiority of Japanese students in international comparisons of achievement in mathematics operations and problem solving may be the result of widespread use in Japan of instructional practices that are similar to mastery learning (Waddington, 1995).

Note also that one other "review," contrary to all of the others, indicated that mastery learning has little to no effect on student achievement (Slavin, 1987). This finding surprised not only scholars familiar with the vast research literature on mastery learning, which consistently demonstrates its positive effects, but also large numbers of practitioners who have experienced its benefits firsthand.

Since its publication, however, others have shown that this review was conducted using techniques of questionable validity (Gamoran, 1987; Hiebert, 1987; Joyce, 1987), employed capricious selection criteria (Anderson & Burns, 1987; Bloom, 1987; Kulik, Kulik, & Bangert-Drowns, 1990b), reported results in a biased manner (Walberg, 1988b), and drew conclusions not substantiated by the evidence presented (Guskey, 1987b, 1988c). Studies designed to examine the specific contentions of this review provide still further evidence that its results are inaccurate and misleading (Anderson, 1989). An excellent discussion and response to this "review" is provided in:

Kulik, J. A., Kulik, C. C., & Bangert-Drowns, R. L. (1990b). Is there better evidence on mastery learning? A response to Slavin. *Review of Educational Research, 60*(2), 303–307.

Gathering Data on Student Affect

Another important consideration of learning outcomes is the way that students typically feel about the subject they are studying, their teacher, their school, learning in general, and themselves. These feelings are referred to generally as *student affect* (Anderson, 1981b). Although affective outcomes typically receive far less attention than cognitive or achievement outcomes, most teachers strongly believe they are a vital part of what is learned in school.

The relationship between learning and student affect is reciprocal in nature; that is, affect influences learning, and learning influences affect. A student who feels confident, is interested in the subject, and is frequently praised by the teacher will probably be a successful learner. In turn, a student who has success in learning is likely to express increased confidence, greater interest in the subject, and generally more positive attitudes toward learning (Anderson & Anderson, 1982).

Mastery learning theory recognizes the strong influence that student affect can have on learning (Bloom, 1971c, 1976). The feelings and attitudes toward learning that students have when they enter a course of study certainly affect their learning success. And, as Bloom (1977) pointed out, success in one unit influences students' feelings and attitudes toward learning in the next unit. Success in a second unit adds further enhancement. By providing more students with successful learning experiences in each unit, the mastery learning process thus can have a strong and systematic influence on student affect (Block, 1984; Guskey & Pigott, 1988).

A wide variety of important affective outcomes can be assessed, including academic self-esteem, interest in the subject, attitudes, preferences, attributions, anxiety, and general mental health (Anderson, 1981b). For our purposes here, however, we will concentrate on only two: academic self-esteem and interest in the subject.

DIRECTIONS: Choose from among the following responses the one that comes closest to your feeling about each statement.

A	B	C	D	E
Strongly Agree	Agree	Not Sure	Disagree	Strongly Disagree

1. I am proud [or ashamed] of my work in this class.
2. This is a subject that I understand [or confuses me] easily.
3. I usually do well [or poorly] on class assignments.
4. The teacher often praises [or criticizes] my class work.
5. I feel good [or bad] most of the time I am in this class.

Figure 7.1 Examples of items used to measure academic self-esteem (a negative version of each item would use the corresponding word in brackets)

Academic Self-Esteem

Students' subjective perceptions of themselves as learners in academic settings is generally referred to as *academic self-esteem* (Anderson, 1981b). Someone with positive academic self-esteem feels confident and self-assured in learning situations, while someone with negative self-esteem feels incompetent and uncertain. Information on students' academic self-esteem can be gathered in many ways, including observations, interviews, open-ended questions (e.g., I feel best in school when . . .), and closed-item questions in which alternatives are fixed or arranged on a scale (Bloom, Madaus, & Hastings, 1981). A short questionnaire with items such as those in Figure 7.1 is probably the most common technique (the negative version of each item is shown in brackets). Excellent published instruments are also available to assess students' academic self-esteem (see, for example, Coopersmith, 1967).

To encourage students to answer honestly, teachers often ask students not to put their names on the questionnaires. Or sometimes teachers will ask each student to create a fictitious name to record on this and future questionnaires, which allows individual change to be assessed while providing students with some degree of anonymity.

Even when students remain anonymous and only class averages are available, however, valuable information is gained. Changes from the beginning to the end of the term in average class responses or differences among class sections can help teachers learn whether students, in general, developed increased confidence in themselves, felt more self-assured in learning situations, or gained a greater sense of self-worth.

One word of caution. Many students have highly categorical perceptions of learning and of themselves as learners; that is, a student may feel confident in learning to read, but uncertain or doubtful in learning mathematics, or vice versa. Because of these categorical perceptions, experiencing greater learning success in one subject may have little transfer to students' perceptions of themselves as learners in other subject areas. Thematic instruction and integrated curriculums that combine topics from various academic disciplines may lessen these perceptions, but a teacher still may find that positive change in academic self-esteem is specific to the subject in which students have experienced increased success. In addition, changes in academic self-esteem generally occur gradually and may not be evident when measured over a relatively short period of time. Nevertheless, even modest changes can be important.

Interest in the Subject

Interest is a feeling that impels a person to seek out things (Anderson, 1981a). Persons who are interested in a subject want to find out more about it, understand it better, or enhance their skills in that area. Information about students' interest in a subject can be gathered in a variety of ways similar to those used for academic self-esteem. Again, a short questionnaire with items similar to those in Figure 7.2 is probably the most common technique.

Just as with measures of academic self-esteem, teachers often do not ask students to record their names on the questionnaire. Instead, they use a fictitious name or number. And, like measures of academic self-esteem, changes in interest also tend to be subject-specific; that is, students who attain greater success in learning a particular subject are apt to express increased interest in it. At the same time, they may not express interest in other subjects or in learning in general. Teachers can use certain procedures, however, to enhance transfer and generalization in addition to using thematic instruction and integrated curriculums. These are discussed in detail in Chapter 8.

For additional information on student affect and procedures for measuring these outcomes, the following resources are recommended:

Anderson, L. W. (1981b). *Assessing affective characteristic in the schools.* Boston: Allyn & Bacon.

Bloom, B. S., Madaus, G. F., & Hastings, J. T. (1981). "Evaluation techniques for affective objectives." Chapter 1 in *Evaluation to improve learning.* New York: McGraw-Hill.

Krathwohl, D. R., Bloom, B. S., & Masia, B. B. (1964). *Taxonomy of educational objectives, Handbook II: Affective domain.* New York: McKay.

Popham, W. J. (1988). "Assessing the elusive: Measurement of affect." Chapter 7 in *Educational evaluation* (2nd ed.). Englewood Cliffs, NJ: Prentice-Hall.

DIRECTIONS: Choose from among the following responses the one that comes closest to your feeling about each statement.

A	B	C	D	E
Strongly Agree	Agree	Not Sure	Disagree	Strongly Disagree

1. I would [not] like to learn more about this subject.
2. The things we learn in this class are interesting [boring] to me.
3. I would like to spend more [less] time in this class.
4. I would like to take more [fewer] classes on this subject.
5. I enjoy [dislike] doing extra work for this class.

Figure 7.2 Examples of items used to measure interest in a subject (a negative version of each item would use the corresponding word in brackets)

Results From Studies on Student Affect

Studies and evaluations of the implementation of mastery learning have tapped a wide range of affective outcomes. These include students' affect toward the subject they are studying (Anania, 1981; Anderson, Scott, & Hutlock, 1976; Block & Tierney, 1974; Burke, 1983; Dillashaw & Okey, 1983; Nordin, 1979; Tenenbaum, 1982), their feelings about the importance of the subject (Blackburn & Nelson, 1985), their affect toward school (Cabezon, 1984), their academic self-esteem (Anderson, Scott, & Hutlock, 1976; Cabezon, 1984; Tenenbaum, 1982; Yildiran, 1977) their grade expectations (Denton, Ory, Glassnap, & Poggio, 1976), and their attributions for learning outcomes (Duby, 1981; Guskey, Benninga, & Clark, 1984). Results from these studies indicate that mastery learning procedures have an overall positive effect on affective outcomes, although typically not as large as they have on cognitive or achievement outcomes. Students who learn under mastery learning conditions generally like the subject they are studying, are more confident of their abilities in that subject, feel the subject is more important, and accept greater responsibility for their learning than students who learn under nonmastery conditions.

Two issues should be kept in mind when interpreting these affective results. First, nearly all of these studies assessed affective change over relative short periods of time. Because affective characteristics can be difficult to alter in a short time, studies conducted over longer periods could potentially yield larger effects. On the other hand, these favorable results may be partly attributable to a Hawthorne effect; that is, the novelty of the mastery learning procedures might have led to temporary expressions of enthusiasm by students. If so, then longer duration studies could yield smaller effects. Clearly, this issue needs more study (Guskey & Pigott, 1988).

Additional Outcomes of Interest

Other outcomes also may be of interest in an evaluation. For example, we might be interested in evaluating involvement in learning, course-completion rates, attendance, or discipline problems. Because these outcomes can be important in certain situations, we will briefly discuss each and offer suggestions for measurement.

Involvement

The amount of time students are engaged in learning is strongly related to their level of achievement. The more time students are involved in high quality learning activities, the more they tend to learn (Denham & Lieberman, 1980). This has led some educators to suggest lengthening the school day or adding more days to the school calendar (Wiley, 1976). Doing so, however, can be costly. And, as we discussed in the previous chapter, research studies have shown that students who spend the same amount of time in class vary greatly in the proportion of time they are actively engaged in learning (Anderson, 1976; Bloom, 1976). Some students are involved, or "on task," for more than 80 percent of the class period, while others are involved for no more than 20 percent of that time. If more students were involved in learning for a larger portion of the time they spend in class, then learning outcomes undoubtedly would be enhanced.

A consistently high rate of student involvement is one result frequently noted in mastery learning classes. Anderson (1973, 1975b, 1976), for example, found that students in mastery learning classes maintained a high level of involvement throughout the term or semester. This situation is quite different from most traditional classrooms, where students' involvement often declines steadily. Because mastery learning helps students attain the learning prerequisites they need for each new unit, they are prepared to learn new concepts and skills, experience less frustration in their learning, and are more likely to become involved in classroom activities.

Measures of involvement generally are made by having classroom observers watch a random sample of students and judge their behavior at regular time intervals as either on-or off-task. In many classes, class sessions are videotaped to make a permanent record for observation. Although these direct observations of students are limited to overt displays of involvement, they can yield a fairly accurate estimate of the proportion of time that students spend in learning. Involvement data also can be gathered from student self-reports (see

Hecht, 1977) or through the use of "stimulated recall" methods in which students are asked to report what they were doing or thinking at various points in a lesson (see Anania, 1981). When assured of their anonymity, students' self-reports and stimulated recall data provide helpful information that teachers can use to check the accuracy of their subjective judgments about student involvement.

Attendance

Most students enter classrooms at the beginning of the school year with the expectation of new and different things: new teachers, new subjects, new books, and maybe a new chance at learning success. These expectations typically last at least until the first quiz or assessment, which students regard as an evaluation device on which they have a single chance at success. If they are unsuccessful and receive a low grade on that first quiz or assessment, many see little chance of success later. And because students tend to avoid situations that offer little chance of success, attendance problems often begin to occur.

In mastery learning classes, students learn that the first assessment is not their only chance at success. They discover that assessments can be learning tools that inform and guide them in correcting their learning difficulties. They also know that they will have a second chance at success. Because this process typically helps more students become successful, mastery learning class attendance rates are usually higher than those in more traditional classes (Clark, Guskey, & Benninga, 1983). In addition, attendance data at both the class and school levels are fairly easy to collect for evaluation purposes because attendance records are a part of regular classroom and school procedures.

Course-Completion Rates

Institutions of higher education and some high schools often find that a fairly large number of students withdraw, drop out, or otherwise fail to complete the courses in which they enroll. Although these high withdrawal rates have many causes, most studies find one major reason is students' lack of successful learning experiences (Pantages & Creedan, 1978; Guskey, 1988d). Studies of mastery learning at the college level, however, find that courses using mastery learning methods have much higher completion rates than do similar courses taught by other methods. Guskey and Monsaas (1979), for example, found that the application of mastery learning in first-year courses brought a nearly 10 percent average increase in course-completion rates across nine different subject areas. Another study by Jones, Gordon, and Schechtman (1975) yielded similar results. This evidence suggests that helping students to be more successful in their learning may influence their persistence in learning activities and increase their chances of completing their courses and programs of study.

Discipline Problems

Like attendance problems, most discipline problems begin to occur after the first instructional unit is completed and the first quiz or assessment is administered. Furthermore, research by Kounin (1970) and others shows that the vast majority of discipline problems involve students who are having academic difficulties and experiencing few learning successes. Many teachers report, however, that discipline problems are dramatically reduced in mastery learning classes (Guskey & Kifer, 1995). Certainly having more students experience success contributes to this reduction. In addition, the cooperative atmosphere among students, the focus on clearly specified learning goals, and the expectation that all students can attain those goals serve to maintain a more positive classroom climate that, in turn, reduces discipline problems. Evaluations that include discipline measures generally entail teachers keeping daily records of problems or disruptions. In some cases, records of office referrals are also used.

Meaningful Comparisons

Once decisions are made about what specific data or information to gather for the evaluation, meaningful comparisons must be planned. Evaluation generally implies a determination of relative merit or worth. In other words, is one option better or worse than another option or options? This judgment requires some form of comparison. In regard to mastery learning, we need to compare the changes that result from its use with those that were attained previously or that result from other types of instruction. If the application of mastery learning does not result in more positive student learning outcomes, then the extra work it requires might not be worthwhile. However, if more positive student learning outcomes do result, then these advantages can be meaningfully assessed.

Single-Teacher Comparisons

Many mastery learning applications are planned in such a way that teachers can conduct their own individual comparisons and small-scale evaluations. This is especially common at the secondary and college levels where teachers teach several sections of the same course (Guskey, 1981b). Typically, they randomly choose one section in which to use mastery learning. The other sections are then taught by whatever methods or procedures the teacher has used in the past. Preinstruction data often are gathered to determine if students in each section have comparable entry-level skills. The principal difference in the way the class sections are taught is simply the introduction of feedback, corrective, and enrichment procedures in the mastery learning class.

At the end of a semester or school term, all class sections are administered the same summative examination or assessment and the same affective instruments. Evaluation comparisons are then made. This sort of comparison allows each teacher to evaluate directly the usefulness of the mastery learning process.

This approach has one drawback, however. Because teachers are generally sensitive to even subtle changes in their students' learning progress or involvement in instruction, many quickly detect positive differences in the mastery section. When this occurs, they often abandon the "control" procedures and implement mastery learning in all class sections, believing that it would be "immoral" for them to deny the process to other students (Stahman, 1980). Although this may confound the evaluation design, one would be foolish to argue against it.

Another procedure that some teachers use compares the results from their current classes with those from previous classes. Ensuring that students in present and past classes are comparable in terms of their entry-level skills is a major problem with comparisons of this type, however. In addition, these comparisons are only meaningful if current students are administered the same examinations or assessments as were used in the past.

In most evaluations, one of the first and most important comparisons to make is between the average summative examination or assessment score attained by each class section. An average score is computed by adding the scores of all students in the section and dividing that sum by the number of scores added (that is, the number of students who took the assessment in that section). Most teachers find that the average score attained by students in the mastery section is substantially higher than the average score of students in other sections. For example, Jones, Gordon, and Schechtman (1975) used this technique and found that in biology and mathematics classes, the average summative examination score in mastery sections was more than 20 percent higher than the average score in nonmastery sections.

A second useful evaluation comparison is the proportion of students who receive various letter grades in each class section. Teachers generally find that when the same criteria-referenced grading standards are used with all sections, a larger percentage of students receives high course grades (A or B) in the mastery section than in other sections of the same course. Similarly, a smaller percentage of students in the mastery section receives low course grades (D or F).

When mastery learning is initially implemented, differences in high course grades seldom reach the 20 to 80 percent difference that Bloom (1968) originally proposed. However, increases from 20 percent to as much as 60 percent are not uncommon. For example, in an evaluation of a pilot mastery learning project in the Chicago public schools, Guskey, Englehard, Tuttle, and Guida (1978) found that 57 percent of students in English class sections taught by mastery learning procedures received a final grade of A or B, compared to only 17 percent of students in comparable nonmastery sections. In addition, only 20 percent of students in mastery sections received a final grade of D or F, compared to 45 percent of students in the nonmastery sections.

Affective measures are a third important evaluation comparison. An average score on each measure for each class section can be calculated and compared, as was done with summative assessment results. Again, teachers usually find that students in mastery sections express more positive attitudes about themselves and greater interest in the subject than do students in other sections of the same course (Cragin, 1979; Duby, 1981).

A fourth type of evaluation comparison examines the variation in assessment scores, course grades, and affective measures. Mastery learning theory predicts not only that more students will learn well, attain higher levels of achievement, and express more positive attitudes, but also that students will become more similar in terms of these specified learning outcomes. In other words, variation in these outcomes will be reduced. The research of Yildiran (1977) and Clark, Guskey, and Benninga (1983) has noted this reduced variation.

Differences in variation can be compared precisely by computing statistical values known as the *variance* and *standard deviation* for the different measures in each course section. But most teachers use less sophisticated indexes, such as the range of the scores (highest score minus the lowest score) and still generally find less variation in the mastery section.

Multiple-Teacher Comparisons

In many cases, teachers do not teach multiple sections of the same course and so cannot make single-teacher comparisons. The majority of elementary school teachers, for example, spend the entire school day with a single group of students. Although these teachers might compare current results with those from classes taught in previous years, ensuring comparable entry-level skills might prove difficult. To evaluate the effectiveness of mastery learning under these conditions, multiple-teacher comparisons are generally employed. These comparisons contrast the learning outcomes of students taught by teachers using mastery learning and those of students taught by teachers using other techniques.

To make multiple-teacher comparisons, teachers implementing mastery learning typically ask colleagues who teach the same subject or grade level to keep careful records of their students' learning progress. By sharing information, they can then compare procedures and results. This kind of exchange helps each teacher assess the effectiveness of the mastery learning process and find ways to improve implementation techniques.

Multiple-teacher comparisons have both advantages and disadvantages when viewed in relation to single-teacher comparisons. For instance, unintended differences in the way a teacher conducts class sessions or interacts with some students may bias the results of single-teacher comparisons. On the other hand, it is sometimes difficult to separate differences resulting from teaching skill from those resulting from the mastery learning process when different teachers are compared. Multiple-teacher comparisons also do not allow opportunities for teachers to gain comparative evidence as regularly or as immediately as they can through single-teacher comparisons. Furthermore, multiple-teacher comparisons can sometimes lead to an unproductive sense of competition among teachers, unless they are conducted in an open and professional manner. When carefully planned, however, these comparisons do provide meaningful evaluation information.

Preinstruction data are often used in multiple-teacher comparisons, just as in single-teacher comparisons, to determine whether students in different class sections are equivalent in terms of their entry skills. The other evaluation comparisons are the same for both kinds of teacher comparisons. Additional considerations are necessary, however, for multiple-teacher comparisons.

For instance, a comparison of summative examination or assessment results is still critically important. It is meaningful, however, only if the teachers involved agree to administer and score the same summative assessment in the same way. In cases where a department examination, district examination, or standardized assessment in the subject is used, results also can be meaningfully compared. But comparing results from different examinations prepared by different teachers and scored in different ways is inappropriate and pointless. The same is true in comparing course grades, affective results, and measures of variation. For the comparisons to be meaningful, the criteria used in making those comparisons must be identical or at least verifiably equivalent.

Multiple-teacher comparisons were used in evaluating a mastery learning program in New York City public schools (McDonald, 1982). A major portion of this evaluation was based on the scores students attained on statewide assessments called Regents' Examinations, which are prepared and distributed by the New York State Board of Regents. By comparing the examination results of students in classes taught by teachers using mastery learning to the results of students in similar classes taught by other teachers, examiners found that "the number of students passing the Regents' Examination may be anywhere from two to four times the average of other classes in the same school in the same subject" (p. 8). This difference approaches the theoretically proposed 20 to 80 percent difference originally hypothesized by Bloom (1968).

Remember that evaluations conducted in actual school settings will almost always have methodological difficulties because of the lack of experimental control. These difficulties mean that evaluation results must be interpreted cautiously. Still, evaluations that are carefully and thoughtfully planned can yield information that is both valuable and useful.

Summary

Evaluating the effectiveness of the mastery learning process at the classroom or school level involves systematically collecting and analyzing information through thoughtful and meaningful comparisons. A principal source of evaluation information is evidence of student achievement. Such data can be gathered before instruction begins (preinstruction), during the instructional process (formative), and at the end of an instructional sequence (summative). Data about affective outcomes–such as the way students feel about a subject, school, learning in general, or themselves–are also important in evaluating mastery learning.

Hundreds of studies have evaluated the effects of mastery learning on student learning outcomes. Syntheses of this massive body of evidence indicate that the implementation of mastery learning is consistently related to significant improvements in student achievement. Improved student affective outcomes have also been noted, although typically not as large.

Evaluation comparisons of achievement or affective outcomes are generally made through single- or multiple-teacher comparisons. Both procedures involve comparing student learning outcomes attained through mastery learning with those attained through other approaches to instruction. Although most evaluation designs have weaknesses because of the lack of strict experimental control, the information gained through carefully and thoughtfully planned evaluations can enable us to make better decisions about the usefulness and value of the mastery learning process in specific settings.

Activities

1. Develop a plan for evaluating the application of mastery learning in a particular setting. The plan should include each of the following elements:
   a. A clear statement of the purpose of the evaluation and the questions it should answer.
   b. A description of the information to be collected for the evaluation and procedures for gathering that information. This would include the achievement and affective instruments to be used and additional data thought to be important.
   c. A summary of the comparisons to be made in determining the effectiveness of the mastery learning process in that setting.
   d. A general time line for the evaluation that indicates when the various sources of information will be collected and analyzed.
2. Have a colleague check your plan to make sure that the information gathered and the comparisons planned are in line with the purposes of the evaluation and the questions it is designed to answer.

8

Onward and Upward

Up to now, we have focused on the three major steps in implementing mastery learning: *planning, managing,* and *evaluating*. Because these steps are so important, each was analyzed in extensive detail. In this chapter, however, we step back and consider mastery learning in a broader context.

First, we will examine the implementation of mastery learning on a school- or districtwide basis, including a time line for achieving broad-based involvement and positive results. Included is a set of guidelines to ensure high quality implementation and program maintenance. Additional research on the effects of mastery learning is then explored for those readers interested in applications at particular levels or specific subject areas. From there we turn to the procedures teachers use to help students transfer the "learning-to-learn" skills they develop under mastery learning to other subjects and future learning situations. This is followed by a description of several promising additions to the mastery learning process. Finally, we consider ideas on the future of mastery learning and its possible impact on future generations of students and teachers.

Steps to Program Implementation

Mastery learning is used throughout the world today in a wide array of educational environments (Guskey, 1994g, 1995a). Although the essential elements of mastery learning are evident in all of these settings, the process is adapted to fit the special conditions of each context. In like fashion, the implementation of mastery learning programs at the school or district level also must be adapted to fit each particular context. A careful analysis of successful programs shows, however, that they share many operational similarities. In particular, many have followed a similar sequence of implementation steps that not only serves to guarantee high quality applications, but also maintains enthusiasm and support for implementation efforts (see Guskey, Passaro, & Wheeler, 1991).

The following steps characterize many highly successful mastery learning programs, particularly in schools in the United States (also see Figure 8.1):

1. Large-group presentation
2. Survey of interest in professional development
3. Professional development on mastery learning, first year
4. Follow-up and support
5. Reviewing and sharing results
6. Recruiting trainers
7. Training the trainers
8. Professional development on mastery learning, second year
9. Professional development on extending mastery learning
10. Follow-up and support

Large-Group Presentation

Nearly all programs begin with a large-group presentation to all faculty and staff members on the topic of mastery learning. This presentation typically focuses on mastery learning's development, its essential elements, and their classroom application (see Chapter 1). Although this presentation is usually made by a person from outside the school or district who has great expertise in mastery learning, local people with personal experience and excellent presentation skills also can be highly effective. This presentation establishes a common knowledge base and vocabulary on which future discussions can be built. It also helps to dispel rumors and clarify misunderstandings. For these reasons, it is important for all faculty and staff members to attend.

Survey of Interest in Professional Development

An informal survey follows the large-group presentation to determine the extent of interest in a more comprehensive professional development program focusing on mastery learning. This survey simply asks teachers and staff members if they would like to take part in a more extensive training session that will provide the time and opportunity for them to plan for implementation. Participation in training sessions is almost always voluntary, and typically 20 percent to 30 percent of teachers and staff members volunteer to take part. Those who volunteer often are among the most effective and most talented teachers on staff (Guskey, 1988a). Although this may positively bias the success of early implementation efforts, it is unwise to require participation in training at this early stage.

Mastery Learning Implementation Plan

1. Large-Group Presentation
   - Information-sharing session
   - Delivered by outside expert
   - Attendance required
2. Survey of Interest in Professional Development
   - Seek voluntary participation in training
   - Typically, 20% to 30% of staff members volunteer
3. Professional Development on Mastery Learning, First Year
   - Conducted by outside expert
   - Minimum of two to three days
4. Follow-Up and Support
   - Provide opportunities for continued planning and development
   - Monthly follow-up meetings for an hour or so after school
   - Coordinated by building principals
5. Reviewing and Sharing Results
   - Recognize hard work and improvements
   - Encourage increased participation
   - Focus on results, not individuals
6. Recruiting Trainers
   - Rely on those with experience
   - Voluntary involvement
7. Training the Trainers
   - Conducted by outside expert
   - Focus on effective professional development, change, and adult learners
8. Professional Development on Mastery Learning, Second Year
   - Conducted by outside expert
   - Trainers serve as facilitators
   - Minimum of two to three days
9. Professional Development on Extending Mastery Learning
   - Conducted by outside expert
   - Minimum of two or three days
   - May be held in conjunction with first year
10. Follow-Up and Support
    - Continued coordination and support from school leaders
    - Experienced practitioners serve as peer coaches and mentors
    - Trainers conduct local seminars and professional development sessions
    - Outside experts *no longer needed!*

Figure 8.1 Steps in the implementation of successful mastery learning programs

Professional Development on Mastery Learning, First Year

Those teachers and staff members who volunteer are then involved in a mastery learning seminar and workshop. During this time, they work in collaborative teams to organize the materials they will need and plan for implementation. Teams are generally arranged based upon grade-level assignments at the elementary level and subject areas taught at the middle and secondary levels. Although an outside expert usually conducts this initial professional development session, local individuals with personal experience also may be used. A college or university often cosponsors the session so that participants can receive course credit for their participation.

Mastery learning seminars and workshops are generally held during the summer months when teachers are relieved of regular classroom responsibilities. Sometimes, however, sessions are held during the school year and teachers are given release time to attend. This is usually more expensive because it requires paying substitute teachers. Many teachers also are reluctant to be away from their classes for extended times during the school year. The only disadvantage of summer seminars is the delay in implementing newly learned practices. Two or three days are typically required for the seminar, although those cosponsored by a college or university may be extended to one week.

Follow-Up and Support

When teachers return to implement the mastery learning process in their classrooms, they must be provided with regular opportunities for follow-up and support. Brief monthly meetings after school, perhaps for an hour or two, may be all that is needed. These meetings allow teachers to address any problems or difficulties they may have encountered and to share their successes. Problems are generally solved through collaborative efforts, though occasionally advice from experts is sought. In addition, a portion of each meeting is usually set aside for continued cooperative planning and development activities.

Although teachers generally welcome these opportunities to meet with their colleagues, the principal, or another administrator with schoolwide responsibilities, must take the initiative in scheduling and coordinating these meetings. Most teachers' daily schedules are so complicated by classroom responsibilities that they have few opportunities to communicate with their colleagues and set up such meetings. The principal's active involvement also demonstrates support and encourages teachers to persist in their implementation efforts.

Reviewing and Sharing Results

As the teachers who implement mastery learning begin to see positive results, it is important that these be shared with other faculty and staff members. The results may be improved scores on class assessments, higher levels of involvement during class sessions, better homework completion rates, more positive attitudes among students, or any other learning outcome that teachers consider important. When these positive results become well known, the mastery learning process gains credibility. Teachers who were initially doubtful are presented with credible evidence on the value of the process, not from an outside expert, but from colleagues who teach the same students that they teach. As a result, more teachers volunteer to become involved in the process and take advantage of professional development opportunities.

In making these positive results well known, it is crucial that the emphasis be placed on the results, not the people. Although those teachers who first participated may be outstanding and extremely dedicated individuals, their actions, not their personalities, are what made the difference. And what they did can be done by all teachers, if they are provided high quality professional development and appropriate follow-up (Guskey, 1989a).

Recruiting Trainers

With more teachers now interested in implementing mastery learning, a second seminar and workshop must be planned. Teachers and staff members who did not take part in the initial seminar but now want to become involved must know that other professional development opportunities are available to them. Early in this planning process, however, teachers who already have been successful in implementation should be surveyed to determine their interest in becoming mastery learning trainers. Although the decision to become a trainer should be voluntary, those who have gained positive results also have the necessary experiential background. Furthermore, if the mastery learning program is ever to become an integral part of the school or district, it is essential that in-house resources be fully used.

Training the Trainers

Those teachers experienced in implementing mastery learning and interested in becoming trainers must now be trained. This element is critical to any large-scale implementation effort, because a teacher must make the necessary but sometimes difficult transition from successful practitioner to successful trainer.

Often the outside expert is called on again to train the trainers, although the focus of this session is more on process and method than on substance. In other words, although some time may be spent helping trainers extend their knowledge of mastery learning, most of the time is devoted to planning and conducting successful professional development seminars and follow-up sessions. In particular, this session must emphasize the characteristics of effective professional development and change efforts (Fullan, 1991; Guskey, 1994h), along with the special conditions of working with adult learners (Huberman, 1995).

Many such "training trainers" sessions also allow prospective trainers to practice their presentation skills and question-answering techniques, usually in pairs or small groups. Figure 8.2 lists some of the common concerns and most frequently asked questions that trainers must be prepared to address.

Professional Development on Mastery Learning, Second Year

A second mastery learning seminar and workshop is conducted for newly interested teachers and staff members. Participants are still mainly volunteers, although the credible evidence attained by those who were successful in implementation is sometimes used to encourage others who may be reluctant to take part. Sessions again place participants in collaborative teams to organize materials and plan for implementation. An outside expert typically directs the seminar, but the newly trained trainers are actively engaged as facilitators. During the seminar, they work with the participants in small groups, help them in their planning, and answer their questions. In addition, they observe the expert as a trainer, making note of methods and techniques in order to refine their own individual training strategies. If problems or difficult questions arise, they can always call on the expert for assistance. In other words, they are provided with guided practice as a trainer.

As with the first seminar, two or three days are typically required. At the end of each day, a debriefing session is held for the trainers at which they discuss their work with seminar participants, what they noted in observing the expert, and any difficulties they may have experienced. They also discuss the format for the next session and future professional development plans.

Professional Development on Extending Mastery Learning

In addition to the second mastery learning seminar and workshop, a second level of professional development in mastery learning also must be provided for faculty and staff members who are experienced in the process. This seminar provides these mastery learning veterans with a structured opportunity to refine and expand their implementation efforts. It also provides another opportunity for collaborative work with colleagues. These second-level sessions are typically scheduled in conjunction with initial-level professional development seminars. In this way, those with more experience in mastery learning can serve as peer coaches for those who are new to the process.

Follow-Up and Support

At this point, everything is in place for the "institutionalization" of mastery learning (Joyce & Showers, 1988). Principals and other school leaders are

Common Concerns and Questions About Mastery Learning

1. I already do this.
2. Most of my students do well now, so why change?
3. This is just good teaching.
4. It is simply teach-test-reteach-retest.
5. Isn't this simply "teaching to the test"?
6. It doesn't fit my subject (e.g., kindergarten, art, music, physical education, creative writing).
7. It sounds great, but it would be too much work.
8. How much extra time does this take?
9. I won't be able to cover the material.
10. This process isn't fair to my brighter students.
11. It's not fair to give students a "second chance."
12. This isn't what life is like.
13. They don't teach this way in colleges and universities.
14. After all, who knows what "mastery" is?
15. What evidence is there that this works?
16. I can see this working for most of my students, but what about George (a recently "included" student with special needs)?
17. What about students who just want to "pass" and don't care about "mastery"?
18. How will this affect my grouping practices?
19. Are you sure this is not simply this year's "new thing"?
20. Will I have to change my grading policies to use this?
21. Do I count the formative assessments as part of the grade?
22. How much time should I spend on correctives and enrichment?
23. How should I mark the formative assessments?
24. How do I motivate students to do well on the first formative assessment?
25. What do I do with students who don't reach mastery on the second assessment?
26. How should I deal with absentees?
27. Don't students in the corrective group feel bad?
28. Do the same students always show up in the corrective group?
29. How do I manage two groups in the classroom at a time?
30. Where do I find appropriate corrective and enrichment activities?
31. How does this relate to other innovations (e.g., cooperative learning, multiple intelligences, whole language, etc.)?
32. Sure students can reach mastery, but do they retain what they learned?
33. Won't I be accused of grade inflation?
34. What if not all teachers in the department or at a grade level are involved?
35. What happens if next year's teachers don't use this?
36. Should we require all teachers to use it?

Figure 8.2 Common concerns and questions about mastery learning

prepared to support teachers in their implementation efforts and to coordinate follow-up sessions. Teachers experienced in mastery learning can serve as peer coaches and mentors for those who are new to the process. Trainers are prepared to conduct seminars and workshops on site for new teachers and staff members. And, perhaps most important, outside experts are no longer needed. The program can stand on its own and, with appropriate support, continue to grow and develop.

In viewing this ten-step process, remember that it is a multiyear endeavor. Implementing a mastery learning program takes place over years, not over just a few weeks or months. Strong, continued support from all levels of the organization is essential if the true improvements that are possible are to be realized.

Guidelines for Success

It is difficult to make precise statements about the characteristics of successful mastery learning programs. As mentioned earlier, each program is adapted to fit the special conditions of a particular context. But certain procedural guidelines appear to be crucial to program success. These are derived not from the research on mastery learning per se, but from evidence on effective professional development efforts (e.g., Guskey & Huberman, 1995). Like the common sequence of implementation steps described in the previous section, however, these guidelines offer a useful framework for directing the energies of educators interested in implementing high quality mastery learning programs.

The procedural guidelines that direct the implementation efforts in many successful mastery learning programs include the following:

1. Think big, but start small.
2. Work in teams.
3. Use available resources.
4. Integrate programs.

Think Big, But Start Small

There is no easier way to sabotage any improvement effort than to take on too much at one time. In fact, the vast research literature on change shows clearly that the magnitude of change people are asked to make is inversely related to their likelihood of making it (Guskey, 1991). Professionals at all levels generally oppose radical alterations to their procedures. In addition, change often adds extra responsibilities to an already burdensome workload. Successful programs typically approach change in a gradual and incremental fashion (Fullan, 1991).

For mastery learning, this means that beginning on a relatively small scale is best. Classroom applications might start with a single subject area at the elementary level or a single course at the secondary or college level. School applications typically begin with a fourth to a third of the staff taking part. Beginning in a single subject and being able to continue efforts through the year is better than starting in five subject areas and then having to abandon the process after one month because the amount of extra work is overwhelming.

At the same time, modest, narrowly conceived projects seldom bring significant improvement (Guskey, 1994h). To implement mastery learning only in a single unit, for example, is clearly insufficient. "Thinking big" means that implementation must be seen as a sustained, multiyear endeavor that is guided by a grand vision of where we hope to be three to five years into the future, while recognizing the steps required to reach that goal.

Work in Teams

The discomfort that accompanies change is greatly compounded if those involved perceive they have no say in the process or if they feel isolated and detached in their implementation efforts. For this reason, all aspects of the planning and implementation process must involve teams of individuals working together.

When teachers work together in planning for mastery learning, they serve as valuable resources of ideas for one another. The approach one teacher uses for initial instruction in a unit, for example, might be an effective corrective for another teacher who approaches the unit differently. Teaching colleagues are also important resources for alternative approaches to assessment, enrichment activities, motivational strategies, and classroom-management techniques. Experience shows, in fact, that when teachers share development tasks and responsibilities, not only is the amount of work required of each individual substantially reduced, but also the quality of the work produced increases dramatically.

Many teachers even team during their implementation of mastery learning. Especially in elementary schools, teachers at the same level frequently coordinate their schedules to administer formative assessments at the same time. After the assessment is reviewed and scored, students are exchanged across classes. In other words, the students working on correctives go with one teacher, while those involved in enrichment activities go with the other. In large elementary schools, up to five teachers at a level have been known to coordinate their schedules to accommodate such teaming. Although they usually begin with four corrective groups and only one enrichment, this soon changes. In relatively short time, they have four enrichment groups and only one corrective group. Similar teaming also can be accomplished at the secondary level when class schedules permit.

Use Available Resources

Implementation efforts can be made more efficient and effective if available resources are used. Textbooks, for example, should not be abandoned: They are a valuable source of information and activities. Although all textbooks have their limitations, they are an important learning resource for teachers and students alike. Many textbook series also include instruments for checking on students' learning progress. These often can be used as formative assessments, so long as they are well designed and carefully match a teacher's instructional goals (see Chapter 3). Similarly, most successful mastery learning teachers do not develop or create all of their corrective and enrichment activities. Instead, they simply become resourceful in finding suitable activities and making these available to their students. When they enter a teacher supply store or view publishers' displays at educational conferences, for instance, they are actively searching for materials they can use as correctives or enrichments.

Of course, "available resources" means not only materials, but also people. When teams are formed to begin planning for mastery learning, for instance, it is important to include the special educators and resource teachers. Because of their expertise on instructional alternatives, they are a particularly valuable resource for ideas on correctives. Teachers of gifted and talented students also should be included. Their expertise can be especially helpful in planning enrichment activities. Librarians, media specialists, counselors, and school administrators also should be included. They, too, have important instructional expertise and experience that can greatly add to the quality of implementation.

Guidelines for Implementation Success

1. Think big, but start small.
2. Work in teams.
3. Use available resources.
4. Integrate programs.

Integrate Programs

More than any other profession, education seems fraught with innovation. In fact, innovations seem to come and go in education about as regularly as the seasons. Each year, new programs are introduced in schools without any effort to show how they relate to those that came before or after. Furthermore, how these various innovations contribute to a growing professional knowledge base is seldom mentioned. The result is an enormous overload of fragmented, uncoordinated, and ephemeral attempts at change (Fullan & Miles, 1992).

The steady stream of innovations in education leads many practitioners to view all new programs as isolated fads that will soon be gone, only to be replaced by yet another bandwagon (Latham, 1988). This pattern of constant yet unrelated, short-term innovations not only obscures improvement and provokes cynicism, but also imposes a sense of affliction. Having seen a multitude of innovations come in and go out of fashion, veteran teachers frequently calm the fears of less experienced colleagues with the advice, "Don't worry; this, too, shall pass."

If professional development efforts focusing on mastery learning are to succeed, they must include precise descriptions of how mastery learning can be integrated with other existing programs and strategies. Mastery learning must be seen as an integral part of a coherent framework for improvement. Because no single innovation is totally comprehensive, substantial improvements become possible only when several strategies are carefully and systematically integrated. And as Doyle (1992), Sarason (1990), and others emphasize, coordinating programs and combining ideas releases great energy in the improvement process.

In recent years, several researchers have described how mastery learning can be brought together with other innovations to yield impressive results. These include combinations of mastery learning and thinking skills programs (Arredondo & Block, 1990; Kozlovsky, 1990), mastery teaching techniques (Guskey, 1988e), peer tutoring (Grossman, 1985), and cooperative learning (Guskey, 1990a; Mevarech, 1985, 1991; Mevarech & Susak, 1993). In addition, several frameworks for integrating a collection of programs that include mastery learning have been developed. One example is a framework developed by Marzano, Pickering, and Brandt (1990) based on various dimensions of learning. Figure 8.3 (page 202) shows another framework developed by Guskey (1990b) that is built around five major components in the teaching and learning process. Frameworks such as these allow skilled practitioners to see more clearly the linkages among various innovations. They also offer guidance to reformers who seek to pull together programs that collectively address the most pressing problems in a particular context.

A crucial point here is that mastery learning fits well and complements other educational innovations. These linkages and associations, however, must be made clear. As Fullan (1992) stresses, "[S]chools are not in the business of managing single innovations; they are in the business of contending with multiple innovations simultaneously" (p. 19). In other words, mastery learning is likely to be one of several innovations being implemented in a school at any particular time. By recognizing the complementary strengths of different innovations and programs, however, educators are better able to pull together those that collectively address what is most needed in that context.

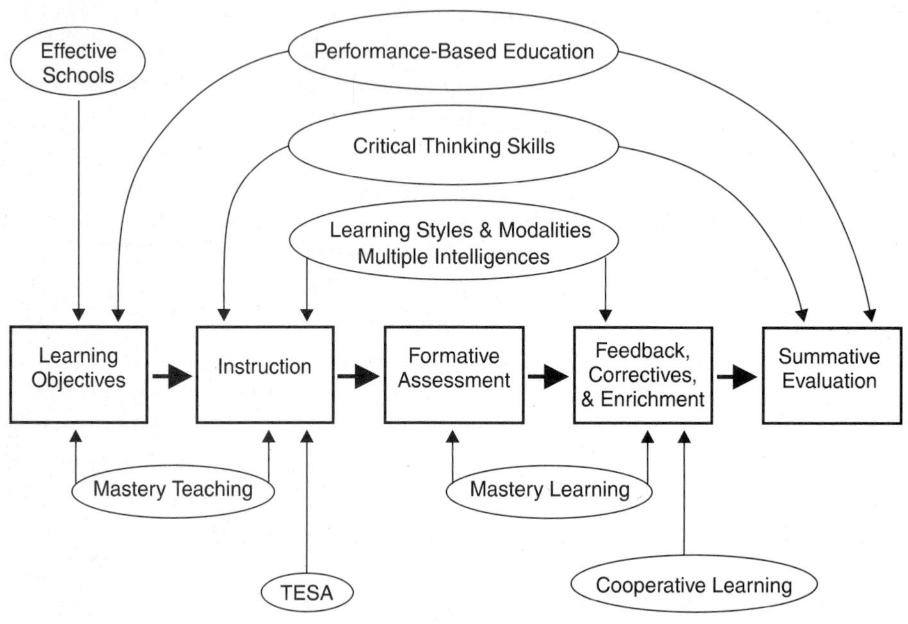

Figure 8.3 The principal strengths of selected innovative strategies (from Guskey, 1990b)

Additional Research on the Effects of Mastery Learning

As discussed in Chapter 7, mastery learning has been widely applied, its effects on student learning have been thoroughly evaluated, and syntheses of this research have been reported in respected education journals. As might be expected, most of this documented evidence focuses on applications in the major academic areas of reading and language arts, mathematics, social studies, science, and foreign languages. It is important to point out, however, that mastery learning also has been successfully applied to instruction across the entire range of grade levels and in a wide variety of subject areas.

The following studies and articles describe the application of mastery learning at different levels of education, with diverse groups of students, and in a variety of subject areas. Although this list is not complete, it does show the diversity of mastery learning's successful applications.

Kindergarten

Puleo, V. T. (1986). *Application of mastery learning theory to full- and half-day kindergarten research.* Unpublished manuscript (ERIC No. ED286623). This paper reviews the key concepts of mastery learning and focuses on the qualities that make it especially suitable for application in kindergarten classes.

First Grade

Lahdes, E. (1982). Mastery learning in theory and practical innovation. *Scandinavian Journal of Educational Research, 27*(2), 89–107. This article describes the results from a Finnish experiment in which mastery learning principles were applied in first-grade classes and yielded exceptionally positive results.

Educationally Disadvantaged

Rachal, A. M. (1991). *Mastery learning in the steel magnolia town.* Paper presented at annual meeting of the International Reading Association, Las Vegas, NV. This paper reports that the application of mastery learning principles in one school district's Chapter I reading programs has consistently yielded positive gains in the academic performance of educationally disadvantaged students.

Gifted Education

Perryman, L. (1986). *Mastery learning and its implications for gifted education programs.* Unpublished manuscript (ERIC No. ED280214). This paper reviews the literature on mastery learning and suggests that the process can benefit gifted students by (1) providing information to determine if gifted students have mastered the essential elements for a particular subject area, and (2) offering stimulating learning alternatives for gifted students once mastery has been demonstrated.

Physical Education

Blakemore, C. L. (1992). Comparison of students taught basketball skills using mastery and nonmastery learning methods. *Journal of Teaching in Physical Education, 11*(3), 235–247. This article describes a study of psychomotor skill development that showed that students taught basketball skills under mastery learning conditions outperformed control students on tests of isolated skills.

Music

Larsen, J. J. (1987). *Teaching basic jazz piano skills: A mastery learning approach.* Paper presented at annual meeting of the American Educational Research Association, Washington, DC. This paper summarizes the evaluation of a short course on jazz piano, and shows that students taught through mastery learning techniques reached high levels of performance and acquired more positive attitudes toward their own improvisational ability.

Geography

Fox, M. F. (1987). A decade of mastery learning: Evolution and evaluation. *Journal of Geography in Higher Education, 11*(1), 3–10. This article describes the superior performance of students taught in a mastery learning format on final course examinations.

Business Education

Whiting, B., & Render, G. F. (1987). Cognitive and affective outcomes of mastery learning: A review of sixteen semesters. *Clearing House, 60* (6), 276–280. This article concludes that mastery learning produces successful learning experiences for at least 80 percent of the students in business and distributive education classes.

Legal Education

Feinman, J. M., & Feldman, M. (1985). Achieving excellence: Mastery learning in legal education. *Journal of Legal Education, 35*(4), 528–551. This article describes the successful application of mastery learning strategies in courses on contracts, torts, and legal research and writing.

Automobile Mechanics

Wentling, T. L. (1973). Mastery versus nonmastery instruction with varying test item feedback treatments. *Journal of Educational Psychology, 65*(1), 50–58. This article summarizes the positive effects of mastery learning techniques on both achievement and retention of learned material in courses on automobile mechanics.

The Transfer of Learning-to-Learn Skills

Research studies have shown that students in mastery learning classes improve their learning-to-learn skills (see, for example, Hecht, 1977). In other words, the mastery learning process appears to help students better organize their learning, use the feedback they receive from the teacher, pace their learning, and work at correcting their learning difficulties. A limitation to these positive findings, however, is that these skills tend to be context-specific; that is, relatively few students seem to carry over such skills to learning in other classes or other subjects.

Recently, however, teachers have had some success in directly teaching students to transfer these improved learning skills to other classes and subject areas. After their students become accustomed to the mastery learning process, these teachers point out the aspects of that process that are responsible for helping to improve learning. They discuss the importance of preparing for the formative assessments, of using the assessments to get information about what is important to learn, and of regularly correcting learning errors. They stress that these are things that the best students have always done and that they are actually the steps involved in learning how to learn. They then ask, "How might you do these things for yourself in classes where mastery learning is not used?" The question initiates a discussion of various ways that students might continue the process on their own, independent of the teacher.

Students can usually come up with a variety of creative mastery learning tactics. Their ideas include making up their own formative assessments, using quizzes and tests as a "guide" for what the teacher wants, studying the things missed on quizzes and assessments as soon as they are returned from the teacher, and saving quizzes and assessments to study for larger examinations. In many cases, the students also suggest paying attention to the teacher for cues as to what is important, raising their hands and asking questions when something is unclear, and asking friends to explain concepts they do not understand. Although some of these ideas may go beyond the formal mastery learning process, all are learning-to-learn skills that students can apply in any learning situation.

When students are explicitly shown the general utility of these aspects of the mastery learning process, they seem better able to transfer such skills to other classes and to other subject areas. Usually, they already have discovered the value of these techniques for their learning and have gained some sense of the rewards they bring in higher achievement and better grades. Being able to transfer these strategies to other learning situations also provides students with skills they will need throughout their lives. In fact, the most important benefits that mastery learning can offer students may be a clear understanding of how they can improve their learning, as well as a sense of confidence in learning situations.

Promising Additions to the Mastery Learning Process

The literature on mastery learning has grown at a fantastic rate over the past two decades. As we described in the previous chapter, the ERIC system currently lists nearly 2,000 articles related to the topic of mastery learning. Although the application of mastery learning in diverse settings continues to be studied, it is important that we also look beyond mastery learning to find ways of improving student learning even further.

In the early 1980s, two of Benjamin Bloom's doctoral students conducted studies that showed that under the ideal instructional conditions of one-to-one tutoring, the average student attains a level of achievement that typically is reached by only the top 2 percent of students under more traditional, group-based approaches to instruction (Anania, 1981; Burke, 1983). Achieving these results, however, required resources far beyond those that are available to most schools. For example, few schools can afford to provide each student with an excellent tutor for a major portion of the school day. Still, knowing that such results are possible led Bloom to search for ways to approximate these results in group-based classrooms. He also challenged other educators to join in the search (Bloom, 1984a, 1984b).

Several of Bloom's students took up the challenge. Using mastery learning as a basis, they explored procedures that teachers might use to further enhance their students' learning. Among these efforts, two of the most promising are a study on improving students' mastery of higher level skills (Mevarech, 1980) and another on enhancing students' prerequisite cognitive skills (Leyton, 1983).

Improving Mastery of Higher Level Skills

Mevarech (1981) was keenly interested in students' acquisition of higher level cognitive skills, particularly the abilities to make applications, analyze problems, and synthesize what is learned. These skills are typically harder to teach and are more difficult to assess than lower level skills that require only recall of information. But, at the same time, higher level skills are more exciting for students to learn and are generally retained for a longer period of time.

The purpose of Mevarech's study was to determine the effects of different teaching methods and the effects of feedback and corrective procedures on students' mastery of higher level cognitive skills. Four groups of students were studied. Two groups were taught mathematics problem solving using direct procedures (algorithms), while the other two groups were taught by discovery techniques that encouraged students to develop their own problem-solving strategies (heuristics). Then mastery learning feedback and corrective procedures were introduced to one algorithm group and one heuristic group. In these mastery learning classes, one-third of the items on all formative assessments were designed to measure higher level cognitive skills. After several units of instruction, students in all four groups were assessed on their mastery of higher level problem-solving skills. The results are shown in Figure 8.4.

When taught by algorithms, only 12 percent of the students attained mastery (80 percent correct) of the higher level skills. These are typical results from classes taught by most conventional instructional techniques. The discovery or heuristic method resulted in 26 percent of the students reaching mastery on higher level skills. Thus the difference in instructional method resulted in an increase of 14 percent. When feedback and correctives were used with the algorithm method, 41 percent of the students mastered higher level skills. When these procedures were used with the heuristic method, 64 percent attained the mastery criterion. Hence the addition of feedback and corrective procedures resulted in an increase of 29 and 38 percent, respectively.

An intriguing aspect of this study is that these effects appear to be additive; that is, both the different instructional methods and the feedback and corrective procedures contribute to more positive learning outcomes. But the addition of feedback and corrective procedures to the more effective teaching method resulted in substantial improvements above and beyond those provided by the difference in teaching method alone.

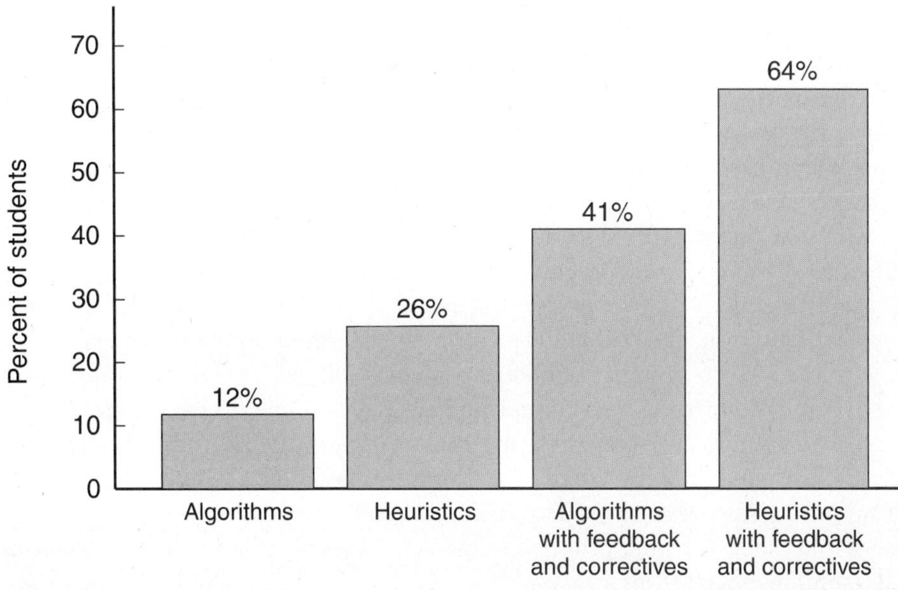

Figure 8.4 The percentage of students in various groups attaining the mastery criterion (80 percent correct) on higher level cognitive items (from Mevarech, 1980)

Changes in teaching methods can be difficult to accomplish, and the results are often short-lived. But adding feedback and corrective procedures is relatively easy, costs little, and, as this study shows, significantly improves students' mastery of higher level skills. And when the feedback and corrective procedures of mastery learning are combined with effective teaching, the improvements in students' learning of higher level cognitive skills can be dramatic.

Enhancing Prerequisite Skills

Mastery learning emphasizes the importance of getting nearly all students to learn the concepts and skills in each learning unit to a high standard. In this way, students are well prepared for future learning tasks. But some students enter mastery learning classes ill-prepared. These are students with deficient "cognitive entry behaviors" (Bloom, 1976). They have not learned the concepts and skills from previous courses well, and they are inadequately prepared for learning in the current course.

Leyton (1983) was interested in procedures that might enhance the entry skills of ill-prepared students. He believed that taking a brief period of time at the beginning of a term or school year to identify and then reteach these necessary skills might greatly enhance students' learning in the course.

To test his idea, Leyton designed a study that also involved four groups of students. All of these students were enrolled in a second-level mathematics or foreign language course. Leyton helped the teachers of these courses prepare assessments that measured students' knowledge of concepts that the teachers considered prerequisites for their courses. Generally, these were concepts the teachers believed should have been mastered by students in the first-level course. The assessments were administered to all four groups of students on the first day of the term. In two groups, Leyton used the assessment results to help students identify and review the concepts they had not learned well. A group review was conducted that covered problems common to many students. This was followed by individualized help on specific difficulties. The assessment and review lasted approximately a week and a half. Then one review group and one nonreview group were taught using mastery learning. The other review and nonreview groups were taught by whatever methods the teachers typically employed. After several units of instruction, all four groups were assessed to determine their learning progress in the course. Figure 8.5 shows the results of this summative assessment.

When conventional teaching methods were used without any review, only 8 percent of the students attained the mastery standard (80 percent correct) on the summative assessment. In classes where the initial prerequisites were reviewed and students were helped to learn these prerequisites well before instruction on the new material began, 28 percent reached mastery. Review sessions thus led to a 20 percent increase.

The introduction of mastery learning resulted in 43 percent of the students attaining the mastery standard. This was an increase of 35 percent over conventional methods. However, when the review sessions were combined with mastery learning, 61 percent of the students attained mastery, an increase of 53 percent. Viewed in another way, the combination of review plus mastery learning resulted in more than seven times the number of students reaching the mastery standard than under conventional methods.

Leyton also found that the effects of review and mastery learning seem to be additive; that is, the review sessions brought about a 20 percent increase in the number of students reaching mastery in both conventional and mastery learning classes. The mastery learning process with or without review resulted in approximately a 35 percent increase. However, when the review and mastery learning were combined, the results were approximately equal to the sum of these effects–nearly a 55 percent increase.

Another interesting aspect of Leyton's study is that the results attained in classes where both the review and mastery learning were used come close to approximating the results attained under the conditions of individual tutoring. In other words, when review and mastery learning are combined in a classroom

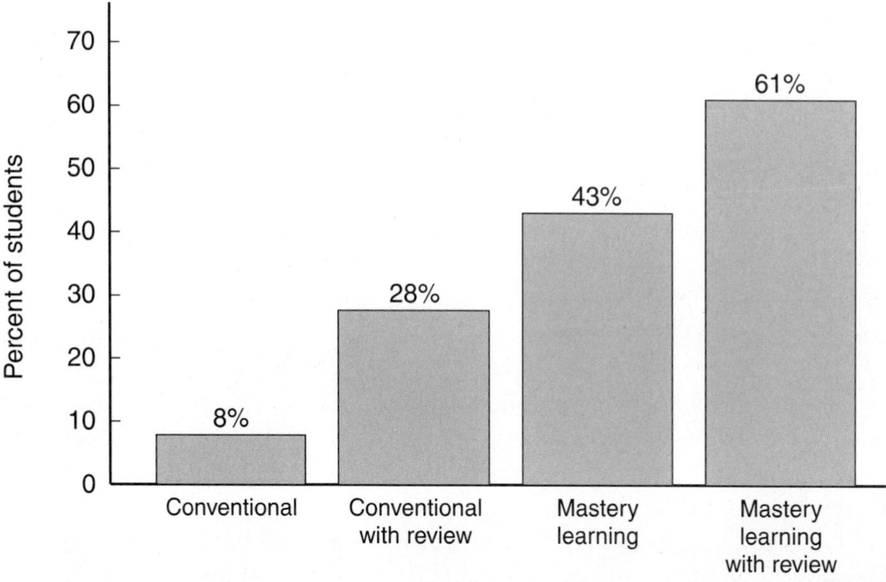

Figure 8.5 The percentage of students in various groups attaining the mastery criterion (80 percent correct) on a summative assessment (from Leyton, 1983)

setting, the average student attains a level of learning that is above the ninetieth percentile for students taught by conventional methods. Thus the introduction of this combination of procedures in the classroom setting results in achievement levels that are close to those attained through individual tutoring, and at far less expense.

Leyton's study was conducted in only a few subject areas and under tightly controlled conditions, so we must be cautious in interpreting the results and in making generalizations. Nevertheless, the findings are extremely promising.

The Future of Mastery Learning in the Schools

Most teachers are skeptical of innovations in education, and with good reason. Their experience indicates that most innovations, although they may be sound in theory, are impractical for use in many classroom settings. Furthermore, few innovations are the panacea they are often described to be.

Even though it has been widely used for many years now, mastery learning is sometimes viewed as just another trend or innovation. But unlike other innovations, mastery learning makes no pretense to being an educational cure-all. There are many classroom problems it will not solve. For instance, mastery learning will not provide a teacher with the necessary management skills to direct the activities of twenty-five or more students. Nor does it offer solutions for dealing with the wide variety of classroom disruptions that impede teachers' instructional efforts. However, it does offer a useful tool that incorporates many of the elements known to be a part of effective teaching. It can help teachers organize their instruction and ensure congruence among learning goals, instructional techniques, and procedures for assessing or evaluating students' learning. It provides a mechanism through which teachers can offer students regular feedback on their learning progress and guidance in correcting learning difficulties. Most important, it is a way for teachers to have more students experience success in their learning and gain the many benefits that come from that success.

Few teachers initially believe that mastery learning will bring about significant improvements in their students' learning. This is especially true of experienced classroom veterans. But typically those who are intrigued enough by the process to try it quickly see a positive change. As students catch on to mastery learning, they become more involved during class sessions. They begin to use the results from their formative assessments and often start helping one another with learning problems. These changes surprise but delight many teachers. And in most cases, changes such as these are all that is needed to convince teachers that the mastery learning process will work for them (Guskey, 1984, 1989b).

Mastery learning stems from an exceptionally optimistic view of the potential of education. The theory of mastery learning stresses that *all* students can learn well when appropriate instructional conditions are provided. This is not to say that all students can or should master subjects like topology or nuclear physics. It does mean, however, that all students can learn to read and comprehend what they have read, can learn to solve problems requiring higher level mathematics skills, and can learn to write in a clear and concise manner. The instructional conditions under which many students now learn are clearly inappropriate for them. Although the mastery learning process may not be a perfect solution to this problem, it is clearly a step in the right direction.

Today, strong support for mastery learning comes from parents, teachers, and school administrators throughout the world. Equally strong support comes from educational researchers whose studies on the elements of effective instruction consistently describe procedures that closely parallel mastery learning (Brophy & Good, 1986; Walberg, 1986; Weinert & Helmke, 1995). Although some researchers have criticized mastery learning (Glickman, 1979; Mueller, 1976), their criticism has consistently involved minor points of specific applications–not the basic mastery learning process. Overall, mastery learning has an unusually broad base of support.

Another promising aspect of mastery learning is that it provides a unique vehicle for cooperation within educational institutions. Planning for the implementation of mastery learning typically involves teachers, school administrators, and sometimes parents working together for the common goal of improved student learning. The process builds on teachers' professional expertise and allows school administrators the opportunity to serve as instructional leaders in their schools. Furthermore, mastery learning provides opportunities for parents and business leaders to become more closely involved with their children's education. An excellent example of this kind of cooperation occurred in the New York City public schools, where the mastery learning program was collaboratively sponsored by the board of education, the United Federation of Teachers, and an independent group of business leaders called the New York City Economic Development Council (Cooke, 1979).

One needs only to talk to teachers or students in mastery learning classes to verify that the future of mastery learning is indeed bright. Few teachers choose to abandon the mastery learning process after they have tried it in their classes for even a short time. In fact, they often begin to consider ways in which they might add to the process to gain still greater success. This has been referred to as the "multiplier effect" of mastery learning (Guskey, Barshis, & Easton, 1982). In several instances, students became so excited about their learning success under mastery learning that they petitioned their school principal to have more teachers use the process (Guskey, 1980a). As word of this kind of enthusiasm about learning spreads, interest in mastery learning will certainly grow. Although educators cannot afford to waste their time and energy experimenting with innovations that have little practical utility, they also cannot afford to neglect a process that offers such positive and meaningful results.

Conclusion

There is little doubt that teaching is one of the most difficult and challenging of all professions. Furthermore, the responsibilities of teaching can sometimes be overwhelming. In the face of these challenges and responsibilities, teachers often lose sight of the tremendous influence they have on their students. Teachers not only affect what and how their students learn, but also shape in large part their students' attitudes toward learning and how they feel about themselves as learners. Mastery learning offers teachers a way to make the best and most positive use of that influence. It gives teachers a powerful tool that increases their effectiveness in helping more of their students learn well and gain the many positive benefits of learning success.

The mastery learning process is certainly not perfect. It may not help all students master everything they are taught. Nevertheless, strong evidence shows that it can sharply reduce the variation among students in terms of their mastery of specified learning goals, as well as greatly increase the efficiency and effectiveness of students' learning skills. Realizing outcomes as positive as these has dramatically altered the perspectives of many theorists about the potential of education.

Mastery learning is based on the philosophical premise that *all students can learn well.* Although lofty and extremely optimistic, this same premise is the basis of the majority of today's educational reform efforts. Many teachers find this premise difficult to accept, especially experienced classroom veterans who know firsthand the challenges and difficulties of teaching. Its significance in directing our efforts, however, cannot be neglected.

The important consequences of accepting the premise that all students can learn well were put into perspective several years ago during a televised interview with educator Mortimer Adler on the public television show "Firing Line." Interviewer William F. Buckley challenged Adler and the educational philosophy he advocated by sternly asking, "Are you sure all children can learn?"

Adler's immediately replied, "No, I am not sure. But I don't believe you are sure that all children cannot. And I prefer to live with my hope, rather than your doubt!" It is precisely that perspective that must guide all of our endeavors in education.

Questions for Discussion

1. What strategies or procedures could be used to make teachers and school administrators more aware of strategies such as mastery learning?
2. What problems might discourage teachers from using mastery learning in their classrooms? How might these problems be averted?
3. What are the major advantages of mastery learning from the perspective of a classroom teacher? a school administrator? a board member? a parent? a student? What problems or difficulties might be seen from each perspective?
4. How might the mastery learning process be further improved? How could evidence be gathered to demonstrate this improvement?

Part II

Examples of Materials for Implementing Mastery Learning

The following chapters contain materials prepared in large part by teachers who use mastery learning in their classes. These teachers have adapted the essential elements of mastery learning to fit the learning needs of their students and the unique conditions of their classrooms. At the same time, they have maintained the integrity of the mastery learning principles. In every case, these educators have been highly successful in helping nearly all of their students learn well and reach a high level of performance.

Each chapter is a sample unit for a particular topic or subject area. As such, each contains a table of specifications, formative assessments, correctives, and enrichment activities. These units vary widely, however, in their scope and level of detail, primarily because of subject area and grade-level differences. But also reflected are differences in the personal preferences and teaching styles of the teachers who prepared the materials. In some cases, the materials have been adapted to provide a comparable format across all units. For the sake of completeness, additions also have been made to several units.

These units are not necessarily exemplary models. Undoubtedly, all could be further refined. Nevertheless, they do provide working examples of the procedures described in the preceding chapters. Hopefully they will add clarity and understanding to those descriptions.

9

Elementary Mathematics and Science

Unit Description and Critique

The following unit was prepared for an elementary mathematics and science class. The unit focuses on various aspects of measurement and is typically taught in the second or third grade. At this level, the unit might require about two weeks of class time, or ten instructional days.

The unit's table of specifications is relatively brief and clearly lists the unit objectives. This is typical of early elementary units, which are generally shorter and cover fewer objectives than do units for more advanced grades. Note, however, that the items on the formative assessment emphasize higher level learning skills. Apparently, the teachers judged these skills to be of greatest importance in the unit. The addition of the scoring table, which lists the specific learning goals of the unit, further clarifies the unit's focus.

Comparing the table of specifications with the formative assessments shows that they are well matched. Formative assessments A and B are also well designed and parallel. The scoring rubrics for the problem-solving items on the formatives helps to clarify their intent. The correctives are brief and might be improved by offering greater detail. The same is true of the enrichment activities, particularly because they are likely to require some degree of supervision from the teacher. Still, it is a thoughtfully planned and well-designed unit.

Sample materials in Chapter 9 were prepared by Mary Kay Hunt, Lakeside Elementary School, Indianapolis, Indiana 46229.

Table of Specifications				
Knowledge of		Translations	Applications	High Level Skills
Terms	Facts			
Measurement Inches Feet Yards Centimeters Decimeters Meters	Customary and metric units used to measure length	Determine the best measurement estimate related to the length of real-life objects (4) (10)	Measure objects to determine length in inches or centimeters (1) (7)	Compare and contrast the customary units of measurement: inches, feet, and yards (21)
Cup Pint Quart Liter	Customary and metric units used to measure volume	Determine the best measurement estimate related to the volume of real-life objects (2) (6) (12) (17)	Measure quantities to determine volume in cups or liters	Compare and contrast the metric units of measurement: centimeters, decimeters, and meters (20)
Pound Kilogram	Customary and metric units used to meaure weight and mass	Determine the best measurement estimate related to the weight of real-life objects (11) (13) (16)	Measure objects to determine weight in pounds or kilograms	Solve length and weight problems that involve demonstrations of math skills and explanations of solutions (18) (19)
Fahrenheit Celsius–Centigrade		Read a thermometer using °F and °C (3) (9) (14) Determine the best measurement estimate related to temperature (15)		Explain solutions to length and weight problems (22) (23)

Measurement

Formative Assessment A

Name ____________________ Date ____________

Directions: For this assessment you will need the following instruments and materials in the classroom—*inch ruler, centimeter ruler, weight scales, the small vase, the brick,* and *the pair of shoes.* Be sure to write your answer on the line under each question.

1. Use your inch ruler. How long is the yarn?

   ____

2. Which object can hold more than one liter?

   a cup a bowl a fish tank

   ____

3. What is the temperature?

   30 20 10 0 °C

   ____

4. Estimate the length of a pencil. If it were a real pencil, would it be about 6 inches, 6 feet, or 6 yards?

   ____

5. Use the scales. How many pounds does the brick weigh?

   ____

6. What is the best estimate of the volume of the vase?

   1 cup 1 pint 1 quart

   ____

7. Use your centimeter ruler. How long is the ribbon?

   ____

8. Use the scales to find out how many kilograms the shoes weigh.

   ____

9. What is the temperature?

   100 90 80 70 60 50 °F

   ____

10. Estimate the length of a real couch. Is it 2 centimeters, 2 decimeters, or 2 meters?

    ____

11. What is the best estimate for the weight of a toy car?

    Less than 1 kilogram
    More than 1 kilogram

    ____

12. What is the best estimate for the volume of a pan?

    3 pints 30 quarts

    ____

Measurement—Formative Assessment A

13. What is the best estimate for the weight of a real dog?

    less than 1 pound
    more than 1 pound

    ____

14. What is the temperature?

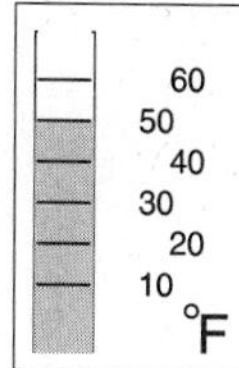

    ____

15. What is the best estimate of the temperature of a cup of soup?

    30° F 100° F

    ____

16. What is the best estimate of the weight of a bag of apples?

    3 pounds 23 pounds

    ____

17. What is the best estimate of the volume of a glass of water?

    Less than 1 liter
    More than 1 liter

    ____

Use addition or subtraction to solve the following problems.

18. Jim sold 9 pounds of red grapes. He sold 5 pounds of green grapes. How many pounds of grapes did he sell in all?

    ____

19. Ann has 17 feet of cloth. She uses 8 feet of the cloth. How much does she have left?

    ____

Use centimeters or meters to complete the following.

20. Tim wants to make a toy boat for his baby brother's wading pool. He wants to be sure he has enough wood for the boat. Would he measure the boat in centimeters or meters?

    ____

Use inches or feet to answer the following.

21. Jill is decorating for a party. She wants to make paper placemats. Would she measure the placemats in inches or feet?

    ____

22. If you were going to have a party for 6 friends, how much paper would you need for placemats? Show how you would solve this problem. Explain your answer.

23. Describe how inches and feet are alike and different. When would you use these measurements?

Scoring Rubrics

Measurement—Formative Assessment A

Item 22

A. If you were going to have a party for 6, how much paper would you need for placemats?

EXEMPLARS:

1 + 1 + 1 + 1 + 1 + 1 = 6 feet	2 + 2 + 2 + 2 + 2 + 2 = 12 feet
6 × 1 = 6 feet	2 × 6 = 12 feet

Give 1 point for either version or a response that justifies the answer through the logic provided.

B. Explain your answer.

EXEMPLARS:

I use 6 feet of paper because I am going to make each placement 1 foot long, so 6 placemats that are 1 foot long means I need 6 feet of paper.

Six placemats that are 2 feet wide in length makes 12 feet of paper.

Score 1 point for either version of the exemplar or for a response that logically justifies the answer given.

Item 23

A. Describe how inches and feet are alike and different. When would you use these measurements?

EXEMPLAR:

They are alike in that they measure lengths of objects or distances. They are different because they are used to measure objects or distances of larger or smaller size. Inches are used for measuring small objects like a pencil. Feet are used in measuring objects that are too big to measure in inches, such as the size of a room.

Score 2 points for the response that justifies the answer with logical responses.

Scoring Table

Measurement: Formative A _____ Formative B _____

Name ____________________

Goals	Items	Criteria Score	No. Correct
A. Measure or estimate length in customary units or metric units.	1 4 7 10	3/4	/4
B. Measure or estimate weight in customary units or metric units.	5 8 11 13 16	4/5	/5
C. Measure or estimate volume in customary units or metric units.	2 6 12 17	3/4	/4
D. Read a thermometer.	3 9 14 15	3/4	/4
E. Solve story problems requiring addition or subtraction.	18 19	1/2	/2
F. Solve story problems using measurement of length.	20 21	1/2	/2
G. Explain and solve story problems using length (rubric score).	22a 22b 23a 23b	3/4	/4
Total Score			**/25**
Percentage			**%**

Correctives

Use peer tutors to give individual students added help as needed with specific skills that were troublesome on the assessment. These activities might include the following.

A. Measure objects within the room in inches or centimeters.

B. Estimate and then measure the length, weight, or volume of objects in the room.

C. Use thermometers to estimate and then measure the temperature in degrees Celsius and Fahrenheit. The thermometer is placed in conditions such as ice water or warm water so that students have opportunities to measure varying temperatures.

D. Use the computer measurement software program to reinforce the above activities now presented on a one-to-one basis with a student who is strong in the area of measurement. This allows peer tutors to give "tidbits" that may help the student who is having difficulty grasp the concept better and master the skills.

After the peer tutors have assisted the students with a hands-on approach, allow the student to complete another worksheet with another peer tutor nearby. This will allow the student engaged in correctives to build confidence and reassurance before taking Formative Assessment B.

Enrichment Activities

The enrichment activities allow students who have mastered the skills of measurement to expand their knowledge and explore other areas. Students may pick one of the activities, or the teacher may choose to set up the activities in learning stations and have students rotate through the stations. Students who have mastered the unit also may wish to work with classmates as peer tutors.

A. Math trivia: game board activity

B. Making paper placemats for the "Friday Treat Day Activities." Students will use butcher paper to design and create placemats for "group" mates to be used at the treat day parties.

C. Measuring and cutting paper, string, and so on. Students will prepare materials to be used in creating their own "useful" creation projects. They may create whatever they want from a collection of materials in the "odds and ends" container. The requirements are that the student must:

   1. have a use for the creation;
   2. explain to the class why or how it works;
   3. explain why it is important; and
   4. explain how the object was created and how the measurements are important to the design.

These activities may require more time to complete than the time allowed at the end of the unit. For this reason, they may be carried over to completion at the end of the next unit.

Measurement

Formative Assessment B

Name ______________________ Date ______________________

Directions: For this assessment, you will need the following instruments and materials in the classroom—*inch ruler, centimeter ruler, weight scales, modeling clay, a bag of candy,* and *a toy boat.* Be sure to write your answer on the line under each question.

1. Use your inch ruler. How long is the yarn?

____

2. Which object can hold more than one liter?

   a juice box   a bath tub   a bowl

____

3. What is the temperature?

70
60
50
40
30
20
°F

____

4. Estimate the length of a crayon. If it were a real crayon, would it be about 3 yards, 3 feet, or 3 inches in length?

____

5. Use the scales: How many pounds does the package of modeling clay weigh?

____

6. What is the best estimate of the volume of a mug?

   1 quart   1 pint   1 cup

____

7. Use your centimeter ruler. How long is the ribbon?

____

8. Use the scales to find out how many kilograms the bag of candy weighs.

____

9. What is the temperature?

40
30
20
10
0
°C

____

10. Estimate the length of the science table. Is it 3 meters, 3 decimeters, or 3 centimeters?

____

11. What is the best estimate for the weight of a basketball?

   Less than 1 kilogram
   More than 1 kilogram

____

12. What is the best estimate for the volume of a fish tank?

   3 pints   30 quarts

____

Measurement—Formative Assessment B

13. What is the best estimate for the weight of the toy boat?

    less than 1 pound
    more than 1 pound

    ____

14. What is the temperature?

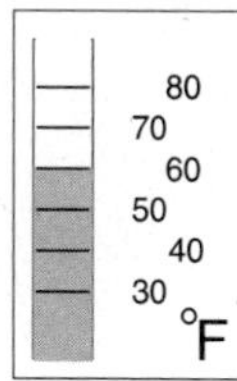

    ____

15. What is the best estimate of the temperature of a glass of ice water?

    40° F   80° F

    ____

16. What is the best estimate of the weight of our science book?

    2 pounds   20 pounds

    ____

17. What is the best estimate of the volume of a trash can?

    Less than 1 liter
    More than 1 liter

    ____

Use addition or subtraction to solve the following.

18. Sean has 8 blue cars. He bought 7 red cars. How many cars does he have in all?

    ____

19. Gloria had 14 crayons. She lost 6 crayons. How many crayons does she have left?

    ____

Use centimeters or meters to complete the following.

20. Karen wants to make a pair of pants. She wants to be sure she has enough material. Should she measure the material for the pants in centimeters or meters?

    ____

Use inches or feet to answer the following.

21. Pam is going to paint a picture. The paper for the picture comes in rolls. Would she measure the paper in inches or feet?

    ____

22. Pam is going to give her pictures to 5 friends. How much paper will she need for the pictures? Show how you would solve this problem. Explain your answer.

23. Describe how centimeters and decimeters are alike and different. When would you use these forms of measurement?

Scoring Rubrics

Measurement—Formative Assessment B

Item 22

A. How much paper will Pam need for the pictures?

EXEMPLARS:

5 + 5 + 5 + 5 + 5 = 25 inches	1 + 1 + 1 + 1 + 1 = 5 feet
5 × 5 = 25 inches	5 × 1 = 5 feet

Give 1 point for either version or a response that justifies the answer through the logic provided.

B. Explain your answer.

EXEMPLARS:

If Pam makes each picture 5 inches long and she has 5 friends, she will need 5 × 5 = 25 inches of paper altogether.

If Pam makes each picture 1 foot in length, and she has 5 friends, 5 × 1 = 5 feet of paper is what she needs altogether.

Score 1 point for either version of the exemplar or for a response that logically justifies the answer given.

Item 23

A. Describe how centimeters and decimeters are alike and different. When would you use these measurements?

EXEMPLAR:

They are alike in that they measure lengths of objects or distances. They are different because they are used to measure objects or distances of larger or smaller size. Centimeters are used for measuring small objects such as a crayon or a book. Decimeters are used in measuring objects that are too big to measure in centimeters, such as a door or a rug.

Score 2 points for the response that justifies the answer with logical responses.

10

Elementary Language Arts

Unit Description and Critique

This unit was developed for use in elementary language arts classes. Specifically, it is designed to teach second-grade students the concept of story "setting," and it is part of a series of literature units that focus on story plot components. Generally, this unit is taught early in the school year and is a basis for future units that focus on other story characteristics. It is also a relatively short unit, requiring only two or three instructional days. This length is not unusual at this level, however, especially considering that this concept is the foundation for other, more advanced literary concepts.

The unit's table of specifications is quite brief but clearly lists the unit objectives. This, too, is typical of early elementary units. The formative assessments focus on the application level and include a well-designed scoring rubric. The corrective and enrichment activities are also carefully designed, and the practice exercise to be used to prepare students for the second formative assessment is an excellent addition to the unit.

Although to some teachers this unit may appear to be too short or too narrow in scope, it seems well suited for this level and the instructional framework planned. As an essential first step in guiding students' understanding of story plot components, it is particularly well designed.

Sample materials in Chapter 10 were prepared by Donna M. Bowar, Garretson, South Dakota 57030.

Table of Specifications			
Knowledge of		Translations	Applications
Terms	Facts		
Component	Parts of a story are referred to as story components	Read a story and determine the setting	Write a story that includes a description of the setting
Setting When	Setting tells when and where the story takes place		
Where	Setting is usually described at the beginning of the story		

Language Arts—Grade Two

Formative Assessment A—Setting

Name ______________________ Date ________________________

Directions: Write a paragraph that describes the setting of a story. Use capital letters and punctuation (periods and question marks). If you are unsure of the correct spelling of words, spell them the way they sound.

____

____

____

____

____

____

____

____

____

Scoring Rubric

Setting Formative Assessments

Score 3: High Pass

Student

- uses both components of a setting in writing a story part–when and where a story takes place.
- writes several sentences using capital letters and end punctuation.
- uses spelling (both real and inventive) that does not inhibit the reader's understanding.

Score 2: Pass (Correctives Optional)

Student

- uses one component of a setting in writing a story part–when or where a story takes place.
- expresses complete thoughts, although sentences may be fragments or run-on.
- uses spelling (both real and inventive) that, for the most part, does not inhibit the reader's understanding.

Score 1: Needs Correctives

Student

- does not use either component of a setting when writing a story part.
- expresses self in ways that inhibit the reader's understanding.
- does not demonstrate understanding of sound or symbol relationships.

Score 0: No Response (Needs Correctives with Special Assistance)

Correctives

Students engaged in correctives typically work in teams. The following activities are designed to help them clarify their understanding of the concept of "setting" and strengthen their own writing skills.

A. Read the book, *Peace at Last* by Jill Murphy, with your partner. Draw a picture and write two sentences about the setting of the story.

B. Choose one of the setting cards from the setting surprise box. Draw a picture of it.

Students may take Formative Assessment B as soon as they complete their corrective work.

Enrichment Activities

Students who have mastered the concept of "setting" may pick one of these activities, or they may engage in several if time permits.

A. Work on the correctives with one of your classmates who does not understand the concept of "setting."

B. Read *The Little Island* by Golden McDonald and Leonard Weisgard. Draw four pictures of the little island–one in spring, one in summer, one in autumn, and one in winter.

C. Make a Setting Web.

Language Arts—Grade Two

Corrective A—*Setting*

Name ____________________ Date _______________

Directions: 1. Read the book, *Peace at Last,* by Jill Murphy.

2. Draw a picture of the setting in the story.

3. Write two sentences about the setting in the story.

1. ____

____

2. ____

____

Language Arts—Grade Two

Corrective B—*Setting*

Name ____________________ Date ______________

Directions: 1. Choose a card from the Setting Surprise Box.
2. Draw a picture of it.
3. Tell *when* and *where* your setting takes place.

When? ____

____

Where? ____

____

Language Arts—Grade Two

Enrichment B—*Setting*

Name ____________________ Date ______________

Directions: 1. Read *The Little Island* by Golden McDonald and Leonard Weisgard.

2. Draw four pictures of the little island—one in spring, one in summer, one in autumn, and one in winter.

Language Arts—Grade Two

Enrichment C—*Setting*

A Setting Web

Name ______________________ Date ______________________

Directions: Circle one time, one season, and write the year you want in the box. Then answer the questions in the large boxes below.

A long time ago	Today	Many years from now

Season

Spring	Summer	Autumn	Winter

Year

What does this place look like?	What is the name of this place?	Who goes to this place?

Best part about this place?	Worst part about this place?

Language Arts—Grade Two

Practice Exercise on *Setting*

Name ______________________ Date ________________________

Directions: 1. Read each question carefully.
2. Circle the letter of the correct answer.

1. The setting of a story tells
   a. how many people are in the story.
   b. where the story takes place.
   c. what will happen next.
2. The setting of a story also
   a. comes at the end of the story
   b. tells what the character's problem is.
   c. tells when the story takes place.
3. Read this story part:

   I like to go for walks in the woods and look for animals. This morning I saw two rabbits, a robin, and a turtle.

What is the setting in this story part? Remember a setting usually tells us two things.

1. ____

2. ____

Language Arts—Grade Two

Formative Assessment B—*Setting*

Name ______________________ Date ______________________

Directions: Write a paragraph that describes the setting of a story. Use capital letters and punctuation (periods and question marks). If you are unsure of the correct spelling of words, spell them the way they sound.

____

____

____

____

____

____

____

____

____

11

Goal Setting

Unit Description and Critique

This unit is entitled "Goal Setting" and is designed for use at the upper elementary or middle school level. It would be most beneficial to teach at the beginning of the school year so that students may see improvement in their goal areas, but it may be used at any time. The goal sheets, scoring rubric, and other assessment sheets all were designed by teachers and may be adapted to fit individual needs.

As the table of specifications shows, this unit emphasizes the higher level skill areas of application and synthesis. It is used by teachers to help students develop their own school-related goal plans and then work to achieve their goals. The assessment is similar to what would be used in a writing class; that is, students' goal plans are assessed based on the specific criteria indicated in the scoring rubric. Their revised plans then constitute the second formative assessment. The assessment process also involves students' writing group goals and critiquing goals under the teacher's supervision.

Most teachers use this unit initially to help students develop short-term goals that can be achieved in one to two weeks. In this way, students can assess their plan and experience success. Self-assessment questions are provided as closure to the unit.

The corrective activity consists of student conferences that can be conducted by the teacher or by another student who achieved mastery. The intent of the corrective activity is to guide the students through self-reflection and improve their original goal-setting plan. Enrichment activities revolve around goal setting and provide a variety of options.

Although this unit is not specific to any particular subject area, teachers at almost any level of education will probably find it useful. It is also an excellent example of how broadly the principles of mastery learning can be applied.

Sample materials in Chapter 11 were prepared by Erica Chamberlain and Betty Arnold, Charlevoix-Emmet Intermediate School District, Charlevoix, Michigan 49720.

Table of Specifications						
Knowledge of				Translations	Applications	Analyses and Syntheses
Terms	Facts	Rules and Principles	Processes and Procedures			
Goal: target; something you want to achieve or change; an aim **Time line:** dates for accomplish-ments **Resources:** people, technology, or materials that help you achieve your goal **Adjust:** make changes in order to continue progress on your goal **Obstacles:** people or things that may hinder progress toward your goal **Rubric:** scoring checklist	Goals must be specific, personal, sequential, measurable, and realistic. Long-range goals take longer than a year to achieve. Short-range goals take a year or less to achieve. Goal formation requires the identification of personal strengths and weaknesses.	Goals must be ■ written, ■ stated positively, and ■ stated in clear and under-standable language **Goal rubric** is a set of guidelines for goal writing shared with students.	Process of identifying personal strengths and weaknesses Prioritizing goals in order of importance and immediacy **Goal Process:** 1. Set goal. 2. Devise plan. 3. Measure progress. 4. Set time lines. 5. Rewards and benefits 6. Obstacles 7. Evaluate and monitor.	Identify well-written vs. poorly written goals. Develop group goal plans and implement plans in cooperative groups. Critique group plan using the goal rubric.	Explain the benefits of setting goals. Write an individual goal plan and implement the plan.	Analyze own and others' goal plans and critiques. Revise goal plans using the goal rubric. Complete the self-assessment.

Goal Plan

Name ______________________________ Date ________________________

Goal or Aim

Completion Date ____

Results, or How I Will I Know I've Reached My Goal?

Resources:

People: ____

Materials: ____

Obstacles:

1.
2.
3.

Endurance Strategies:

1.
2.
3.

Steps to Complete the Goal

	Date
Step 4	_______
Step 3	_______
Step 2	_______
Step 1	_______

Starting Date: __________________________

Goal Rubric

This rubric should be given to students before their individual goal plans are developed. Teachers may want to use this rubric as part of a class session to rate sample goals and discuss the criteria thoroughly. In this way, students will have a clearer understanding of the teacher's expectations.

The rubric also may be used as a guideline or checklist for students when they are in the process of developing their goal plan. Points are assigned according to each student's performance in the three areas listed in the rubric. Students may use self-assessment or peer assessment in evaluating their plans. Mastery is set at 80 percent (or a score of 7 out of 9 possible points).

Goal Rubric			
Rating	**Goal Statement**	**Goal Plan**	**Evaluation**
Excellent Points: 3	■ Reflects area needed ■ Clearly understandable aim ■ Achievable and realistic	■ States steps and resources needed ■ States time line ■ Includes thorough evaluation	■ Completed all steps of the goal plan ■ Achieves goal
Acceptable Points: 2	■ Area not a priority ■ Not stated in specific terms ■ Long-term goals not broken down	■ Some steps left out or resources limited ■ Time line unrealistic ■ Evaluation unclear	■ Followed most steps in the goal plan ■ Showed improvement
Marginal Points: 1	■ Reflects area where goal is not needed ■ Goal unclear or underestimated ■ Goal overestimated	■ Inappropriate sequence of steps ■ Time line incomplete ■ Minimal or incomplete evaluation	■ Followed few goal steps ■ Little improvement
Unacceptable Points: 0	■ No goal	■ No steps ■ No time line ■ No evaluation	■ Did not follow steps ■ Showed no improvement
Self			
Peer			
Teacher			
TOTAL			

Correctives

Using the goal rubric, the teacher or a fellow student would interview the student using the following questions. Not every question needs to be addressed.

Question	**Response** Yes	Not Yet
1. Can you explain your goal?		
2. Do you believe your goal is realistic and a high priority for you at this time?		
3. Can you tell me about your plan?		
4. How do you think you can improve your plan?		
5. Are there any obstacles that occurred that you didn't anticipate?		
6. Can you think of any possible solutions?		
7. Can you develop an alternative plan?		
8. Can you relate this goal to others you've had?		

Comments

____

____

____

____

Enrichment Activities

The enrichment activities are for students whose goal plans met the criteria listed in the goal rubric. Students may pick one of these activities or engage in several if time permits.

A. Students may confer with another student who has not achieved mastery.

B. Students may elect to talk to a person they admire and interview him or her about their goals.

C. Students may read about a person they admire and summarize his or her major goals.

D. Students may write another goal and analyze it.

E. Students may create an acrostic or poster, write a poem, or devise a rap about goal setting.

Goal Questions for Self-Assessment

These questions are designed to allow students to reflect on the goal-setting process after achieving mastery in the unit. Their purpose is to help students process what they have done and to internalize the metacognitive strategies involved. Teachers also can use these questions to determine how well students are able to explain and assess their thinking through the goal-setting process.

1. What were you supposed to do in the goal-setting process?
2. What was your favorite part of goal setting?
3. What was your least favorite part of goal setting?
4. If you wrote another goal, is there anything you would do differently?
5. Given the rubric, how would you score yourself?
6. Is there a new goal you would like to achieve?

12

Middle School Algebra

Unit Description and Critique

This unit covers signed numbers for a first-level algebra class. It is one of the first units taught in the semester and usually requires about five to seven class days to complete.

The table of specifications is divided by horizontal lines. These indicate the topics and objectives that are covered in each daily lesson. The numerals on the table correspond to items on the formative assessment. These indicate that the teacher is most interested in students' ability to make translations and applications, because the majority of the items on the assessments involve these skills.

Formative Assessment A is well organized. Items on the assessment have been arranged considering both cognitive level and item type. The criteria by which the items in the latter part of the assessment are to be scored, however, remain somewhat unclear. For example, will partial credit be given?

The corrective exercises are specific for each item and appear right on the assessment. These include a class date when the objective measured by the item was explained, a reference to pages in the textbook where the objective is discussed, and additional problems that measure the same objective. Students can therefore begin working on their correctives immediately after the assessment is checked. Corrective exercises not completed in class are then assigned for homework. The double answer sheet offers both students and teacher a record of the assessment results.

Sample materials in Chapter 12 were prepared by Janet Slavin, New York City Public Schools, Brooklyn, New York 11201.

The enrichment activities provide students with several possible alternatives. While all are related to the subject, they are not necessarily tied to the content of this unit, which is fine. In addition, all of these enrichment activities would seem to be rewarding and involve higher level cognitive skills.

Formative assessment B is closely parallel to assessment A, although the two assessments are not matched item for item. Apparently, the item arrangement was changed on assessment B to avoid the possibility of students memorizing answers to items by their location on the assessment. Although this does not change the degree to which the assessments are parallel, it does make matching formative assessment B to the unit's table of specifications more difficult. Formative assessment B also appears shorter than assessment A, but this is simply because the correctives are not included on this assessment. Both assessments cover the same identical objectives.

The unit could be improved by providing greater specification on scoring for the items in the latter part of the formative assessments. Still, it is an excellent example for middle school algebra classes.

Table of Specifications
Algebra I—Unit: Signed Numbers

Knowledge of			Translations	Applications
Terms	**Facts**	**Rules and Principles**		
Real number line	Zero is included in the set of signed numbers, although it is written without a sign.	"+" and "–" are both signs of operation and also direction.	(11b) Draw a real number line and locate given points.	Solve verbal problems using the number line.
Signed numbers	All signed numbers are ordered on the real number line.	(11b) Any number is $>$ numbers to its left $<$ numbers to its right on the number line.	(6) (12) Represent given situations by signed numbers	(13) Describe opposites of given situations.
Integers: positive negative	(5) $\lvert x \rvert$ represents the absolute value of x.		(3) Given a number, state its opposite.	
Opposites Absolute value		Absolute values of any pair of opposite numbers are the same.	(2) Given a number, state its absolute value. (14b) Given the absolute value of a number, find another number with the same absolute value.	

Table of Specifications
Algebra I—Unit: Signed Numbers, continued

Knowledge of			Translations	Applications
Terms	**Facts**	**Rules and Principles**		
			Find sums using the number line.	Solve verbal problems by adding signed numbers on the number line.
(4) Additive identity Additive inverse	For every signed number a: $a + 0 = a$ $a + (-a) = 0$	Rules for adding two or more signed numbers	(1) Given a number, state its additive inverse. (17a) Add two signed numbers using the rules. (17b) Add three or more signed numbers using the rules.	(16) Solve verbal problems involving the addition of two or more signed numbers.

Table of Specifications Algebra I—Unit: Signed Numbers, continued				
Knowledge of			Translations	Applications
Terms	Facts	Rules and Principles		
(10) Multiplicative identity Multiplicative inverse (reciprocal)	(9) For every signed number *a*: $a \times 0 = 0$ $0 \times a = 0$ For every signed number *a*: $a \times 1 = a$ $a \times \frac{1}{a} = 1$	Rules for multiplying two or more signed numbers.	(8) Given a number, state its multiplicative inverse. (18a) Find the product of two or more signed numbers. (18b) Find the value of powers.	
		Rules for subtracting signed numbers.	(19) Subtract given signed numbers.	(15) Solve verbal problems involving subtraction of signed numbers.
	Zero divided by any nonzero number is zero. (7) Division by zero is not defined.	Rules for dividing signed numbers. (14a) For every signed number *a*: $\frac{0}{a} = 0$ $\frac{a}{0}$ = Not defined	(20) Divide given signed numbers.	

Algebra I: Signed Numbers

Formative Assessment A with Correctives

Name ______________________ Date ______________

This formative assessment is intended to give you feedback on how successfully you have mastered the important concepts in this unit. After each item in the assessment are exercises, listed in parentheses. The first number listed is the date the concept was discussed in class so you can refer to your class notes. Next are listed several problems from the textbook that you should complete.

Please be sure in answering the questions that your record each answer TWICE, on BOTH halves of the answer sheet. When you complete the assessment, tear the answer sheet in half. One half is turned in; the other half is your record of answers.

I. Directions: Match each item in column A with the appropriate item from column B. Place the letter of the item from column B in the space provided on the answer sheet. The items in column B may be used more than once. (20 points)

COLUMN A

1. Additive inverse of +8
   (9/15. Read p. 37. Do problems 1–5.)
2. Absolute value of –7
   (9/13. Read p. 32. Do problems 7–10.)
3. Opposite of +7/8
   (9/13. Read p. 32. Do problems 3–6.)
4. Additive identity
   (9/15. Read p. 37. Do problems 1–5.)
5. [+7]
   (9/13. Read p. 32. Do problems 7–10.)
6. Withdrawal of 8 dollars from the bank
   (9/14. Read p. 35. Do problems 16–20.)
7. (+7) ÷ 0
   (9/21. Read p. 51. Do problems 1–5.)
8. Multiplicative inverse of +7/8
   (9/17. Read p. 44. Do problems 6–10.)
9. Product of +8 and 0
   (9/16. Read p. 40. Do problems 11–16.)
10. Multiplicative identity
    (9/17. Read p. 44. Do problems 1–3)

COLUMN B

a. Not defined
b. 0
c. $-\frac{7}{8}$
d. $+\frac{7}{8}$
e. 1
f. $-\frac{8}{7}$
g. $+\frac{8}{7}$
h. –7
i. +7
j. –8
k. +8

II. Directions: Answer each of the following questions in the space provided on the answer sheet. (80 points)

11a. Draw a real number line, labeling the integers from –10 through +10.
(9/13. Read p. 32. Do problems 1–2.)

b. Which is the smallest integer among the following?

–6, +5, –2, +1, $+\frac{1}{2}$

(9/13. Read p. 32. Do problems 3–6.)

12. Represent the following as a signed number:

a. A deposit of 400 dollars in the bank
(9/14. Read p. 35. Do problems 16–24.)

b. 100 feet below sea level
(9/14. Read p. 35. Do problems 16–24.)

13. Describe in words the OPPOSITE of:

a. A rise in price of 10 dollars
(9/14. Read p. 35. Do problems 10–15.)

b. 30 degrees south of the equator
(9/14. Read p. 35. Do problems 10–15.)

14a. What is the numerical value of 0 ÷ (–4)?
(9/21. Read p. 51. Do problems 1–5.)

b. Name two numbers whose absolute value is 5.
(9/21. Read p. 51. Do problems 1–4.)

15. Represent a change in temperature from 12 degrees above zero to 13 degrees below zero as a signed number.
(9/20. Read p. 47. Do problems 15–21.)

16. In a football game, a team gains 8 yards on the first play, loses 3 yards on the second play, and gains 7 yards on the third play. What is the net result of the three plays?
(9/20. Read p. 47. Do problems 26, 28, and 29.)

17. Add:
    a. $(-12) + (-6) = ?$
    b. $(-11) + (+15) + (-6) + (+2) = ?$
    (9/15. Do problems 11–15 on p. 37.)

18. Multiply:
    a. $(-8)\ (-6)\ (+3) = ?$
    b. $(-2)^3 = ?$
    (9/17. Do problems 11–15 on p. 44.)

19. Subtract:
    a. $(+26) - (-18) = ?$
    b. $\begin{array}{r} -2 \\ \underline{-21} \end{array}$
    (9/20. Do problems 16–19 on p. 47.)

20. Divide:
    a. $(-45) \div (-5) = ?$
    b. $\frac{-144}{-12}$
    (9/21. Do problems 11–15 on p. 51.)

Algebra I

Formative Assessment Answer Sheet

Student's Answer Sheet

Name ____________________

Date ____________________

I. 1. ________ 6. ________

2. ________ 7. ________

3. ________ 8. ________

4. ________ 9. ________

5. ________ 10. ________

II. 11a.

b. ________

12a. ________ b. ________

13a. ____________________

b. ____________________

14a. ________ b. ________

15. ____________________

16. ____________________

17a. ________ b. ________

18a. ________ b. ________

19a. ________ b. ________

20a. ________ b. ________

Teacher's Answer Sheet

Name ____________________

Date ____________________

I. 1. ________ 6. ________

2. ________ 7. ________

3. ________ 8. ________

4. ________ 9. ________

5. ________ 10. ________

II. 11a.

b. ________

12a. ________ b. ________

13a. ____________________

b. ____________________

14a. ________ b. ________

15. ____________________

16. ____________________

17a. ________ b. ________

18a. ________ b. ________

19a. ________ b. ________

20a. ________ b. ________

Enrichment Activities

The following is a list of enrichment activities for those of you who attained mastery on formative assessment A. You may choose any one of these activities, or you may develop an enrichment activity of your own. Those developed on your own must be approved by the teacher before you begin.

1. Computer number games 127, 131, 134, and 135.
2. Create your own number games on the computer.
3. Serve as a peer tutor for students working on corrective assignments.
4. Plan for an algebra competition by developing questions that could be asked of opposing teams.
5. Create your own enrichment activities about some aspect of signed numbers of algebra in general.

Algebra I: Signed Numbers

Formative Assessment B

Name ______________________________ Date ____________________

This formative assessment is intended to give you feedback on how successfully you have mastered the important concepts in this unit. Please be sure in answering the questions that your record each answer TWICE, on BOTH halves of the answer sheet. When you complete the assessment, tear the answer sheet in half. One half is turned in; the other half is your record of answers.

I. Directions: Match each item in column A with the appropriate item from column B. Place the letter of the item from column B in the space provided on the answer sheet. The items in column B may be used more than once. (20 points)

COLUMN A	**COLUMN B**
1. Opposite of –4/5	a. Not defined
2. Additive identity	b. 0
3. Product of –4 and 0	c. $-\frac{4}{5}$
4. Absolute value of +5	d. $+\frac{4}{5}$
5. A deposit of 5 dollars in the bank	e. 1
6. Additive inverse of –4	f. $-\frac{5}{4}$
7. Multiplicative identity	g. $+\frac{5}{4}$
8. [–5]	h. –4
9. Multiplicative inverse of –4/5	i. +4
10. (–5) ÷ 0	j. –5
	k. +5

II. Directions: Answer each of the following questions in the space provided on the answer sheet. (80 points)

11a. Draw a real number line, labeling the integers from –12 through +12.

b. Which is the smallest integer among the following?

+10, $+\frac{1}{2}$, –1, –5, –8

12. Represent the following as a signed number:
    a. 3,000 feet above sea level
    b. 45 degrees north of the equator
13. Describe in words the OPPOSITE of:
    a. 50 miles east
    b. A temperature of 48 degrees above zero

14a. What is the numerical value of 0 ÷ (+5)?
  b. Name two numbers whose absolute value is 8.

15. A person wants to buy a car costing $6,500 but has saved only $4,000. Represent this person's financial position as a signed number.

16. One evening the temperature is recorded as 13 degrees above zero. Two hours later it has dropped by 8 degrees. Three hours later it has dropped another 9 degrees. What is the temperature at this last time?

17. Add:
    a. (–15) + (–17) = ?
    b. (+23) + (–18) + (+12) + (–25) = ?

18. Multiply:
    a. (–7)(–4)(–3) = ?
    b. $(-3)^2 = ?$

19. Subtract:
    a. (–17) – (–14) = ?
    b. $\begin{array}{r} -34 \\ \underline{-17} \end{array}$

20. Divide:
    a. (–72) ÷ (–9) = ?
    b. $\begin{array}{r} -108 \\ \underline{+12} \end{array}$

13

High School Language Arts

Unit Description and Critique

The following unit was prepared for a high school level world literature class. It is designed to enhance students' ability to define tragedy, as well as broaden their backgrounds in Shakespearean literature. The entire unit requires about four to five weeks of class time, because it involves reading and analyzing the play *Macbeth.* As such, it is quite a bit longer than the typical mastery learning unit. Most teachers would probably break this unit into two shorter units, perhaps administering a summative assessment at the end of the five-week period.

This unit is typically introduced in the latter part of the fall semester after several shorter units that focus on time periods leading up to the Shakespearean. The table of specifications for the unit is quite extensive and includes terminology specific to *Macbeth,* as well as that generally associated with the concept of tragedy.

From the table of specifications and the formative assessments, we can see that the introduction of terminology is important at the beginning of the unit. As the unit progresses, however, reading of the play takes on greater significance. Throughout the unit, students are asked to interpret the universal ideas inherent in all tragedy within the context of the play. As the unit progresses, students also

---

Sample materials in Chapter 13 were prepared by Glen David Young, Littlefield Public Schools, Alanson, Michigan 49706.

are asked to incorporate their knowledge of current events and to determine how news stories fit the characteristics of tragedy.

The correctives in the unit take several forms. Most students are required to research the background for answers to questions missed, to more fully incorporate current events as an explanation of tragedy, or to go back through the play looking for details to fill in gaps in their understanding. These activities can be completed individually or in teams. Enrichment activities also take several forms. Undoubtedly, the most popular is an activity in which students are asked to transform the Shakespearean drama into a modern format, adapting both the language and cultural nuances. In addition, students are encouraged to delve further into both Shakespeare and the historical character of Macbeth.

This unit could be strengthened by more closely illustrating the connections between the learning goals outlined in the table of specifications and the items included in the formative assessments, as well as providing more explicit directions for the enrichment activities. However, the unit is a good example for high school language arts.

Table of Specifications						
Knowledge of				**Translations**	**Applications**	**Analyses and Syntheses**
Terms	**Facts**	**Rules and Principles**	**Processes and Procedures**			
Tragedy Tragic hero Tragic flaw Catharsis Deceit Nepotism Prophecy Blank verse Imagery Soliloquy Aside Stage conventions Dramatic Irony Inquiry Legend Foil Elizabethan	Play based on Holinshed's *Chronicles.* Aristotle first defined tragedy. Tragedy contains three universal themes: ■ isolation, ■ overwhelming passion, and ■ dissolution of natural order and its reestablishment.	Blank verse is unrhymed iambic pentameter. Hero must suffer punishment that is considered severe relative to his or her flaw. Tragic hero must be generally considered a decent, well-known, and well-liked individual who succumbs to a tragic flaw. Tragic flaw must be a character flaw, such as greed, envy, or avarice.	The hero must first be portrayed in a positive light. Audience must experience catharsis, or emotional release, as a result of the hero's tribulations and eventual downfall.	Describe the difference between a classic tragedy and a tragic event. Translate into modern language and discuss the meaning of specific critical passages from *Macbeth.* Describe how current events fit the outline of a tragedy.	Explain how current tragedies may become legends over time. Explain more recent examples of nepotism. Examine stage conventions in other dramatic works. Examine the use of dramatic irony in other dramatic works.	Compare and contrast *Macbeth* with other Shakespearean tragedies. Compare and contrast Shakespeare's tragedy to that of Sophocles.

Tragedy—Macbeth

Formative Assessment A

Name ______________________________ Date ____________________

This assessment is designed to let you know how well you have learned the concepts we have covered in this unit. Read carefully the directions to each section before answering. Make sure you answer every question.

Part I: True or False. Circle the T for each answer that is true and the F for those that are false. Each correct answer counts for 1 point.

T F 1. Macbeth is both the Thane of Cawdor and the Thane of Glamis at the opening of Act One.

T F 2. Isolation is an example of a theme common in all tragedy.

T F 3. A tragic hero must possess superhuman powers.

T F 4. Catharsis means the audience experiences what the character in the play experiences, and that the audience feels an emotional release.

T F 5. A soliloquy takes place with only one actor on stage.

Part II: Short Answer. Answers to these questions will be judged complete if they contain the necessary information in the context of at least one or two complete sentences. A complete answer is worth 2 points.

1. What are the elements necessary to make someone a tragic hero or heroine?
2. What two dramatic conventions are designed to give the audience insights into what specific characters are thinking or feeling?
3. What prophecies do the three witches have for Macbeth's friend Banquo?
4. Explain what blank verse is and how it is important in the play.
5. What two heirs of Duncan stand between Macbeth and the throne?

Page 2

Part III: Interpreting the Language. In your own words, rewrite the following passage from Act One of the play *Macbeth.* A translation will be judged complete if you have all the key points, correctly identify the characters mentioned, and come within a reasonable approximation of the events being explained. A complete answer will count for 5 points.

Soldier: "Doubtfully it stood;
As two spent swimmers that do cling together
And choke their art. The merciless Macdonwald—
Worthy to be a rebel—for to that
The multiplying villainies of nature
Do swarm upon him,—from the Western isles
Of kerns and gallowglasses is supplied;
And fortune, on this damned quarrel smiling,
Show'd like a rebel's whore. But all's too weak:
For brave Macbeth,—well he deserves that
Disdaining fortune, with his brandish'd steel,
Like valour's minion,
Carv'd out his passage till he fac'd the slave. . . ."

Correctives

To correct errors made on the first part of the formative assessment, students are directed to review the questions they missed and explain where they were able to find the information to correct their answers. Resources of information include the text, class notes, any videos watched, or other sources the teacher has cited or may have used during classroom discussions. For current event information, newspapers and magazines are used. Although students may work together on their correctives, every student who did not reach the mastery standard of 85 percent correct is required to hand in an individualized corrective assignment.

Those students who had difficulties with the second part of the formative assessment complete the following exercise that pertains to blank verse and the translation of Shakespearean language.

Corrective Assignment

For each of the following four examples determine first whether it is an example of blank verse. Indicate "Blank Verse" or "Not Blank Verse" in the space below the last line of each selection. Then rewrite each passage in your own words. When you have completed this exercise, you will be ready to attain mastery on Formative Assessment B.

1. That God forbid, that made me first your slave,
   I should in thought control your times of pleasure;
   Or at your hand the account of hours to crave,
   Being your vassal bound to stay your leisure.

2. When I have seen by Time's fell hand defac'd
   The rich-proud cost of outworn buried age;
   When sometime lofty towers I see downras'd,
   And brass eternal, slave mortal rage.

3. To cut the head off and hack the limbs,
   Like wrath in death and envy afterwards;
   for Antony is but a limb of Caesar.

4. As virtuous men pass mildly away,
   And whisper to their souls, to go,
   Whilst some of their sad friends do say,
   The breath goes now, and some say, no.

Enrichment Activities

The following activities are for those students who attained the mastery level of 85 percent or better on the formative assessment. You may choose to do any of the following activities, or you may choose an activity of your own. If you choose something of your own, you must have the teacher approve the activity before you begin.

1. Write a modern-day version of the first act of *Macbeth.* Remember that your characters should be people of great importance, as they were in the play. Therefore, you may want to include current political figures. Make the language your own, and be sure to write your version as if it were to be acted on stage.

2. Look at the phenomenon of fortune-telling. Conduct an informal survey of your classmates and find out how many of them have had their fortunes told or how many believe fortune-telling is a waste of time or a hoax. You might ask the following questions:
   a. Have you had your fortune told, or would you like to?
   b. Would you act differently if a fortune teller told you something positive or negative about your future?
   c. Would you want to know what is going to happen in your future?

Keep in mind that these are only examples of questions, and you should also come up with some of your own.

Tragedy—Macbeth

Formative Assessment B

Name ______________________________ Date ____________________

This assessment is designed to let you know how well you have learned the concepts we have covered in this unit. Read carefully the directions to each section before answering. Make sure you answer every question.

Part I: Matching. Match each term definition in column A with the correct term from column B. Each correct answer counts for 1 point.

Column A	Column B
____ 1. An actor stands alone on stage, delivering information important to the audience.	A. Catharsis
	B. Imagery
____ 2. The audience experiences emotional release and empathy for the tragic hero.	C. Thane
____ 3. An actor stands apart from others on stage to give key information to the audience.	D. Foil
	E. Isolation
____ 4. Theme common to all tragedies and evident in Act One of *Macbeth*.	F. Aside
____ 5. Title in Ancient Scotland that is similar to our present-day Mayor or Governor.	G. Soliloquy

Part II: Short Answer. Answers to the these questions will be judged complete if they contain the necessary information in the context of at least one or two complete sentences. A complete answer is worth 2 points.

1. Two dramatic conventions are designed to give the audience insights into what specific characters are thinking and feeling. What are they and how are they used?

Page 2

2. What are the prophecies the three witches have for Macbeth's friend Banquo?

3. What is the definition of blank verse? Why is it important to the play?

4. What prevents Macbeth from taking the throne?

5. Explain how Macbeth meets the initial criteria for a tragic hero of being basically a good person and well thought of in his community.

Part III: Interpreting the Language. In your own words, rewrite the following passage from Act One of *Macbeth.* A translation will be judged complete if you have all the key points, correctly identify the characters mentioned, and come within a reasonable approximation of the events being explained. A complete answer will count for 5 points.

First Witch: "I myself have all the other,
And the very ports they blow,
All the quarters that they know
I' the shipman's card.
I will drain him dry as hay:
Sleep shall neither night nor day
Hang upon his pent-house lid;
He shall live a man forbid:
Weary se'n nights nine times nine
Shall he dwindle, peak and pine:
Through his bark cannot be lost,
Yet it shall be tempest-tost.
Look what I have."

14

High School Foreign Language: Spanish, Level I

Unit Description and Critique

The following unit was developed for a high school first-level Spanish class. Three general topics are covered in the unit: the family, possessives, and numerals and arithmetic. The unit is usually the second or third in the instructional sequence and typically requires five to seven class sessions to complete.

The unit's table of specifications is quite detailed and includes learning objectives as well as instructional procedures the teacher plans to use in the unit. In addition, several activities for students are included. Without numerals corresponding to formative assessment items, however, the relationship between the table and the formative assessments is somewhat difficult to see immediately.

The unit contains an outline for assessment, correctives, and enrichment activities. This outline explains the procedure the teacher follows in implementing these elements in the mastery learning process. It offers an excellent description of the way one teacher implements mastery learning in her classes.

Sample materials in Chapter 14 were prepared by Cecile Baer, New York City Public Schools, Brooklyn, New York 11201.

Formative assessment A clearly is well organized. Items are grouped according to specific topics and objectives, and a mastery level is specified for each grouping. Clear directions are also provided with each group of items.

The correctives have been prepared by the teacher and are also fairly detailed. Separate correctives have been designed for each major grouping of objectives on the assessment. The directions to students involved in corrective work seem quite clear, and because a mastery level is specified for each grouping, students can begin their corrective assignments immediately after the formative assessment is checked. The enrichment activities, which the teacher also has prepared, are directly related to the unit's content and undoubtedly are rewarding to students.

Formative assessment B strongly parallels assessment A and has the same level of detail. Although somewhat different terms are used in various items, the same general objectives are assessed at the same level of difficulty.

This unit represents a great deal of work on the part of the teacher, particularly in developing the corrective and enrichment activities. It is an excellent example of mastery learning materials for a foreign language. The only suggestion for improvement would be to show more explicitly the relationship between the table of specifications and the formative assessments.

Table of Specifications
Spanish Level I—Topic, La Familia

Terms and Facts	Rules and Principles	Translations	Applications
Family members in masculine/feminine pairs: a. el padre—la madre el papá—la mamá b. el hijo—la hija c. el hermano—la hermana d. el abuelo—la abuela e. el primo—la prima f. el tío—la tía g. el nieto—la nieta h. el sobrino—la sobrina i. el esposo—la esposa Also: los padres los hijos Family relationships (e.g., El hijo de mi hermano es mi sobrino.)	Definite articles: el, la, los, and las a. To discuss a masculine, singular relative, such as padre or tío, use *el* to mean "the." b. To discuss a feminine, singular relative, such as madre or tía, use *la* to mean "the." c. To discuss a masculine plural group of relatives, use *los* to mean "the." NOTE: Even if there are women in the group, the group is considered masculine if at least one male is present. d. To discuss a feminine, plural group of relatives, use *las* to mean "the."	From pictures representing family members, students can say, read, and write the names of relatives. Given the masculine form of a relative, students can respond with the corresponding feminine form, and vice versa. Students use *mi* and *mis* when talking about their own family members. Students understand and can reply to questions about family relationships (e.g., when asked, "¿Quién es el padre de su padre?" students respond, "El padre de me padre es mi abuelo."). Students can reply correctly when asked questions involving numbers (e.g., ¿Cuántas personas hay en su familia?).	**Activities** Students make flash cards showing relative pairs; for example: Side 1 el padre Side 2 la madre Students use the flash cards to test each other in learning relative pairs. Students make a personal family tree: El árbol del la familia. Each figure on the tree should be labeled with the appropriate relationship (e.g., mi padre, mi hermana, mi tío, and so on).

Table of Specifications Spanish Level I—Topic, La Familia, continued			
Terms and Facts	**Rules and Principles**	**Translations**	**Applications**
Spanish family names: a. Spanish men, unmarried women, and children usually have two last names: their father's last name, immediately followed by their mother's maiden last name (e.g., Juan Ramos Sánchez gets the name Ramos from his father and the name Sánchez from his mother). b. When a woman marries, she keeps her father's last name, but drops her mother's. Instead, she adds her husband's last name, preceded by *de* (e.g., when Luisa Santiago Romero marries Juan Ramos Sánchez, she becomes Luisa Santiago de Ramos).	Possessive adjectives: *mi, mis,* and *su* a. To discuss a singular relative, use *mi* to show he or she is your relative. b. To discuss a plural group of relatives, use *mis* to show they are your relatives. c. When a question is asked about *su madre,* you respond with *mi madre.* The use of *hay* a. *Hay* means "there are." b. When asked, "¿Cuántas personas hay en su familia?" the response is "Hay _________ personas en mi familia."	Students can look at Spanish family names and determine family relationships. For example, look at these names and tell how each is related to Enrique García Ramírez: Juan García Colón Isabel Ramírez de García Marta García Ramírez Carmen Colón de García María García Colón Answer: Juan es el padre. Isabel es la madre. Marta es la hermana. Carmen es la abuela. María es la tía.	

Table of Specifications Spanish Level I—Topic, Posesión			
Terms and Facts	**Rules and Principles**	**Translations**	**Applications**
The terms: *de, del, de la, de los,* and *de las* The terms: *muchacho—muchacha, muchachos—muchachas* These are general terms for: boy—girl, boys—girls	Possession using forms of *de* a. In English, an apostrophe can be used to show possession (e.g., the boy's father). A longer form would use "of" (the father *of* the boy). b. Spanish uses no apostrophe. Therefore the longer form is always used. c. To show possession, use *de* plus a definite article. However, we cannot say *de* + *el.* Instead, these words are contracted to *del.* d. The four combinations are: *del, de la, de los,* and *de las.* e. No definite article is used before a person's name, so possession is shown simply by using *de* plus the name.	Students can say, read, and write the following five patterns: a. El padre *del* muchacho b. El padre *de la* muchacha c. El padre *de los* muchachos d. El padre *de las* muchachas e. El padre *de* Roberto When given incomplete sentences, students can apply the appropriate possessive forms.	**Activities** Students make flash cards showing possession. For example: **Side 1** muchacho **Side 2** el padre del muchacho Students use the flash cards to test each other on possession.

Table of Specifications Spanish Level I—Topic, Los Números y la Aritmética			
Terms and Facts	**Rules and Principles**	**Translations**	**Applications**
			Activities:
The numbers 1–20 (uno–veinte) The question: ¿Cuántos son _____ y _____? The question: ¿Cuántos son _____menos _____? Questions about one's age: ¿Cuántos años tiene usted? Questions about the age of others: ¿Cuántos años tiene su hermano? Questions about counting: ¿Cuántas personas hay en su familia? ¿Cuántos alumnos hay en la clase de español?	When counting in a series, the number for one is *uno.* However, when followed by a noun, the number becomes *un.* In addition, the word for "and" or "plus" is *y.* In subtraction, the word for "minus" is *menos.* In telling age in Spanish, we say, *Tengo _____ años,* which literally means, "I have _____ years." The numbers between 16 and 19 can be written correctly in two ways: *diez y seis* and *dieciséis.* The Spanish word for "how much" or "how many" is *cuántos* (masculine) and *cuántas* (feminine).	Students can ask and answer questions about addition and subtraction. Students can ask and answer questions about their age and the ages of friends and relatives. Students can ask and answer questions about how many persons are in their family, class, and so on.	Students make flash cards showing numbers, addition, and subtraction. Students use the flash cards to test each other.

Outline for Assessment, Correctives, and Enrichment

The following outline is based on a three-day assessment, corrective, and enrichment period for a class that meets daily from 10:00 to 10:45 A.M. At the conclusion of each unit of instruction, the following activities take place:

Day 1	10:00–10:25	All students take formative assessment A.
	10:25–10:45	a. Students hand in answer sheets and begin textbook-based correctives and enrichment. b. Students who need more time finish assessment A.
	Homework:	Go over your assessment paper and make corrections.
Day 2	10:00–10:05	Teacher congratulates pupils who achieved mastery (90 percent or higher) on assessment A and returns the corrected answer sheets.
	10:05–10:10	Students come to the front of the room to pick up materials if needed and then join one of five groups: a. *Teacher-led corrective group.* This group reviews the answers on assessment A and receives additional explanations and reinforcement. b. *Individualized corrective group.* Each student works alone, using the corrective worksheet as a guide. Students may also choose to play individualized language games. c. *Peer-tutoring corrective group.* Students work in pairs or in small groups with one mastery student. d. *Individualized enrichment group.* Each student works alone on planned enrichment activities or a special project. e. *Peer enrichment group.* Students work on group games, activities, or special projects, or serve as peer tutors for students working on correctives.
	Homework:	Study for assessment B or continue enrichment activities.
Day 3	10:00–10:25	a. Students take formative assessment B. b. Mastery students continue enrichment activities individually or in teams.
	10:25–10:45	Teacher quickly goes over assessment B and begins presenting the next unit to the entire class.
	Homework:	First assignment from the new unit.

SPANISH LEVEL I

Formative Assessment A

Name ______________________________ Date ____________________

I. DICTADO (10 points: Mastery = No more than 3 errors)

LISTEN as the teacher reads each sentence to you. On the second reading, WRITE the sentence. Then LISTEN a third time and make any corrections.

Note: The following sentences appear on the teacher's copy only.

1. Yo tengo tres hermanos.
2. Mi prima tiene catorce años.
3. En la clase de español, hay doce alumnos.

II. LA FAMILIA

A. *Opposites* (15 points: Mastery = 4 or more correct)
Next to each word write its gender opposite.

4. el hijo ____________________
5. la madre ____________________
6. el abuelo ____________________
7. la sobrina ____________________
8. el hermano ____________________

B. *Relatives* (10 points: Mastery = 4 or more correct)
Complete these sentences:

9. La hermana de mi madre es mi ____________________.
10. El hijo de mi tío es mi ____________________.
11. La madre de mi madre es mi ____________________.
12. El hijo de mi hermano es mi ____________________.
13. La hija de mis padres es mi ____________________.

C. *Spanish names* (10 points: Mastery = 4 or more correct)

Enrique García Ramírez is the son of José García Pérez and Dolores Ramírez de García. How are these people related to Enrique?

14. María García Ramírez es la ____________________ de Enrique.
15. Juan García Gonzalez es el ____________________ de Enrique.
16. Elene García Pérez es la ____________________ de Enrique.

If Marta Gonzalez Romero marries Pedro Rojas García, Marta's married name will be:

17. Marta ____.

If Pedro Álvarez Santiago and Juanita Colón de Álvarez have a son named Alfredo, his complete name will be:

18. Alfredo ____.

III. LA ARITMÉTICA (45 points: Mastery = 12 or more correct)

Write the arithmetic problems listed below and give the correct answers. Be sure to write all numbers in Spanish.

19. 10 + 4 = ? _____ y _____ son _____.
20. 12 + 7 = ? _____ y _____ son _____.
21. 11 + 5 = ? _____ y _____ son _____.
22. 8 – 2 = ? _____ menos _____ son _____.
23. 20 – 3 = ? _____ menos _____ son _____.

IV. POSESIÓN (10 points: Mastery = 4 or more correct)

Fill in the missing word or words to complete these expressions.

24. (Pedro's father) El padre _______________ Pedro
25. (The girl's father) El padre _______________ muchacha
26. (The boys' father) El padre _______________ muchachos
27. (The girls' father) El padre _______________ muchachas
28. (The boy's father) El padre _______________ muchacho

SPANISH LEVEL I

Corrective Activities

Use your book, worksheets, and homework assignments as references and complete the following activities.

Topic I: LA FAMILIA

1. Review your family flash cards and divide them into two piles.
   Pile 1: the ones you know
   Pile 2: the ones you don't remember
2. Write each word from Pile 2 three times.
3. Play a game of family flash cards with a friend.
4. Complete the following drill about your family:
   a. El padre de mi padre es mi ____________________.
   b. La madre de mi madre es mi ____________________.
   c. El hermano de mi padre es mi ____________________.
   d. La hermana de mi padre es mi ____________________.
   e. El hijo de mis padres es mi ____________________.
   f. La hija de mis padres es mi ____________________.
   g. El hijo de mi tío es mi ____________________.
   h. La hija de mi tía es mi ____________________.
   i. El hijo de mi hermano es mi ____________________.
   j. La hija de mi hermana es mi ____________________.
5. All these people are related:
   Juan Ramos Sánchez
   Emilio Ramos Gomez
   Pablo Ramos Perez
   Pedro Ramos Sánchez
   Luisa Gomez de Ramos
   Isabel Ramos Gomez
   Carmen Sánchez de Ramos
   Anita Ramos Sánchez

   Tell how they are related to each other:
   a. Juan es el ____________________ de Emilio.
   b. Luisa es la ____________________ de Isabel.
   c. Carmen es la ____________________ de Isabel.

d. Pablo es el ____________________ de Emilio.

e. Pedro es el ____________________ de Juan.

f. Anita es la ____________________ de Isabel.

g. Juan es el ____________________ de Luisa.

h. Isabel es la ____________________ de Emilio.

i. El hijo de mi hermano es mi ____________________.

j. Isabel es la ____________________ de Luisa.

6. Read these questions aloud and select the correct answer to each. Place the number of the correct answer on the line following the question.

Questions

a. ¿Cuántos personas hay en su familia? _______________

b. ¿Quién es el padre de su padre? _______________

c. ¿Quién es el hijo de sus padres? _______________

Answers

1. El hijo de mis padres es mi hermano.
2. Hay _______________ personas en mi familia.
3. El padre de mi padre es mi abuelo.

Topic II: DE, DEL, DE LA, DE LOS, DE LAS—POSESIÓN

1. Match the Spanish expression in Column A with its English equivalent in Column B.

COLUMN A	COLUMN B
a. la casa de la muchacha	1. the boys' house
b. la casa de Ana	2. the girl's house
c. la casa de los muchachos	3. the boy's house
d. la casa del muchacho	4. the girls' house
e. la casa de las muchachas	5. Ana's house

2. Translate into English:
   a. El padre de Emilio ____________________
   b. La madre del muchacho ____________________
   c. El tío de las muchachas ____________________

3. Translate into Spanish:
   a. The girl's grandfather ____________________
   b. The boys' aunt ____________________
   c. Pedro's brother ____________________

Topic III: LOS NÚMEROS Y LA ARITMÉTICA

1. Read aloud the numbers from 1 to 20.

2. Copy each number two times.

3. Read aloud these arithmetic problems:
   a. Quince y cinco son veinte.
   b. Trece menos dos son once.

4. Go through your number and arithmetic flash cards. Divide them into two piles.
   Pile 1: those numbers and problems that you don't know
   Pile 2: those numbers and problems that you don't remember

5. Write each number or problem from Pile 2 three times.

6. Play a game of number or problem flash cards with a friend.

7. Write out these arithmetic problems in Spanish and answer them.
   a. $12 + 3 = ?$ _____ y _____ son _____.
   b. $15 - 4 = ?$ _____ menos _____ son _____.
   c. $8 + 2 = ?$ _____ y _____ son _____.

8. Match the following questions with their answers and place the number of the correct answer on the line following the question.

   Questions

   a. ¿Cuántas personas hay en su familia? __________
   b. ¿Cuántos hermanos tiene usted? __________
   c. ¿Cuántas hermanas tiene usted? __________
   d. ¿Cuántos alumnos hay en la clase de español? __________
   e. ¿Cuántos años tiene usted? __________
   f. ¿Cuántos años tiene su hermano? __________

   Answers

   1. Yo tengo __________ años.
   2. Yo tengo __________ hermanos.
   3. Hay __________ personas en mi familia.
   4. Mi hermano tiene __________ años.
   5. Hay __________ alumnos en la clase de español.
   6. Yo tengo __________ hermanas.

9. Write out these problems in numbers.

   a. Quince y dos son diez y siete. ____________________
   b. Nueve y tres son doce. ____________________
   c. Veinte menos once son nueve. ____________________
   d. Cinco y tres son ocho. ____________________
   e. Catorce menos ocho son seis. ____________________

SPANISH LEVEL I

Enrichment Activities

LA FAMILIA

Word jumble: Rearrange the letters for each word and write the word in the box. Then combine all the letters in circles to form a surprise message in English about you!

JAHI

DREAM

NBOOSIR

OTI

MEAHNAR

Surprise message: ___ ___ ___ ___ ___ ___ ___ ___! (Do you agree?)

Word grid: See if you can fit all of these words into the grid.

tío
hijo
madre
nieto
padre
primo
abuelo
esposo
familia
hermano
sobrino

Letter grid: Complete each Spanish sentence. Then read the words that appear vertically to form a surprise answer in Spanish about the people who are most important to you.

1. El hijo de mi padre es mi __________. 1. _ _ _ |_| _ _ _
2. El hermano de mi padre es mi __________. 2. _ |_| _
3. Mi padre es el __________ de mi madre. 3. _ |_| _ _ _
4. El hijo de mi tío es mi __________. 4. |_| _ _ _
5. La señora Gomez es la madre de Elena. Elena es la __________ de la señora Gomez. 5. _ _ _ |_|
6. Pablo es el hijo del señor Martinez. El señor Martinez es el __________ de Pablo. 6. _ _ |_| _ _
7. Ana es la hija de la señora Pérez. La señora Pérez es la __________ de Ana. 7. _ _ _ |_| _
8. El padre de mi padre es mi __________. 8. _ _ _ |_| _ _
9. El hijo de mi hermano es mi __________. 9. |_| _ _ _ _

The surprise answer is: ______________________________.

Squares: This game is similar to tic-tac-toe. One player uses the circle as a symbol, and the other player uses the X. The first player selects any square and says and then writes the answer. If both players agree that the answer is correct, then Player 1 gets the square. Player 2 then has a turn. If an incorrect answer is given, it must be erased or crossed out, and the box remains open. The first player to get three squares horizontally, vertically, or diagonally is the winner.

Translate into English:

abuelo __________	prima __________	padre __________
hermano __________	tío __________	sobrina __________
familia __________	madre __________	hija __________

Translate into Spanish:

father __________	aunt __________	daughter __________
wife __________	cousin __________	grandson __________
nephew __________	grandmother __________	uncle __________

LOS NÚMEROS Y LA ARITMÉTICA

More squares:

Write the number in Spanish.

7 __________	4 __________	15 __________
12 __________	20 __________	14 __________
13 __________	9 __________	11 __________

Write the answer in Spanish.

8 + 9 = __________	20 – 13 = __________	10 – 4 = __________
18 – 11 = __________	3 + 2 = __________	12 – 5 = __________
19 – 6 = __________	8 + 7 = __________	17 – 2 = __________

Word search: Can you find all the words listed below hidden in this puzzle?

O	P	E	A	C	I	N	C	O	L
R	E	V	F	A	B	I	U	C	J
E	T	G	H	T	N	M	A	H	O
M	E	R	Z	O	N	E	T	O	S
U	I	D	E	R	E	T	R	E	S
N	S	O	N	C	E	N	O	Q	E
O	B	S	O	E	E	I	P	R	I
A	C	D	I	E	Z	E	U	T	S
Q	U	I	N	C	E	V	E	U	N

uno	diez
dos	once
tres	doce
cuatro	trece
cinco	catorce
seis	quince
siete	veinte
ocho	numero
nueve	

SPANISH LEVEL I

Formative Assessment B

Name ______________________________ Date ____________________

I. DICTADO (10 points: Mastery = No more than 3 errors)

LISTEN as the teacher reads each sentence to you. On the second reading, WRITE the sentence. Then LISTEN a third time and make any corrections.

Note: The following sentences appear on the teacher's copy only.

1. En mi familia, hay cinco personas.
2. Yo tengo quince años.
3. En la clase de español, hay diez y nueve alumnas.

II. LA FAMILIA

A. *Opposites* (15 points: Mastery = 4 or more correct)
Next to each word write its gender opposite.

4. la prima ____________________
5. el padre ____________________
6. la hermana ____________________
7. el sobrino ____________________
8. la hija ____________________

B. *Relatives* (10 points: Mastery = 4 or more correct)
Complete these sentences:

9. El hermano de mi padre es mi ____________________.
10. La hija de mi tía es mi ____________________.
11. El padre de mi padre es mi ____________________.
12. La hija de mi hermana es mi ____________________.
13. El hijo de mis padres es mi ____________________.

C. *Spanish names* (10 points: Mastery = 4 or more correct)

Ana Romero Colón is the daughter of Roberto Romero Hernández and Magdalena Colón de Romero. How are these people related to Ana?

14. Pedro Romero Colón es el ____________________ de Ana.
15. Miguel Romero Hernández es el ____________________ de Ana.
16. Marta Hernández de Romero es la __________________ de Ana.

If Roberto Pidal Ruiz and Anita Jiménez de Ruiz have a daughter named Elena, what is Elena's complete name?

17. Elena ____.

If Luisa Rojaz Diaz marries Pedro Figueroa Perez, what is Luisa's married name?

18. Luisa ____.

III. LA ARITMÉTICA (45 points: Mastery = 12 or more correct)

Write the arithmetic problems listed below and give the correct answers. Be sure to write all numbers in Spanish.

19. 9 + 8 = ? _____ y _____ son _____.
20. 7 + 6 = ? _____ y _____ son _____.
21. 15 + 5 = ? _____ y _____ son _____.
22. 14 – 3 = ? _____ menos _____ son _____.
23. 12 – 2 = ? _____ menos _____ son _____.

IV. POSESIÓN (10 points: Mastery = 4 or more correct)

Fill in the missing word or words to complete these expressions.

24. (The boy's mother) La madre __________________ muchacho
25. (The girls' mother) La madre __________________ muchachas
26. (The girl's mother) La madre __________________ muchacha
27. (The boys' mother) La madre __________________ muchachos
28. (María's mother) La madre __________________ María

References

Airasian, P. W. (1969). *Formative evaluation instruments: A construction and validation of tests to evaluate learning over short time periods.* Doctoral dissertation, University of Chicago.

Airasian, P. W. (1971). The role of evaluation in mastery learning. In J. H. Block (Ed.), *Mastery learning: Theory and practice* (pp. 77–88). New York: Holt, Rinehart & Winston.

Airasian, P. W. (1994). *Classroom assessment* (2nd ed.). New York: McGraw-Hill.

Anania, J. (1981). *The effects of quality of instruction on the cognitive and affective learning of students.* Unpublished doctoral dissertation, University of Chicago.

Anderson, L. W. (1973). *Time and school learning.* Unpublished doctoral dissertation, University of Chicago.

Anderson, L. W. (1975a). *Time to criterion: An experimental study.* Paper presented at annual meeting of the American Educational Research Association, Washington, DC.

Anderson, L. W. (1975b). Student involvement in learning and school achievement. *California Journal of Educational Research, 26* (1), 53–62.

Anderson, L. W. (1976). An empirical investigation of individual differences in time to learn. *Journal of Educational Psychology, 68* (2), 226–233.

Anderson, L. W. (1981a). Instruction and time-on-task: A review. *Journal of Curriculum Studies, 13,* 289–303.

Anderson, L. W. (1981b). *Assessing affective characteristic in the schools.* Boston: Allyn & Bacon.

Anderson, L. W., & Anderson, J. C. (1982). Affective assessment is necessary and positive. *Educational Leadership, 39* (7), 524–525.

Anderson, L. W., & Burns, R. B. (1987). Values, evidence, and mastery learning. *Review of Educational Research, 57* (2), 215–223.

Anderson, L. W., & Burns, R. B. (1989). *Research in classrooms: The study of teachers, teaching and instruction.* New York: Pergamon Press.

Anderson, L. W., & Jones, B. J. (1981). Designing instructional strategies which facilitate learning for mastery. *Educational Psychologist, 16,* 121–138.

Anderson, L. W., & Scott, C. C. (1978). The relationship among teaching methods, student characteristics and student involvement in learning. *Journal of Teacher Education, 29* (3), 52–57.

Anderson, L. W., Ryan, D. W., & Shapiro, B. J. (1989). *The IEA classroom environment study.* Oxford, England: Pergamon.

Anderson, L. W., Scott, C. C., & Hutlock, J. (1976). *The effects of a mastery learning program on selected cognitive, affective and ecological variables in grades 1 through 6.* Paper presented at annual meeting of the American Educational Research Association, San Francisco.

Anderson, R. W. (1989). *The effects of group-based mastery learning and enhanced cognitive entry behaviors on algebra achievement.* Paper presented at annual meeting of the American Educational Research Association, San Francisco.

Anderson, S. A. (1994). Staff development and implementation of mastery learning: A field study. *Outcomes, 13* (2),12–20.

Angoff, W. H. (1971). Scales, norms, and equivalent scores. In R. L. Thorndike (Ed.), *Educational measurement* (2nd ed.) (pp. 508–600). Washington, DC: American Council on Education.

Arlin, M. N. (1973). *Rate and rate variance trends under mastery learning.* Unpublished doctoral dissertation, University of Chicago.

Arlin, M. N. (1982). Teacher responses to student time differences in mastery learning. *American Journal of Education, 90* (3), 334–352.

Arlin, M. N. (1984a). Time variability in mastery learning. *American Educational Research Journal, 21* (1), 103–120.

Arlin, M. N. (1984b). Time, equality, and mastery learning. *Review of Educational Research, 54* (1), 65–86.

Armstrong, T. (1994). *Multiple intelligences in the classroom.* Alexandria, VA: Association for Supervision and Curriculum Development.

Aronson, E., Stephan, C., Sikes, J., Blaney, N., & Snapp, M. (1978). *The jigsaw classroom.* Beverly Hills, CA: Sage.

Arredondo, D. E., & Block, J. H. (1990). Recognizing the connections between thinking skills and mastery learning. *Educational Leadership, 47* (5), 4–10.

Ausubel, D. P. (1963). *The psychology of meaningful verbal learning.* New York: Grune & Stratton.

Ausubel, D. P. (1979). In defense of advance organizers: A reply to the critic. *Review of Educational Research, 48* (2), 251–257.

Ausubel, D. P. (1980). Schemata, cognitive structure, and advance organizers: A reply to Anderson, Spiro, and Anderson. *American Educational Research Journal, 17* (3), 400–404.

Baker, E. L. (1970). Project for research on objective-based evaluation. *Educational Technology, 10* (8), 56–59.

Bangert, R. L., Kulik, J. A., & Kulik, C. C. (1983). Individualized systems of instruction in secondary schools. *Review of Educational Research, 53* (2), 142–158.

Barber, C. (1979). Training principals and teachers for mastery learning. *Educational Leadership, 37* (2), 126–127.

Bargh, J. A., & Schul, Y. (1980). On the cognitive benefits of teaching. *Journal of Educational Psychology, 72* (4), 593–604.

Baron, J. B., & Sternberg, R. J. (Eds.) (1987). *Teaching thinking skills: Theory and practice.* New York: W. H. Freeman.

Benjamin, R. (1981). All kids can learn: Mastery learning. Chapter 2 in *Making schools work* (pp. 37–68). New York: Continuum.

Beyer, B. K. (1995). *How to conduct a formative evaluation.* Alexandria, VA: Association for Supervision and Curriculum Development.

Blackburn, K. T., & Nelson, D. (1985). *Differences between a group using traditional format with mastery learning and a group using traditional format only in developmental mathematics courses at the university level: Implications for teacher education programs.* Paper presented at annual meeting of the American Educational Research Association, Chicago.

Blakemore, C. L. (1992). Comparison of students taught basketball skills using mastery and nonmastery learning methods. *Journal of Teaching in Physical Education, 11* (3), 235–247.

Block, J. H. (1970). *The effects of various levels of performance on selected cognitive, objective, and time variables.* Doctoral dissertation, University of Chicago.

Block, J. H. (1972). Student learning and the setting of mastery performance standards. *Educational Horizons, 50* (4), 183–191.

Block, J. H. (1974). Mastery learning in the classroom: An overview of recent research. In J. H. Block (Ed.), *Schools, society, and mastery learning* (pp. 27–69). New York: Holt, Rinehart & Winston.

Block, J. H. (1983). Learning rates and mastery learning. *Outcomes, 2* (3), 18–23.

Block, J. H. (1984). Making school learning activities more playlike: Flow and mastery learning. *Elementary School Journal, 85* (1), 65–75.

Block, J. H. (Ed.) (1971). *Mastery learning: Theory and practice.* New York: Holt, Rinehart & Winston.

Block, J. H. (Ed.) (1974). *Schools, society and mastery learning.* New York: Holt, Rinehart & Winston.

Block, J. H., & Anderson, L. W. (1975). *Mastery learning in classroom instruction.* New York: Macmillan.

Block, J. H., & Burns, R. B. (1976). Mastery learning. In L. S. Shulman (Ed.), *Review of research in education* (Vol. 4, pp. 3–49). Itasca, IL: Peacock.

Block, J. H., & Tierney, M. L. (1974). An exploratory study of two corrective procedures used in mastery learning approaches to instruction. *Journal of Educational Psychology, 66* (6), 962–967.

Block, J. H., Efthim, H. E., & Burns, R. B. (1989). *Building effective mastery learning schools.* New York: Longman.

Bloom, B. S. (1964). *Stability and change in human characteristics.* New York: Wiley.

Bloom, B. S. (1968). Learning for mastery. *Evaluation Comment* (UCLA-CSIEP), *1* (2), 1–12.

Bloom, B. S. (1971a). *Individual differences in school achievement: A vanishing point?* Bloomington, IN: Phi Delta Kappan International.

Bloom, B. S. (1971b). Mastery learning. In J. H. Block (Ed.), *Mastery learning: Theory and practice* (pp. 47–63). New York: Holt, Rinehart & Winston.

Bloom, B. S. (1971c). Affective consequences of school achievement. In J. H. Block (Ed.), *Mastery learning: Theory and practice* (pp. 13–28). New York: Holt, Rinehart & Winston.

Bloom, B. S. (1974). An introduction to mastery learning theory. In J. H. Block (Ed.), *Schools, society and mastery learning* (pp. 3–14). New York: Holt, Rinehart & Winston.

Bloom, B. S. (1976). *Human characteristics and school learning.* New York: McGraw-Hill.

Bloom, B. S. (1977). Affective outcomes of school learning. *Phi Delta Kappan, 59* (3), 193–198.

Bloom, B. S. (1978). New views of the learner: Implications for instruction and curriculum. *Educational Leadership, 35* (7), 563–576.

Bloom, B. S. (1982). The master teachers. *Phi Delta Kappan, 63* (10), 664–668, 715.

Bloom, B. S. (1984a). The 2-sigma problem: The search for methods of group instruction as effective as one-to-one tutoring. *Educational Researcher, 13* (6), 4–16.

Bloom, B. S. (1984b). The search for methods of group instruction as effective as one-to-one tutoring. *Educational Leadership, 41* (8), 4–18.

Bloom, B. S. (1987). A response to Slavin's "Mastery learning reconsidered." *Review of Educational Research, 57* (4), 507–508.

Bloom, B. S. (1988). Helping all children learn in elementary school and beyond. *Principal, 67* (4), 12–17.

Bloom, B. S., Engelhart, M. D., Furst, E. J., Hill, W. H., & Krathwohl, D. R. (1956). *Taxonomy of educational objectives. Handbook I: Cognitive domain.* New York: McKay.

Bloom, B. S., Hastings, J. T., & Madaus, G. F. (1971). *Handbook on formative and summative evaluation of student learning.* New York: McGraw-Hill.

Bloom, B. S., Madaus, G. F., & Hastings, J. T. (1981). *Evaluation to improve learning.* New York: McGraw-Hill.

Bloom, S. (1976). *Peer and cross-age tutoring in the schools.* Washington, DC: National Institute of Education.

Blum, R. E. (1981). *Goal based education: Profiles, programs, & products.* Portland, OR: Northwest Regional Educational Laboratory.

Blum, R. E., & Butler, J. A. (1981). *A directory of goal based approaches to education.* Portland, OR: Northwest Regional Educational Laboratory.

Bortnick, R. (1995). Interactive learning and hypermedia technology. In J. H. Block, S. T. Everson, & T. R. Guskey (Eds.), *School improvement programs* (pp. 77–90). New York: Scholastic.

Boysen, T. C. (1992). *Transformations: Kentucky's curriculum framework.* Frankfort, KY: Kentucky Department of Education.

Bracey, G. W. (1994). Grade inflation? *Phi Delta Kappan, 76* (4), 328–329.

Brandt, R. (1992). On outcome-based education: A conversation with Bill Spady. *Educational Leadership, 50* (4), 66–70.

Brandt, R. S. (1986). On the expert teacher: A conversation with David Berliner. *Education Leadership, 44* (2), 4–9.

Brooks, J. G., & Brooks, M. G. (1993). *In search of understanding: The case for constructivist classrooms.* Alexandria, VA: Association for Supervision and Curriculum Development.

Brophy, J. E. (1981). On praising appropriately. *Elementary School Journal, 81* (5), 269–278.

Brophy, J. E. (1992). Probing the subtleties of subject-matter teaching. *Educational Leadership, 49* (7), 4–8.

Brophy, J. E., & Good, T. L. (1986). Teacher behavior and student achievement. In M. C. Wittrock (Ed.), *Handbook of research on teaching* (3rd ed., pp. 328–375). New York: Macmillan.

Bruner, J. S. (1960). *The process of education.* New York: Vintage.

Burke, A. J. (1983). *Students' potential for learning contrasted under tutorial and group approaches to instruction.* Unpublished doctoral dissertation, University of Chicago.

Burns, R. B. (1986). Accumulating the accumulated evidence on mastery learning. *Outcomes, 5* (2), 4–10.

Burns, R. B. (1987). *Models of instructional organization: A casebook on mastery learning and outcome-based education.* San Francisco: Far West Laboratory for Educational Research and Development.

Cabezon, E. (1984). *The effects of marked changes in student achievement patterns on the students, their teachers, and their parents: The Chilean case.* Unpublished doctoral dissertation, University of Chicago.

Callaway, R. (1988). *A study of teachers' planning.* Paper presented at annual meeting of the American Educational Research Association, New Orleans, LA.

Cameron, J., & Pierce, W. D. (1994). Reinforcement, reward, and intrinsic motivation: A meta-analysis. *Review of Educational Research, 64*(3), 363–423.

Canady, R. L., & Hotchkiss, P. R. (1989). It's a good score! Just a bad grade. *Phi Delta Kappan, 71*(1), 68–71.

Cangelosi, J. S. (1990). Grading and reporting student achievement. Chapter 9 in *Designing tests for evaluating student achievement* (pp. 196–213). New York: Longman.

Carbo, M., Dunn, R., & Dunn, K. (1986). *Teaching students to read through their individual learning styles.* Reston, VA: Prentice-Hall.

Carnine, D., Grossen, B., & Silbert, J. (1995). Direct instruction to accelerate cognitive growth. In J. H. Block, S. T. Everson, & T. R. Guskey (Eds.), *School improvement programs* (pp. 129–152). New York: Scholastic.

Carroll, J. B. (1963). A model for school learning. *Teachers College Record, 64,* 723–733.

Cartwright, C. A., & Cartwright, G. P. (1984). *Developing observation skills.* New York: McGraw-Hill.

Chan, K. S. (1981). *The interaction of aptitude with mastery versus non-mastery instruction: Effects on reading comprehension of grade three students.* Unpublished doctoral dissertation, University of Western Australia.

Chan, K. S., & Cole, P. G. (1986). *An aptitude-treatment interaction in a mastery learning model of instruction.* Paper presented at annual meeting of the American Educational Research Association, San Francisco.

Chion-Kenney, L. (1994). Negotiating the challenge of outcome-based education. *The School Administrator, 51* (8), 8–19.

Christie, N., & Savers, D. L. (1989). *Using microcomputers to implement mastery learning with high-risk and minority adolescents.* Paper presented at annual meeting of the American Educational Research Association, San Francisco.

Clark, C. R., Guskey, T. R., & Benninga, J. S. (1983). The effectiveness of mastery learning strategies in undergraduate education courses. *Journal of Educational Research, 76* (4) 210–214.

Coffman, W. E. (1971). Essay examinations. In R. L. Thorndike (Ed.), *Educational measurement* (2nd ed.). Washington, DC: American Council on Education.

Cohen, P. A., & Kulik, J. A. (1981). Synthesis of research on the effects of tutoring. *Educational Leadership, 39* (3), 227–229.

Cohen, S. A. (1987). Instructional alignment: Searching for the magic bullet. *Educational Researcher, 16* (8), 16–20.

Cooke, L. M. (1979). Why business supports mastery learning. *Educational Leadership, 37* (2), 124–125.

Cooper, H. (1989). Synthesis of research on homework. *Educational Leadership, 47* (3), 85–91.

Cooper, H. (1994). *The battle over homework: An administrator's guide to setting sound and effective policy.* Thousand Oaks, CA: Corwin Press.

Cooper, J. M. (Ed.) (1990). *Classroom teaching skills.* Lexington, MA: D.C. Heath.

Cooper, M., & Leiter, M. (1981). *Three peer-initiated and delivered staff development models for mastery learning.* Paper presented at annual meeting of the American Educational Research Association, New York.

Coopersmith, S. (1967). *Self-esteem inventory.* Davis, CA: Department of Psychology, University of California.

Cragin, J. M. (1979). *A study of the effects of mastery learning on self-concept and attitudes.* Unpublished doctoral dissertation, University of Arkansas.

Cruickshank, D. R., Bainer, D., & Metcalf, K. (1995). *The act of teaching.* New York: McGraw-Hill.

Csikszentmihalyi, M., & McCormack, J. (1986). The influence of teachers. *Phi Delta Kappan, 67* (6), 415–419.

Cunningham, R. D. (1991). Modeling mastery learning through classroom supervision. *NASSP Bulletin, 75* (536), 83–87.

Deci, E. L. (1971). Effects of externally mediated rewards on intrinsic motivation. *Journal of Personality and Social Psychology, 18* (1), 105–115.

Del Seni, D. (1981). Mastery learning from the perspective of an intermediate school principal. *IMPACT on Instructional Improvement, 17* (2), 25–31.

Denham, C., & Lieberman, A. (Eds.). (1980). *Time to learn.* Washington, DC: National Institute of Education, U.S. Department of Education.

Denton, J. J., & Seymour, J. G. (1978). The influence of unit pacing and mastery learning strategies on the acquisition of higher order intellectual skills. *Journal of Educational Research, 71* (3), 267–271.

Denton, W. L., Ory, J. C., Glassnap, D. R., & Poggio, J. P. (1976). *Grade expectations within a mastery learning strategy.* Paper presented at annual meeting of the American Educational Research Association, San Francisco.

Dillashaw, F. G., & Okey, J. R. (1983). Effects of a modified mastery learning strategy on achievement, attitudes, and on-task behavior of high school chemistry students. *Journal of Research in Science Teaching, 20* (2), 203–211.

Dollard, J., & Miller, N. E. (1950). *Personality and psychotherapy.* New York: McGraw-Hill.

Doyle, D. P. (1992). The challenge, the opportunity. *Phi Delta Kappan, 73* (7), 512–520.

Doyle, W., & Good, T. L. (Eds.) (1982). *Focus on teaching.* Chicago: University of Chicago Press.

Drake, S. M. (1993). *Planning integrated curriculum: The call to adventure.* Alexandria, VA: Association for Supervision and Curriculum Development.

Duby, P. B. (1981). *Attributions and attribution change: Effects of a mastery learning instructional approach.* Paper presented at annual meeting of the American Educational Research Association, Los Angeles.

Dunn, R., & Dunn, K. (1975). *Educator's guide to individualizing instructional programs.* West Nyack, NY: Parker.

Dunn, R., & Dunn, K. (1978). *Teaching students through their individual learning styles: A practical approach.* Reston, VA: Reston Publishing.

Dyke, W. E. (1988). *The immediate effect of a mastery learning program on the belief systems of high school teachers.* Paper presented at annual meeting of the American Educational Research Association, New Orleans.

Ebel, R. L. (1972). *Essentials of educational measurement.* Englewood Cliffs, NJ: Prentice-Hall.

Evertson, C. M., Anderson, L. M., & Brophy, J. E. (1978). *Texas junior high school study: Final report of process-outcome relationships* (Vol. 1. Research Report No. 4061). Austin, TX: Research and Development Center for Teacher Education, University of Texas at Austin.

Farnsworth, B. J., & Wilkinson, J. C. (1987). A fully integrated management system for tracking student mastery. *Technological Horizons in Education, 15* (4), 96–100.

Feinman, J. M., & Feldman, M. (1985). Achieving excellence: Mastery learning in legal education. *Journal of Legal Education, 35* (4), 528–551.

Fiske, E. B. (1980). New teaching method produces impressive gains. *The New York Times,* March 30, pp. 1 & 37.

Fitzpatrick, K. A. (1985). *Group-based mastery learning: A Robin Hood approach to instruction?* Paper presented at annual meeting of the American Educational Research Association, Chicago, IL.

Flavell, J. H. (1971). Stage-related properties of cognitive development. *Cognitive Psychology, 2,* 421–453.

Forman, G. (1987). The constructivism perspective. In J. L. Roopnarine & J. E. Johnson (Eds.), *Approaches to early childhood education* (pp. 71–84). Columbus, OH: Merrill

Fox, M. F. (1987). A decade of mastery learning: Evolution and evaluation. *Journal of Geography in Higher Education, 11* (1), 3–10.

Fullan, M. G. (1991). *The new meaning of educational change.* New York: Teachers College Press.

Fullan, M. G. (1992). Visions that blind. *Educational Leadership, 49* (5), 19–20.

Fullan, M. G., & Miles, M. B. (1992). Getting reform right: What works and what doesn't. *Phi Delta Kappan, 73* (10), 745–752.

Gage, N. (1978). *The scientific basis of the art of teaching.* New York: Teachers College Press.

Gagne, R. M. (1985). *The conditions of learning* (4th ed.). New York: Holt, Rinehart & Winston.

Gagne, R. M., & Driscoll, M. P. (1988). *Essentials of learning for instruction* (2nd ed.). Englewood Cliffs, NJ: Prentice-Hall.

Gamoran, A. (1987). Organization, instruction, and the effects of ability grouping: Comment on Slavin's "best-evidence synthesis." *Review of Educational Research, 57* (3), 341–345.

Gardner, H. (1983). *Frames of mind: The theory of multiple intelligences.* New York: Basic Books.

Gartner, A. J., & Riessman, R. (1994). Tutoring helps those who give, those who receive. *Educational Leadership, 52* (3), 58–60.

Glaser, R. (1966). *The program for individually prescribed instruction.* Pittsburgh, PA: University of Pittsburgh.

Glass, G. V., & Stanley, J. C. (1970). *Statistical methods in education and psychology.* Englewood Cliffs, NJ: Prentice-Hall.

Glickman, C. D. (1979). Mastery learning stifles individuality. *Educational Leadership, 37* (2), 100–102.

Good, T. L., & Grouws, D. (1979). The Missouri teacher effectiveness program. *Journal of Educational Psychology, 71* (3), 355–362.

Goodlad, S., & Hirst, B. (1989). *Peer tutoring.* New York: Nichols Publishing.

Goodman, K. (1987). *What's whole in whole language?* New York: Scholastic Inc.

Gram, P. (1974). Some criticisms of mastery learning. *Today's Education, 63,* 88–91.

Gregorc, A. F. (1985). *Inside styles: Beyond the basics.* Maynard, MA: Gabriel Systems.

Gronlund, N. E. (1993). *How to make achievement tests and assessments* (5th ed.). Boston: Allyn & Bacon.

Gronlund, N. E. (1995). *How to write and use instructional objectives.* Englewood Cliffs, NJ: Prentice-Hall.

Grossman, A. S. (1985). Mastery learning and peer tutoring in a special program. *Mathematics Teacher, 78* (1), 24–27.

Guerin, G. R., & Maier, A. S. (1983). *Informal assessment in education.* Palo Alto, CA: Mayfield.

Guskey, T. R. (1980a). What is mastery learning? *Instructor, 90* (3), 80–84.

Guskey, T. R. (1980b). Mastery learning: Applying the theory. *Theory into Practice, 19* (2), 104–111.

Guskey, T. R. (1981a). Mastery learning: An introduction. *IMPACT on Instructional Improvement, 17* (2), 25–31.

Guskey, T. R. (1981b). The implementation and evaluation of mastery learning programs. In R. S. Caponigri (Ed.), *Proceedings of the second annual national mastery learning conference* (pp. 62–67). Chicago: City Colleges of Chicago.

Guskey, T. R. (1982a). The theory and practice of mastery learning. *The Principal, 27* (4), 1–12.

Guskey, T. R. (1982b). The effects of change in instructional effectiveness upon the relationship of teacher expectations and student achievement. *Journal of Educational Research, 75* (6), 345–349.

Guskey, T. R. (1983). Clarifying time related issues. *Outcomes, 3* (1), 5–7.

Guskey, T. R. (1984). The influence of change in instructional effectiveness upon the affective characteristics of teachers. *American Educational Research Journal, 21* (2), 245–259.

Guskey, T. R. (1985a). *Implementing mastery learning.* Belmont, CA: Wadsworth.

Guskey, T. R. (1985b). Bloom's mastery learning: A legacy for effectiveness. *Educational Horizons, 63* (2), 90–92.

Guskey, T. R. (1985c). The effects of staff development on teachers' perceptions about effective teaching. *Journal of Educational Research, 78* (6), 378–381.

Guskey, T. R. (1985d). The contributions of mastery learning. *Outcomes, 4* (3), 1–10.

Guskey, T. R. (1986). Staff development and the process of teacher change. *Educational Researcher, 15* (5), 5–12.

Guskey, T. R. (1987a). The essential elements of mastery learning. *Journal of Classroom Interaction, 22* (2), 19–22.

Guskey, T. R. (1987b). Rethinking "Mastery learning reconsidered." *Review of Educational Research, 57* (2), 225–229.

Guskey, T. R. (1988a). Teacher efficacy, self-concept, and attitudes toward the implementation of instructional innovation. *Teaching and Teacher Education, 4* (1), 63–69.

Guskey, T. R. (1988b). Exceptionally effective college teachers. Ch. 2 in *Improving student learning in college classrooms* (pp. 15–30). Springfield, IL: Charles Thomas.

Guskey, T. R. (1988c). Response to Slavin: Who defines best? *Educational Leadership, 46* (2), 26–27.

Guskey, T. R. (1988d). *Improving student learning in college classrooms.* Springfield, IL: Charles C. Thomas.

Guskey, T. R. (1988e). Mastery learning and mastery teaching: How they complement each other. *Principal, 68* (1), 6–8.

Guskey, T. R. (1989a). Every teacher can be the best. *Vocational Education Journal, 64* (1), 20–22.

Guskey, T. R. (1989b). Attitude and perceptual change in teachers. *International Journal of Educational Research, 13* (4), 439–453.

Guskey, T. R. (1990a). Cooperative mastery learning strategies. *Elementary School Journal, 91* (1), 33–42.

Guskey, T. R. (1990b). Integrating innovations. *Educational Leadership, 47* (5), 11–15.

Guskey, T. R. (1991). Enhancing the effectiveness of professional development programs. *Journal of Educational and Psychological Consultation, 2* (3), 239–247.

Guskey, T. R. (1994a). Bloom's "Learning for Mastery" revisited: Modern perspectives and misinterpretations. *Outcomes, 13* (1), 16–39.

Guskey, T. R. (1994b). Defining the differences between outcome-based education and mastery learning. *The School Administrator, 51* (8), 34–37.

Guskey, T. R. (1994c). Responding to the critics of outcome-based education. *Outcomes, 13* (2), 21–27.

Guskey, T. R. (1994d). What you assess may not be what you get. *Educational Leadership, 51* (6), 51–54.

Guskey, T. R. (1994e). Making the grade: What benefits students. *Educational Leadership, 52* (2), 14–20.

Guskey, T. R. (Ed.) (1994f). *High stakes performance assessment: Perspectives on Kentucky's educational reform.* Thousand Oaks, CA: Corwin Press.

Guskey, T. R. (1994g). Mastery learning. In L. W. Anderson (Ed.), *International Encyclopedia of Education, Vol. 6* (2nd ed., pp. 3625–3631). Oxford, England: Pergamon Press.

Guskey, T. R. (1994h). Results-oriented professional development: In search of an optimal mix of effective practices. *Journal of Staff Development, 15* (4), 42–50.

Guskey, T. R. (1995a). Mastery learning. In J. H. Block, S. T. Everson, & T. R. Guskey (Eds.), *School improvement programs* (pp. 91–108). New York: Scholastic.

Guskey, T. R. (1995b). Integrating school improvement programs. In J. H. Block, S. T. Everson, & T. R. Guskey (Eds.), *School improvement programs* (pp. 453–472). New York: Scholastic.

Guskey, T. R. (1996). Reporting on student learning: Lessons from the past–Prescriptions for the future. In T. R. Guskey (Ed.), *Communicating student learning: 1996 Yearbook of the Association for Supervision and Curriculum Development* (pp. 13–24). Alexandria, VA: Association for Supervision and Curriculum Development.

Guskey, T. R., Barshis, D., & Easton, J. Q. (1982). The multiplier effect: Exploring new directions in community college research. *Community and Junior College Journal, 52* (8), 22–25.

Guskey, T. R., Benninga, J. S., & Clark, C. R. (1984). Mastery learning and students' attributions at the college level. *Research in Higher Education, 20* (4), 491–498.

Guskey, T. R., & Block, J. H. (1991). The Missouri miracle: A success story about statewide collaboration to improve students' learning. *Outcomes, 10* (2), 28–43.

Guskey, T. R., & Easton, J. Q. (1983). The characteristics of very effective teachers in urban community colleges. *Community/Junior College Research Quarterly, 7* (3), 265–274.

Guskey, T. R., Englehard, G., Tuttle, K., & Guida, F. (1978). *A report on the pilot project to develop mastery courses for the Chicago Public Schools.* Chicago: Center for Urban Education, Chicago Board of Education.

Guskey, T. R., & Gates, S. (1986). Synthesis of research on the effects of mastery learning in elementary and secondary classrooms. *Educational Leadership, 45* (8), 73–80.

Guskey, T. R., & Huberman, M. (Eds.) (1995). *Professional development in education: New paradigms and practices.* New York: Teachers College Press.

Guskey, T. R., & Kifer, E. (1995). *Evaluation of a high school block schedule restructuring program.* Paper presented at annual meeting of the American Educational Research Association, San Francisco.

Guskey, T. R., & Monsaas, J. A. (1979). Mastery learning: A model for academic success in urban junior colleges. *Research in Higher Education, 11* (3), 263–274.

Guskey, T. R., Passaro, P. D., & Wheeler, W. (1991). Missouri's Thorpe Gordon School: A model for school improvement. *Principal, 71* (1), 36–38.

Guskey, T. R., Passaro, P. D., & Wheeler, W. (1995). Mastery learning in the regular classroom: Help for at-risk students with learning disabilities. *Teaching Exceptional Children, 27* (2), 15–18.

Guskey, T. R., & Pigott, T. D. (1988). Research on group-based mastery learning programs: A meta-analysis. *Journal of Educational Research, 81* (4), 197–216.

Haddock, T. T. (1982). Microcomputer makes mastery learning possible. *The Individualized Learning Letter, Micro-Ed Digest, 11* (4), 1 & 7.

Harmin, M. (1994). *Inspiring active learning: A handbook for teachers.* Alexandria, VA: Association for Supervision and Curriculum Development.

Harnadek, A. (1978). *Mindbenders: Deductive thinking skills.* Pacific Grove, CA: Critical Thinking Press & Software.

Harris, L., & Associates (1992). *The Metropolitan Life survey of the American teacher 1992. The second year: New teachers' expectations and ideals.* New York: Metropolitan Life Insurance Co.

Harrow, A. J. (1972). *A taxonomy of the psychomotor domain.* New York: McKay.

Hau-sut, H. (1990). *A study of mastery learning and its effects on science achievement, retention, attitudes, and self-concepts with special focus on educationally disadvantaged students.* Master's thesis, Chinese University of Hong Kong.

Hecht, L. W. (1977). *Isolation from learning supports and processing of group instruction.* Unpublished doctoral dissertation, University of Chicago.

Heikkenen, H., & Dunkleberger, G. E. (1985). On disk with mastery learning. *Science Teacher, 52* (7), 26–28.

Henrysson, S. (1971). Gathering, analyzing, and using data on test items. In R. L. Thorndike (Ed.), *Educational measurement* (2nd ed.) (pp. 130–159). Washington, DC: American Council on Education.

Hiebert, E. H. (1987). The context of instruction and student learning: An examination of Slavin's assumptions. *Review of Educational Research, 57* (3), 337–340.

Hopkins, C. D., & Antes, R. L. (1990). *Classroom measurement and evaluation.* Itasca, IL: Peacock.

Horak, V. M. (1981). A meta-analysis of research findings on individualized instruction in mathematics. *Journal of Educational Research, 74* (4), 249–253.

Huberman, M. (1995). Professional careers and professional development: Some intersections. In T. R. Guskey & M. Huberman (Eds.), *Professional development in education: New paradigms and practices* (pp. 193–224). New York: Teachers College Press.

Huberman, M., & Miles, M. B. (1984). *Innovation up close: How school improvement works.* New York: Plenum.

Hunter, M. (1979). Diagnostic teaching. *Elementary School Journal, 80* (1), 41–46.

Hunter, M. (1982). *Mastery teaching.* El Segundo, CA: TIP Publications.

Jacobs, H. H. (Ed.) (1989). *Interdisciplinary curriculum: Design and implementation.* Alexandria, VA: Association for Supervision and Curriculum Development.

Johnson, D. W., & Johnson, R. T. (1989). *Cooperation and competition: Theory and research.* Edina, MN: Interaction Book Co.

Johnson, D. W., & Johnson, R. T. (1994). *Joining together: Group theory and group skills* (5th ed.). Boston: Allyn & Bacon.

Johnson, D. W., & Johnson, R. T. (1995). Cooperative learning. In J. H. Block, S. T. Everson, & T. R. Guskey (Eds.), *School improvement programs* (pp. 25–56). New York: Scholastic.

Johnson, D. W., Johnson, R. T., & Holubec, E. J. (1994). *Cooperative learning in the classroom.* Alexandria, VA: Association for Supervision and Curriculum Development.

Johnson, D. W., Skon, L., & Johnson, R. T. (1980). Effects of cooperative, competitive, and individualistic conditions on children's problem-solving performance. *American Educational Research Journal, 17* (1), 83–93.

Johnson, R. T., Johnson, D. W., & Tauer, M. (1979). The effects of cooperative, competitive, and individualistic goal structures on students' attitudes and achievement. *Journal of Psychology, 102,* 191–198.

Jones, B. F., & Monsaas, J. A. (1979). *Improving reading comprehension: Embedding diverse strategies within a mastery learning environment.* Paper presented at annual meeting of the American Educational Research Association, San Francisco.

Jones, E. L., Gordon, H. A., & Schechtman, G. L. (1975). *Mastery learning: A strategy for academic success in a community college.* Los Angeles: ERIC Clearinghouse for Junior Colleges.

Joyce, B. (1987). A rigorous yet delicate touch: A response to Slavin's proposal for "best-evidence" reviews. *Educational Researcher, 16* (4), 12–14.

Joyce, B., & Showers, B. (1988). *Student achievement through staff development.* New York: Longman.

Karnes, F. A., & Collings, E. C. (1980). *Handbook of instructional resources and references for teaching the gifted.* Boston: Allyn & Bacon.

Katims, M., & Jones, B. F. (1985). Chicago mastery learning reading: Mastery learning instruction and assessment in inner-city schools. *Journal of Negro Education, 54* (3), 369–387.

Keller, F. S. (1968). Goodbye, teacher. . . . *Journal of Applied Behavioral Analysis, 1,* 78–89.

Kentucky Department of Education (1992). *Kentucky Instructional Results Information System: Writing assessment portfolio.* Frankfort, KY: Kentucky Department of Education.

Kim, H., et al. (1969). *A study of the Bloom strategies for mastery learning* (in Korean). Seoul: Korean Institute for Research in the Behavioral Sciences.

Kim, H., et al. (1970). *The Mastery Learning Project in the middle schools* (in Korean). Seoul: Korean Institute for Research in the Behavioral Sciences.

Klausmeier, H. J. (1971). The multi-unit elementary school and individually guided education. *Phi Delta Kappan, 53* (3), 181–184.

Klausmeier, H. J., and others (1968). *Individually guided education in the multi-unit school: Guidelines for implementation.* Washington, DC: Office of Education (DHEW), Bureau of Research.

Knight, T. (1981). Mastery learning: A report from the firing line. *Educational Leadership, 39* (2), 134–136.

Kounin, J. S. (1970). *Discipline and group management in classrooms.* New York: Holt, Rinehart & Winston.

Kozlovsky, J. D. (1990). Integrating thinking skills and mastery learning in Baltimore County. *Educational Leadership, 47* (5), 6.

Krathwohl, D. R., Bloom, B. S., & Masia, B. B. (1964). *Taxonomy of educational objectives. Handbook II: Affective domain.* New York: McKay.

Kulik, C. C., & Kulik, J. A. (1987). Mastery testing and student learning: A meta-analysis. *Journal of Educational Technology System, 15* (3), 325–345.

Kulik, C. C., Kulik, J. A., & Bangert-Drowns, R. L. (1990a). Effectiveness of mastery learning programs: A meta-analysis. *Review of Educational Research, 60* (2), 265–299.

Kulik, J. A., & Kulik, C. C. (1989). Meta-analysis in education. *International Journal of Educational Research, 13* (3), 221–340.

Kulik, J. A., Kulik, C. C., & Bangert-Drowns, R. L. (1990b). Is there better evidence on mastery learning? A response to Slavin. *Review of Educational Research, 60* (2), 303–307.

Kulik, J. A., Kulik, C. C., & Cohen, P. A. (1979). A meta-analysis of outcome studies of Keller's personalized system of instruction. *American Psychologist, 34* (4) 307–318.

Lahdes, E. (1982). Mastery learning in theory and practical innovation. *Scandinavian Journal of Educational Research, 27* (2), 89–107.

Lamwers, L. L., & Jazwinski, C. H. (1989). A comparison of three strategies to reduce student procrastination in PSI. *Teaching of Psychology, 16* (1), 8–12.

Langeheine, R. (1992). *State mastery learning: Dynamic models for longitudinal data.* Paper presented at annual meeting of the American Educational Research Association, San Francisco.

Larsen, J. J. (1987). *Teaching basic jazz piano skills: A mastery learning approach.* Paper presented at annual meeting of the American Educational Research Association, Washington, DC.

Latham, G. (1988). The birth and death cycles of educational innovations. *Principal,* 68 (1), 41–43.

Leinhardt, G., & Seewald, A. M. (1981). Overlap: What's tested, what's taught. *Journal of Educational Measurement, 18* (1), 85–96.

Levine, D. U., & Associates (1985). *Improving student achievement through mastery learning programs.* San Francisco: Jossey-Bass.

Leyton, F. S. (1983). *The extent to which group instruction supplemented by mastery of initial cognitive prerequisites approximates the learning effectiveness of one-to-one tutorial methods.* Unpublished doctoral dissertation, University of Chicago.

Linn, R. L., & Gronlund, N. E. (1995). *Measurement and assessment in teaching* (7th ed.). Englewood Cliffs, NJ: Prentice-Hall.

Linn, R. L., Baker, E. L., & Dunbar, S. B. (1991). Complex, performance-based assessment: Expectations and validation criteria. *Educational Researcher, 20* (8), 15–21.

Little, J. W. (1982). Norms of collegiality and experimentation: Workplace conditions of school success. *American Educational Research Journal, 19* (3), 325–340.

Lombardi, T. P., Nuzzo, D. L., Kennedy, K. D., & Foshay, J. (1994). Perceptions of parents, teachers and students regarding an integrated education inclusion program. *High School Journal, 77,* 315–321.

Lortie, D. C. (1975). *Schoolteacher: A sociological study.* Chicago: University of Chicago Press.

Luiten, J., Ames, W., & Ackerson, G. (1980). A meta-analysis of the effects of advance organizers on learning and retention. *American Educational Research Journal, 17* (2), 211–218.

Lysakowski, R. S., & Walberg, H. J. (1981). Classroom reinforcement in relation to learning: A quantitative analysis. *Journal of Educational Research, 75* (1), 69–77.

Lysakowski, R. S., & Walberg, H. J. (1982). Instructional effects of cues, participation, and corrective feedback: A quantitative synthesis. *American Educational Research Journal, 19* (4), 559–578.

Madaus, G. F., Kellaghan, T., & Schwab, R. L. (1989). *Teach them well.* New York: Harper & Row.

Martin, M. A. (1978). The application of spiraling to the teaching of grammar. *TESOL Quarterly, 12* (2), 151–161.

Marzano, R. J. (1992). *A different kind of classroom: Teaching with dimensions of learning.* Alexandria VA: Association for Supervision and Curriculum Development.

Marzano, R. J., Pickering, D. J., & Brandt, R. S. (1990). Integrating instructional programs through dimensions of learning. *Educational Leadership, 47* (5), 17–24.

Marzano, R. J., Pickering, D., & McTighe, J. (1993). *Assessing student outcomes.* Alexandria, VA: Association for Supervision and Curriculum Development.

McCarthy, B. (1987). *The 4MAT system: Teaching to learning styles with right/left mode techniques,* 2nd ed. Barrington, IL: Excel, Inc.

McDonald, F. J. (1982). *Mastery learning evaluation project: Interim report.* New York: Division of High Schools, New York City Board of Education.

McDonald, F., & Elias, P. (1976). *The effects of teaching performance on pupil learning; Vol. 1, Final Report. Beginning Teacher Evaluation Study, Phase 2, 1974–1976.* Princeton, NJ: Educational Testing Service.

McLaughlin, M. W. (1978). Implementation as mutual adaptation: Change in classroom organization. In D. Mann (Ed.), *Making change happen* (pp. 19–31). New York: Teachers College Press.

Mehrens, W. A., & Lehmann, I. J. (1991). *Measurement and evaluation in education and psychology* (4th ed.). New York: Holt, Rinehart & Winston.

Mevarech, Z. R. (1980). *The role of teaching learning strategies and feedback-corrective procedures in developing higher cognitive achievement.* Unpublished doctoral dissertation, University of Chicago.

Mevarech, Z. R. (1981). *Attaining mastery on higher cognitive achievement.* Paper presented at annual meeting of the American Educational Research Association, Los Angeles.

Mevarech, Z. R. (1985). The effects of cooperative mastery learning strategies on mathematical achievement. *Journal of Educational Research, 78* (6), 372–377.

Mevarech, Z. R. (1986). The role of a feedback-corrective procedure in developing mathematics achievement and self-concept in desegregated classrooms. *Studies in Educational Evaluation, 12* (2), 197–203.

Mevarech, Z. R. (1989). *Learning mathematics in different "mastery" environments.* Paper presented at annual meeting of the American Educational Research Association, San Francisco.

Mevarech, Z. R. (1991). Learning mathematics in different mastery environments. *Journal of Educational Research, 84* (4), 225–231.

Mevarech, Z. R., & Susak, Z. (1993). Effects of learning with cooperative-mastery method on elementary students. *Journal of Educational Research, 86* (4), 197–205.

Mevarech, Z. R., & Werner, S. (1985). Are mastery learning strategies beneficial for developing problem solving skills? *Higher Education, 14* (4), 425–432.

Millman, J. (1981). Student achievement as a measure of teacher competence. In J. Millman (Ed.), *Handbook of teacher evaluation* (pp. 146–166). Beverly Hills, CA: Sage.

Millman, J., & Darling-Hammond, L. (Eds.). (1990). *The new handbook of teacher evaluation: Assessing elementary and secondary school teachers.* Newbury Park, CA: Sage.

Mitchell, D. E., & Spady, W. G. (1978). Organizational context for implementing outcome-based education. *Educational Researcher, 7* (7), 9–17.

Moles, O. C. (1982). Synthesis of recent research on parent participation in children's education. *Educational Leadership, 40* (2), 44–47.

Morrison, H. C. (1926). *The practice of teaching in the secondary school.* Chicago: University of Chicago Press.

Mortimer, K., Van Wingerden, C., Zahn, G., Meyers, D., & Passaro, P. (1995). Successful strategies for the inclusive classroom. *Outcomes, 14* (1), 35–45.

Mueller, D. J. (1976). Mastery learning: Partly boon, partly boondoggle. *Teachers College Record, 78* (1), 41–52.

Murnane, R. J. (1981). Interpreting the evidence on school effectiveness. *Teachers College Record, 83* (1), 19–35.

Natriello, G. (1987). The impact of evaluation processes on students. *Educational Psychologist, 22* (2), 155–175.

Nordin, A. B. (1979). *The effects of different qualities of instruction on selected cognitive, affective, and time variables.* Unpublished doctoral dissertation, University of Chicago.

O'Neil, J. (1993). Making sense of outcome-based education. *Instructor, 102* (5), 46–47.

O'Neil, J. (1994). Aiming for new outcomes: The promise and the reality. *Educational Leadership, 51* (6), 6–10.

Orlich, D. C., et al. (1990). *Teaching strategies: A guide to better instruction.* Lexington, MA: Heath.

Ornstein, A. C. (1995). *Strategies for effective teaching* (2nd ed.). Dubuque, IA: Brown & Benchmark.

Owac, P. (1981). *Evaluation report: Recorded messages as a way to link teachers and parents.* St. Louis, MO: CEMREL.

Pajack, E., & Blase, J. J. (1989). The impact of teachers' personal lives on professional role enactment: A qualitative analysis. *American Educational Research Journal, 26* (2), 283–310.

Palincsar, A. S., & Brown, A. L. (1984). Reciprocal teaching of comprehension-fostering and comprehension-monitoring activities. *Cognition and Instruction, 2,* 117–175.

Palincsar, A. S., & Brown, A. L. (1988). Teaching and practicing thinking skills to promote comprehension in the context of group problem solving. *Remedial and Special Education, 2* (1), 53–59.

Pantages, T. J., & Creedan, C. F. (1978). Studies of college attrition: 1950–1975. *Review of Educational Research, 48* (1), 19–101.

Paris, S. G., Wixson, K. K., & Palincsar, A. S. (1986). Instructional approaches to reading comprehension. In E. Z. Rothkof (Ed.), *Review of Research in Education* (Vol. 13, pp. 91–128). Washington, DC: American Educational Research Association.

Passaro, P. D., Guskey, T. R., & Zahn, G. (1994). Using mastery learning to facilitate the full inclusion of students with the most intense educational needs within rural schools. *Rural Special Education Quarterly, 13* (3), 31–39.

Payne, D. A. (1992). *Measuring and evaluating educational outcomes.* New York: Merrill.

Perrone, V. (Ed.) (1991). *Expanding student assessment.* Alexandria, VA: Association for Supervision and Curriculum Development.

Perryman, L. (1986). *Mastery learning and its implications for gifted education programs.* Unpublished manuscript (ERIC No. ED280214).

Polya, G. (1973). *How to solve it.* Princeton, NJ: Princeton University Press.

Popham, W. J. (1987). The merits of measurement-driven instruction. *Phi Delta Kappan, 68* (9) 679–682.

Popham, W. J. (1988). *Educational evaluation* (2nd ed.). Englewood Cliffs, NJ: Prentice-Hall.

Popham, W. J. (1995). *Classroom assessment: What teachers need to know.* Boston: Allyn & Bacon.

Popham, W. J., Cruse, K. L., Rankin, S. C., Sandifer, P. D., & Williams, P. L. (1985). Measurement-driven instruction: It's on the road. *Phi Delta Kappan, 66* (9), 628–634.

Porter, A. C., & Brophy, J. E. (1988). Synthesis of research on good teaching: Insights from the work of the Institute for Research on Teaching. *Educational Leadership, 45* (8),74–85.

Prawat, R. S. (1989). Promoting access to knowledge, strategy, and disposition in students: A research synthesis. *Review of Educational Research, 59* (1), 1–42.

Prawat, R. S. (1992a). Teachers' beliefs about teaching and learning: A constructivist perspective. *American Journal of Education, 100* (3), 354–395.

Prawat, R. S. (1992b). From individual differences to learning communities–Our changing focus. *Educational Leadership, 49* (7), 9–13.

Puleo, V. T. (1986). *Application of mastery learning theory to full-and half-day kindergarten research.* Unpublished manuscript (ERIC No. ED286623).

Purkey, S. C., & Smith, M. S. (1982). Too soon to cheer? Synthesis of research on effective schools. *Educational Leadership, 40* (3), 64–69.

Quilling, M., & Otto, W. (1971). Evaluation of an objective-based curriculum in reading. *Journal of Educational Research, 65* (1), 15–18.

Rachal, A. M. (1991). *Mastery learning in the steel magnolia town.* Paper presented at annual meeting of the International Reading Association, Las Vegas, NV.

Raebeck, B. (1993). *Exploding myths, exploring truths: Humane, productive grading and grouping in the quality middle school.* Paper presented at annual conference and exhibit of the National Middle School Association, Portland, OR.

Raiser, R. A. (1980). Interaction between locus of control and three pacing procedures in a personalized system of instruction course. *Educational Communication and Technology, 28,* 194–202.

Reezigt, B. J., & Weide, M. G. (1990). *The effects of group-based mastery learning on language and arithmetic achievement and attitudes in primary education in the Netherlands.* Paper presented at annual meeting of the American Educational Research Association, Boston, MA.

Reezigt, G. J., & Weide, M. G. (1992). Mastery learning and instructional effectiveness. Paper presented at annual meeting of the American Educational Research Association, San Francisco.

Renzulli, J. S., & Smith, L. H. (1978). *Learning styles inventory.* Storrs, CT: Creative Learning Press.

Rosenshine, B. (1979). Content, time and direct instruction. In P. L. Peterson and H. J. Walberg (Eds.), *Research on teaching: Concepts, findings and implications* (pp. 28–56). Berkeley, CA: McCutchan.

Rosenshine, B. (1986). Synthesis of research on explicit teaching. *Educational Leadership, 43* (7), 60–69.

Rosenshine, B. (1987). Direct instruction. In M. J. Dunkin (Ed.), *International encyclopedia of teaching and teacher education* (pp. 257–262). Oxford, England: Pergamon.

Rosenshine, B. (1993). *Is direct instruction different from expert scaffolding?* Paper presented at annual meeting of the American Educational Research Association, Atlanta, GA.

Rosenshine, B., & Meister, C. (1992). The use of scaffolding for teaching higher-level cognitive strategies. *Educational Leadership, 49* (7), 26–33.

Rosenshine, B., & Meister, C. (1994). Reciprocal teaching. *Review of Educational Research, 64* (4), 479–530.

Rosenshine, B., & Stevens, R. (1986). Teaching functions. In M. C. Wittrock (Ed.), *Handbook of research on teaching* (3rd ed.) (pp. 376–392). New York: Macmillan.

Ross, S. M., & Rakow, E. A. (1981). Learner control versus program control as adaptive strategies for selection of instructional support on math rules. *Journal of Educational Psychology, 73* (5), 745–753.

Rothrock, D. (1982). The rise and decline of individualized instruction. *Educational Leadership, 39* (7), 528–531.

Rubin, L. J. (1985). *Artistry in teaching.* New York: Random House.

Rude, R. T. (1974). Objective-based reading systems: An evaluation. *Reading Teacher, 28* (2), 169–175.

Ryan, D. W. (1985). Preactive and proactive supervision of mastery learning. In D. U. Levine (Ed.), *Improving school achievement through mastery learning programs* (pp. 45–67). San Francisco: Jossey-Bass.

Sarason, S. (1990). *The predictable failure of educational reform.* San Francisco: Jossey-Bass.

Scanlon, R. G. (1966). *Individually prescribed instruction: A manual for the IPI institute.* Washington, DC: Office of Education (DHEW), Bureau of Research.

Schofield, J. W., Eurich-Fulcer, R., & Britt, C. L. (1994). Teachers, computer tutors, and teaching: The artificially intelligent tutor as an agent for classroom change. *American Educational Research Journal, 31* (3), 579–607.

Seymour, J. G. (1977). *The effects of mastery learning on the achievement of higher level cognitive skills.* Unpublished doctoral dissertation, Texas A & M University.

Shavelson, R. J., & Baxter, G. P. (1992). What we've learned about assessing hands-on science. *Educational Leadership, 49* (8), 20–25.

Sherman, J. G. (1992). Reflections on PSI: Good news and bad. *Journal of Behavioral Analysis, 25* (1), 59–64.

Simpson, E. J. (1972). The classification of educational objectives in the psychomotor domain. *The psychomotor domain* (Vol. 3). Washington, DC: Gryphon House.

Slate, J. R., & Charlesworth, J. R. (1989). Information processing theory: Classroom applications. *Reading Improvement, 26* (1), 2–6.

Slavin, R. E. (1987). Mastery learning reconsidered. *Review of Educational Research, 57* (2), 175–213.

Slavin, R. E., & Karweit, N. L. (1984). Mastery learning and student teams: A factorial experiment in urban general mathematics classes. *American Educational Research Journal, 21* (4), 725–736.

Smith, D. L., & Woody, D. (1981). Affective factors as motivators in the middle grades. *Phi Delta Kappan, 62,* 527.

Soled, S W. (1987). *Teaching processes to improve both higher and lower mental process achievement.* Paper presented at annual meeting of the American Educational Research Association, Washington, DC.

Spady, W. G. (1977). Competency-based education: A bandwagon in search of a definition. *Educational Researcher, 6* (1), 9–14.

Spady, W. G. (1978). The concept and implications of competency-based education. *Educational Leadership, 36* (1), 19–22.

Spady, W. G. (1992). It's time to take a close look at outcome-based education. *Outcomes, 11* (2), 6–13.

Spady, W. G., & Mitchell, D. E. (1977). Competency-based education: Organizational issues and implications. *Educational Researcher, 6* (2), 9–15.

Sprouse, J. L., & Webb, J. E. (1994). *The Pygmalion effect and its influence on the grading and gender assignment of spelling and essay assessments.* Master's thesis, University of Virginia.

Stahman, S. (1981). A collaborative, technical support approach toward the implementation of mastery learning. *IMPACT on Instructional Improvement, 17* (2), 19–24.

Stahman, S. (May 6, 1980). *Workshop for mastery learning teachers, April 12, 1980.* Memorandum. New York: Economic Development Council of New York City.

Stallings, J. A., & Stipek, D. (1986). Research on early childhood and elementary school teaching programs. In M. C. Wittrock (Ed.), *Handbook of research on teaching* (3rd ed., pp. 727–753). New York: Macmillan.

Sternberg, R. J. (1994a). Allowing for thinking styles. *Educational Leadership, 52* (3), 36–40.

Stiggins, R. J. (1994a). *Student-centered classroom assessment.* New York: Merrill.

Stiggins, R. J. (1994b). Communicating with report card grades. Chapter 14 in *Student-centered classroom assessment* (pp. 363–396). New York: Macmillan.

Stiggins, R. J. (1995). Assessment literacy for the 21st century. *Phi Delta Kappan, 77* (3), 238–245.

Stiggins, R. J., & Duke, D. L. (1991). *District grading policies and their potential impact on at-risk students.* Paper presented at annual meeting of the American Educational Research Association, Chicago, IL.

Stodolsky, S. S. (1988). *The subject matters.* Chicago: University of Chicago Press.

Stone, C. L. (1983). A meta-analysis of advance organizer studies. *Journal of Experimental Education, 51* (4), 194–199.

Sweedler-Brown, C. O. (1992). The effect of training on the appearance bias of holistic essay graders. *Journal of Research and Development in Education, 26* (1), 24–29.

Szetela, W., & Nicol, C. (1992). Evaluating problem solving in mathematics. *Educational Leadership, 49* (8), 42–45.

Tenenbaum, G. (1982). *A method of group instruction which is as effective as one-to-one tutorial instruction.* Unpublished doctoral dissertation, University of Chicago.

Tennyson, R. D., Park, O., & Christenson, D. L. (1985). Adaptive control of learning time and content sequence in concept learning using computer-based instruction. *Journal of Educational Psychology, 77* (4), 481–491.

Thompson, S. B. (1980). Do individualized mastery and traditional instructional systems yield different course effects in college calculus? *American Educational Research Journal, 17* (3), 361–375.

Thorndike, R. M., Cunningham, G. K., Thorndike, R. L., & Hagen, E. P. (1991). *Measurement and evaluation in psychology and education* (5th ed.). New York: Macmillan.

Tobias, S. (1982). When do instructional methods make a difference? *Educational Researcher, 11* (4), 4–9.

Towers, J. M. (1992). Outcome-based education: Another educational bandwagon. *The Educational Forum, 56* (3), 291–305.

Tyler, R. W. (1949). *Basic principles of curriculum and instruction.* Chicago: University of Chicago Press.

Tyson-Bernstein, H. (1988). The academy's contribution to the impoverishment of American textbooks. *Phi Delta Kappan, 70* (3), 193–198.

Vickery, T. R. (1987). *Evaluating a mastery learning high school.* Paper presented at annual meeting of the American Educational Research Association, Washington, DC.

Waddington, T. (1995). *Why mastery matters.* Paper presented at annual meeting of the American Educational Research Association, San Francisco.

Walberg, H. J. (1984). Improving the productivity of America's schools. *Educational Leadership, 41* (8), 19–27.

Walberg, H. J. (1985). Examining the theory, practice, and outcomes of mastery learning. In D. U. Levine (Ed.), *Improving student achievement through mastery learning programs* (pp. 1–10). San Francisco: Jossey-Bass.

Walberg, H. J. (1986). Syntheses of research on teaching. In M. C. Wittrock (Ed.), *Handbook of research on teaching* (3rd ed., pp. 214–229). New York: Macmillan.

Walberg, H. J. (1988a). Synthesis of research on time and learning. *Educational Leadership, 45* (6), 76–85.

Walberg, H. J. (1988b). Response to Slavin: What's the best evidence? *Educational Leadership, 46* (2), 28.

Walberg, H. J. (1990). Productive teaching and instruction. Assessing the knowledge base. *Phi Delta Kappan, 71* (6), 470–478.

Washburne, C. W. (1922). Educational measurements as a key to individualizing instruction and promotions. *Journal of Educational Research, 5,* 195–206.

Webb, N. M. (1982). Peer interaction and learning in cooperative small groups. *Journal of Educational Psychology, 74* (4), 642–655.

Weinert, F. E., & Helmke, A. (1995). Learning from wise Mother Nature or Big Brother instructor: The wrong choice as seen from an educational perspective. *Educational Psychologist, 30* (3), 135–142.

Wentling, T. L. (1973). Mastery versus nonmastery instruction with varying test item feedback treatments. *Journal of Educational Psychology, 65* (1), 50–58.

Whiting, B., & Render, G. F. (1987). Cognitive and affective outcomes of mastery learning: A review of sixteen semesters. *Clearing House, 60* (6), 276–280.

Whiting, B., Van Burgh, J. W., & Render, G. F. (1995). *Mastery learning in the classroom.* Paper presented at annual meeting of the American Educational Research Association, San Francisco.

Whiting, J. (1985). The use of a computer tutorial as a replacement for human tuition in a mastery learning strategy. *Computers and Education, 9* (2), 101–109.

Wiggins, G. (1989). A true test: Toward more authentic and equitable assessment. *Phi Delta Kappan, 70* (9), 703–713.

Wiggins, G. (1992). Creating tests worth taking. *Educational Leadership, 49* (8), 26–33.

Wiggins, G. (1993). *Assessing student performance.* San Francisco: Jossey-Bass.

Wiggins, G. (1994). Toward better report cards. *Educational Leadership, 52* (2), 28–37.

Wiley, D. E. (1976). Another hour, another day: Quality of schooling, a potent path for policy. In W. J. Sewel, R. M. Hauser, & D. L. Featherman (Eds.), *Schooling and achievement in American society.* New York: Academic Press.

Williams, D. L., & Chavkin, N. F. (1989). Essential elements of strong parent involvement programs. *Educational Leadership, 47* (2), 18–20.

Worthen, B. R., & Sanders, J. R. (1987). *Educational evaluation: Alternative approaches and practical guidelines.* New York: Longman.

Wright, R. G. (1994). Success for all: The median is the key. *Phi Delta Kappan, 75* (9), 723–725.

Wu, W. Y. (1994). *Mastery learning in Hong Kong: Challenges and prospects.* Paper presented at annual meeting of the American Educational Research Association, New Orleans, LA.

Yildiran, G. (1977). *The effects of level of cognitive achievement on selected learning criteria under mastery learning and normal classroom instruction.* Unpublished doctoral dissertation, University of Chicago.

Name Index

Subject Index